The Security Arena in Africa

The labels 'state fragility' and 'civil war' suggest that security within several African countries has broken down. As Tim Glawion observes, however, while people do experience insecurity in some parts of conflict-affected countries, in other areas they live in relative security. Following on from the author's in-depth field research between 2014 and 2018, this book is based on first-hand insights into South Sudan and the Central African Republic during their ongoing civil wars and Somalia's breakaway state of Somaliland. Gaining valuable accounts from the people whose security is at stake, this bottom-up perspective on discussions of peace and security tells vivid stories from the field to explore complex security dynamics, making theoretical insights translatable to real-world experiences and revealing how security is created and undermined in these fragile states.

TIM GLAWION is a political analyst and field researcher focussing on issues of local security within fragile states. He has investigated conflict and peace in the Central African Republic, Democratic Republic of the Congo, Egypt, Kenya, Haiti, South Sudan, and Somaliland. Providing advice to government and civil society organizations, his research is regularly published in journals including *Development and Change* and *Journal of Modern African Studies*.

The Security Arena in Africa

Local Order-Making in the Central African Republic, Somaliland, and South Sudan

TIM GLAWION

German Institute of Global and Area Studies (GIGA)

CAMBRIDGE
UNIVERSITY PRESS

CAMBRIDGE
UNIVERSITY PRESS

University Printing House, Cambridge CB2 8BS, United Kingdom

One Liberty Plaza, 20th Floor, New York, NY 10006, USA

477 Williamstown Road, Port Melbourne, VIC 3207, Australia

314–321, 3rd Floor, Plot 3, Splendor Forum, Jasola District Centre,
New Delhi – 110025, India

79 Anson Road, #06–04/06, Singapore 079906

Cambridge University Press is part of the University of Cambridge.

It furthers the University's mission by disseminating knowledge in the pursuit of
education, learning, and research at the highest international levels of excellence.

www.cambridge.org
Information on this title: www.cambridge.org/9781108493376
DOI: 10.1017/9781108623629

First published 2020

Printed in the United Kingdom by TJ International Ltd, Padstow Cornwall

A catalogue record for this publication is available from the British Library.

Library of Congress Cataloging-in-Publication Data
Names: Glawion, Tim, author.
Title: The security arena in Africa : local order-making in the Central African
Republic, Somaliland, and South Sudan / Tim Glawion.
Description: Cambridge, United Kingdpom ; New York, NY : Cambridge
University Press, 2020. | Includes bibliographical references and index.
Identifiers: LCCN 2019029322 (print) | LCCN 2019029323 (ebook) | ISBN
9781108493376 (hardback) | ISBN 9781108623629 (epub)
Subjects: LCSH: Internal security – Central African Republic. | Internal security –
Somaliland (Secessionist government, 1991–) | Internal security – South Sudan. |
Peace-building – Central African Republic. | Peace-building – Somaliland
(Secessionist government, 1991–) | Peace-building – South Sudan. | Central African
Republic – Politics and government – 2003– | Somaliland (Secessionist government,
1991–) – Politics and government. | South Sudan – Politics and government – 2011–
Classification: LCC HV8275.3.A2 G53 2020 (print) | LCC HV8275.3.A2 (ebook) |
DDC 355/.03306–dc23
LC record available at https://lccn.loc.gov/2019029322
LC ebook record available at https://lccn.loc.gov/2019029323

ISBN 978-1-108-49337-6 Hardback

Contents

Figures

Maps

Tables

Boxes

Acknowledgements

The book cover reads only one name and belies the countless people that have partaken in its creation. For four years, I worked together with Andreas Mehler and Lotje de Vries at the German Institute of Global and Area Studies (GIGA). We had the fortune of gracious funding by the German Science Foundation within the Collaborative Research Center 700 (SFB 700) on Governance in Areas of Limited Statehood. With his encyclopaedic memory, Andreas managed to rein in countless of my thoughts that risked getting carried away. He taught me by example to always bring together the two sides of a story – be it that security actors can also bear insecurity, that deep knowledge of a case should never still one's continued curiosity, and that leadership calls for humility. Furthermore, it is with no exaggeration that I say that this book would not exist without Lotje's guidance. She accompanied me on half of my research trips. She not only taught me the tools of the trade but also its tricks, its pitfalls, and how to learn from inevitable mistakes. Being in the field together with her not only doubled my insights; it quadrupled them. How many times would I have fallen for a rhetorically gifted armed leader's lies, lost my train of thought with evasive state officials, or failed to gain the trust of a sceptical farmer? I am honoured to have had the chance to learn from Andreas and Lotje.

My eternal gratitude goes out to the hundreds of people in the Central African Republic (CAR), South Sudan, Somaliland, and beyond that have entrusted me with their thoughts on such a sensitive topic as are their perceptions of security. I thank in particular the local research assistants that have supported me through geographical guidance, cultural interpretation, language translation, and by keeping me safe while conducting field work. In the CAR, I thank my research colleague Sylvain Batianga-Kinzi for many late nights discussing politics and my research assistants Arthur Lakara, Jean-Noël Yambele

Ndilkissim, Jean Balipio, André Bienvenue Bakpe, as well as my assistants Sylvestre Jean Saint Cyr Dothe, Sylvestre Ningassara, and Alain Kanza for their exceptional motivation and drive. In South Sudan, I thank my research colleague Kenneth Akau Athanasio who guided me not only in whom to talk to and how but also in how to stay safe in the tense environment in which I conducted research in his country. I also thank three South Sudanese research assistants that wrote monthly reports on their localities' security situation but whose names I will keep anonymous for their own security. In Somaliland, I was absolutely delighted to share my adventurous journeys with my research assistants Abdirisaq Aden Abdi, Abdirisaq Boqore, Moxamud Abdi Ismaaciil, and Hassan Abdi Mahamoud, my drivers Abdilahi Indho and Rashid, and my security guards Ahmed and Hussein. All these people and many a local interlocutor have become far more than research subjects – I would like to believe them my friends. My heart is filled with sadness when I think of those people I have met who have lost their lives in Mundri, Raja, and Bangassou or have had to flee their homes due to rising violence in even more places studied in this book.

I wish to cherish their memory by conducting this study in all sincerity and there are more people to thank that made this happen. I express my gratitude to the German taxpayers, to the German Research Foundation (DFG), and to the Collaborative Research Centre (Sonderforschungsbereich, SFB) 700 for generously funding this research over four years. On a practical note, I wish to thank Médecins Sans Frontières, MINUSCA, OCHA, and UNHAS for facilitating air transport in the CAR and UNMISS as well as WFP/UNHAS for doing the same in South Sudan. In Somaliland, I greatly appreciated the assistance of the University of Hargeisa with accommodation, transport, and interpretation and thank in particular Hamse Khayr and Adam Haji Ali of the Institute for Peace and Conflict Studies for their support and the opportunity to teach a course on governance and development.

Back in Europe, I thank Jan Koehler, Christian von Soest, and Markus-Michael Müller for their feedback on the ongoing progress of my thesis. I also thank the participants of several conferences and workshops, particularly Christine Cheng for hosting me at King's College London and Jason Mosley for doing the same at the University of Oxford. Finally, my sincerest gratitude goes out to two anonymous reviewers that have been exceptionally constructive in their feedback of my work and whose suggestions helped bring this manuscript to the next level. Their and countless more scholars' feedback has been critical for embedding this work into the ongoing academic debate.

Last, and most importantly, I wish to thank my friends and family for always being there.

Abbreviations

3 R	Retour, Réclamation, Réhabilitation; Engl.: Return, reclamation, rehabilitation (armed group active in north-western CAR)
AMISOM	African Union Mission in Somalia
Anti-Balaka	Broad term used for a wide array of loosely organized auto-defence groups that fought against the Séléka rebel alliance (CAR)
APRD	Armée Populaire pour la Restauration de la République et la Démocratie; Engl.: Popular army for the restauration of the republic and democracy (near Paoua, CAR)
AU	African Union
CAR	Central African Republic
CAS	Comparative Area Studies
CASAL	Comité d'Appui Spirituel aux Autorités Locales; Engl.: Committee for spiritual support to the local authorities (Paoua, CAR)
CEEAC	Communauté Économique des États de l'Afrique Centrale; Engl.: Economic Community of Central African States (ECCAS)
CEMAC	Communauté Économique et Monétaire de l'Afrique Centrale; Engl.: Economic and Monetary Community of Central Africa
CMPP	Comité de Médiation Pour la Paix; Engl.: Committee for the mediation of peace (Paoua, CAR)
CPA	Comprehensive Peace Agreement (Sudan, South Sudan)
CPMM	Comité de Paix et Médiation de Mbomou; Engl.: Peace and mediation committee of Mbomou (Bangassou, CAR)
DDR	Disarmament, Demobilization and Reintegration

DRC	Democratic Republic of the Congo
EU	European Union
EUFOR-RCA	European Union military operation in the Central African Republic
EUTM-RCA	European Union Training Mission in the Central African Republic
FACA	Forces Armées Centrafricaines
FCFA	Franc de la Coopération Financière en Afrique Centrale; Engl.: Franc of the financial cooperation in Central Africa
FNEC	Fédération Nationale des Éleveurs Centrafricains; Engl.: National federation of Central African herders
GP	Groupe des Patriotes; Engl.: Group of patriots (armed group active near Paoua, CAR)
ICG	International Crisis Group
IGAD	Intergovernmental Authority on Development
IGASOM	IGAD Peace Support Mission in Somalia
IOM	International Organization for Migration
LRA	Lord's Resistance Army
MINUSCA	Mission multidimensionnelle Intégrée des Nations Unies pour la Stabilisation de la République Centrafricaine; Engl.: United Nations Multidimensional Integrated Stabilization Mission in the Central African Republic
MISCA	Mission Internationale de Soutien à la Centrafrique; Engl.: African Union Mission in the CAR
MLPC	Mouvement pour la Libération du Peuple Centrafricain; Engl.: Movement for the liberation of the Central African people (political party, CAR)
MPC	Mouvement Patriotique Centrafricain; Engl.: Central African patriotic movement (armed group active near Paoua, CAR)
NGO	non-governmental organization
NSS	National Security Services, South Sudan
OCHA	Office for the Coordination of Humanitarian Affairs
OFCA	Organisation des Femmes Centrafricaines; Engl.: Organization of Central African women
ONLF	Ogaden National Liberation Front
RCI-LRA	Regional Cooperation Initiative against the LRA

RJ	Révolution et Justice; Engl.: Revolution and justice (armed group active near Paoua, CAR)
RPF	Regional Protection Force (South Sudan)
Sangaris	French military operation from December 2013 to October 2016 (CAR)
Séléka	Sango word for 'Coalition'; Rebel alliance formed in 2012 that briefly took power in March 2013 (CAR)
SNM	Somali National Movement
SONSAF	Somaliland Non State Actors Forum
SPLA	Sudan People's Liberation Army (army of South Sudan, former armed group in Southern Sudan)
SPLA-IO	Sudan People's Liberation Army-in-Opposition (armed group, South Sudan)
SPLM	Sudan People's Liberation Movement (political party, South Sudan)
UN	United Nations
UNDP	United Nations Development Programme
UNHAS	United Nations Humanitarian Air Service
UNHCR	United Nations High Commissioner for Refugees
UNISFA	United Nations Interim Security Force for Abyei (Sudan/South Sudan)
UNMIS	United Nations Mission in Sudan
UNMISS	United Nations Mission in the Republic of South Sudan
UNOSOM	United Nations Operation in Somalia
UNPOL	United Nations Police
UNSC	United Nations Security Council
UPC	Unité pour la paix en Centrafrique; Engl.: Unity for the CAR (armed group active in central CAR)
UPDF	Uganda People's Defence Force
USD	United States Dollars

Introduction

'Unfortunately, I am the prefect', says the man sitting opposite me, half-jokingly.[1] Dressed in basketball shorts and a jersey, the Ugandan army commander rests on a foldable chair in front of his tent. We are almost literally in the geographic heart of Africa, in Obo, a prefectural capital with a population of only 8,000. Obo is situated inland, about 1,000 kilometres from Bangui, the Central African Republic's capital and 2,000 kilometres from the nearest coastline. It is surrounded by forest and fertile soils and is allegedly home to one of the continent's most notorious rebel groups – the Lord's Resistance Army (LRA). The large, smiling man opposite me is talking in his mother tongue, English, and claims to be the political head of this prefecture, where people speak Zande, Sango, and French. Despite the irony in his tone, he might just be right.

The official state prefect of Haut Mbomou, of which Obo is the capital, has a weak local standing. The state receives next to no support from the national government and the local population has accused the prefect of corruption. The Ugandan army commander allows the prefect and other leading state officials to use the army's medical facilities. He even provides the state security forces with fuel and other provisions, which they do not receive from their own government. Local inhabitants are well aware of this arrangement. Naturally, they position the foreign Ugandan army hierarchically above the strongest national security forces as in a chain of command. Within this constellation, Ugandans have a strong grip on security events in Obo, even intervening in abuses by state forces if necessary. However, their massive presence in the fight against the LRA also gives inhabitants the impression that they are living on the front line and thereby raises grave security concerns about potential dangers that lurk in Obo's surroundings.

[1] Interview with UPDF commander, Obo, CAR, 18 March 2015.

1

This book aims to compare the processes of ordering security in nine cases across three conflict-affected countries. By uncovering patterns among local arenas in the Central African Republic (CAR), Somaliland, and South Sudan, I am able to gain generalizable insights into the creation of security and insecurity. Obo is one of nine cases I compare and contrast in regard to actors, processes of ordering, and the impact of ordering on security. In my search for insights from various angles and with minimally preconceived ideas, I witnessed situations on the ground that run counter to official narratives – for example, the Ugandan army commander taking on matters of public security, which should be the role of the state prefect. Because matters on the ground can change quickly (as evidenced by the Ugandan army's abrupt departure in mid-2017), I abstracted insights into security to the analytical level. These answers provide understandings that go beyond one case at one certain point in time.

Such an analysis necessitates finding a concept through which varying local security dynamics can be understood and compared across cases. This includes re-evaluating notions of state, non-state, and intervention and studying the often blurred lines between them. This research avenue also requires scholars to look at local forms of ordering and the way they impact a populace's security perceptions. I thus ask the following question: *what are the effects of varying forms of ordering on perceptions of security in local arenas?*

So far, studies of sub-state security are rare and mostly limited to case studies[2] and statistical analyses.[3] Generalizable qualitative insights into security and insecurity are scarce[4] and a comprehensive concept of local security arenas has yet to be developed.[5] Here, I invite the reader on a journey to understanding security in three countries which, at first sight, appear to be engulfed in conflict: the CAR, South Sudan, and Somaliland (a self-declared independent state in Somalia). I find careless and repressive state institutions, creative non-state forms of security provision and arbitrary violence, peacekeepers drinking beer at the market and others hiding away in their air-conditioned tents, and

---

[2] E.g. Pendle 2014; Vandekerckhove 2011.
[3] E.g. Cederman *et al.* 2011; Fearon & Laitin 2003.
[4] E.g. Reno 1998. This is not counting the many edited volumes on security that use multiple cases but fall short on the comparative side of analysis.
[5] In fact, I found only one social science article with 'security arena' in its title; though the article's author does not specify the concept: Hills 2014a.

a Ugandan army commander claiming to be the head of a foreign country's prefecture.

Going Beyond the Failed States Paradigm

For many international policymakers and academics, the CAR, Somaliland, and South Sudan lack the political institutions necessary to order larger societies as they fall short of Max Weber's widely used definition of the state: 'diejenige menschliche Gemeinschaft, welche innerhalb eines bestimmten Gebietes ... das Monopol legitimer physischer Gewaltsamkeit für sich (mit Erfolg) beansprucht'.[6] According to this concept, a state must have a delineated territory, a specified populace, and a monopoly on the legitimate use of force.[7]

In 1993, Gerald B. Helman and Steven R. Ratner triggered a debate on the 'failed state'.[8] According to Robert I. Rotberg, 'state failure is always associated with intrastate violence'.[9] Others take this a step further by linking failed states to 'the coming anarchy'[10] or 'the spread of pandemics ... criminals and terrorists'.[11] Some authors, therefore, attribute the root causes of many forms of insecurity to the failure of the state.[12] However, the remedy – state monopolization of authority – has an ambiguous effect on security. It can facilitate security provision by offering predictability but a monopoly of authority can also be abused and heighten suffering as documented in the rich literature on authoritarianism.[13] Consequently, some peace- and state-building scholars warn against singularly focussing on state capacity-building as a natural remedy to insecurity.[14] As one research team fittingly put it, 'The calm following the monopolisation of power by one particular actor never meant peace for all, but only for some.'[15]

---

[6] English translation: 'That human community, which rightfully asserts its monopoly over the legitimate use of physical force within a certain territory', Weber 1992 [1919]: 6.

[7] Such legitimacy can be gained through tradition, charisma, or legal rationality. Weber's classification of ideal types of rule has heavily influenced European and American policy and research on statehood ever since. Weber 1922: 19.

[8] Helman & Ratner 1993. More recently among others Acemoglu & Robinson 2012.

[9] Rotberg 2003: 30. See as a counter-argument to conflation of conflict and failed statehood: Aliyev 2017.

[10] Kaplan 1994.   [11] Rice 2005.   [12] E.g. Howard 2010; Rotberg 2003.

[13] E.g. Bellin 2004; Gandhi & Przeworski 2007.

[14] Cf. Schneckener 2010; Schroeder 2010.   [15] Simons *et al.* 2013: 700.

The crux of the 'states with adjectives' literature (e.g. 'failed' or 'weak' states) is a normatively loaded reading of the nature of political order in non-monopolized settings. Authors analyse non-monopolized nations as lesser forms of the ideal state, which is represented by Denmark.[16] This historical propensity towards statehood is based on the seminal work of Charles Tilly, who proposed that 'state structure appeared chiefly as a by-product of rulers' efforts to acquire the means of war'.[17] Such state-making wars would press smaller entities to 'merge into larger units'.[18] A victor's peace was necessary to consolidate states.[19] In Africa, however, colonial powers created boundaries, which were later upheld by international organizations.[20] Furthermore, population pressures were often too low to call for boundary consolidation from within.[21] Thus, while in Europe the state emerged as the most powerful regulator during the Thirty Years War in the seventeenth century,[22] competition in Africa was confined to fixed borders between strongmen who bargained over resources and legitimacy with outside actors rather than their own populations.[23] Catherine Scott thus proposes that state failure describes the historical inability to fill the colonially inherited boundaries with legitimate political order and are thus in effect failed post-colonies.[24] While the failed state concept implies that a once functioning state *has now failed*, political order in the Weberian sense *has never been present* in many parts of the world, particularly in Africa.[25]

Putting all political orders on an imagined continuous path towards an ideal state lumps political entities together that differ considerably. Indeed, numerous state indices rank the three country cases here among the worst in the world, if not *the* worst.[26] However, the political

---

[16] E.g. Krasner & Risse 2014.
[17] Tilly 1990: 14. Interestingly enough, Tilly himself suggested in later chapters of his book that this trajectory is unlikely to repeat itself in the developing world.
[18] Diamond 1999: 283.   [19] Luttwak 1999; Herbst 2004.
[20] Cf. Jackson 1990; Rubin 2005: 96.
[21] Herbst 2000: 11; Diamond 1999: 284; Kraxberger 2012: 109.
[22] Erdmann 2003: 268.   [23] Leander 2004.   [24] Scott 2017.
[25] Engel & Mehler 2005: 91.
[26] Cf. the Fragile States Index: Messner 2017; the indices of the Organisation for Economic Co-operation and Development (OECD, 2015) 'States of Fragility 2015': www.keepeek.com/Digital-Asset-Management/oecd/development/state s-of-fragility-2015_9789264227699-en#; Monty G. Marshall (2017) 'State Fragility and Warfare in the Global System 2016': www.systemicpeace.org/wa rlist/warlist.htm.

trajectories of the three cases, especially with regard to security, could hardly differ more. State forces are virtually non-existent in the CAR, where dozens of fragmented militias roam the country. In South Sudan the government commands a massive repressive apparatus, which it has used to violently intimidate its own citizens and fight heavily armed opposition groups that were once part of the government. Moreover, assigning such labels to entire countries masks variations within those countries. For instance, in the case of Somalia, the south continues to be ravaged by war, while de facto independent Somaliland enjoys relative security.[27] To go beyond the debate on state failure, I developed the concept of the 'security arena', which allowed me to investigate the impact of local ordering struggles on perceptions of security.

Security in the CAR, Somaliland, and South Sudan

Choosing the three 'most fragile' countries in the world – the CAR, South Sudan, and Somaliland (as de jure part of Somalia) – offers particular opportunities to examine divergent security trajectories in countries where the state does not play a dominant role. Having ranked similarly in a prominent fragility index for four years in a row,[28] the three countries would appear to be on like paths in politics and conflict; nevertheless, they have in fact been marked by very distinct recent developments. South Sudan has experienced elevated conflict over long periods of time, whereas the CAR has seen a recent spike in violence. Meanwhile, Somaliland has witnessed a calming of its conflict. Different localities in the three countries provide a wide spectrum of ways to create security or insecurity.

Driven by myriad forms of resistance by southern actors against the oppressive ruling regime in the north, the decades of armed struggle in Sudan have shaped its politics. After a lopsided peace agreement in 2005, South Sudan gained independence in 2011. The new state's institutions are led by former militia leaders-turned-government officials. The security apparatus similarly has its origins in the violent independence struggle and continues to be shaped by the divisions and organizational structures of that era. This characteristic facilitated

---

[27] Glawion *et al.* 2019.
[28] Messner 2017. See online data centre for rankings on all measured years: http://fundforpeace.org/fsi/data/.

the rapid disintegration of the national army after the leadership struggles erupted into violence in December 2013.[29] Today, inhabitants of
the peripheral localities face a heavily resourced central actor that
shows little will to provide public services but goes to great lengths to
suppress resistance. The immense levels of conflict South Sudan has
experienced have spread throughout the young country, triggering
a number of national and local conflict lines, resulting in all sides
committing atrocities against civilians. The overlap between national
and local issues is a main cause of spiralling conflict.

The security situation in the CAR is also marked by high levels of
violence. Successive CAR governments have neglected the country's
peripheries and have reduced state administration and security personnel to extremely low numbers. In 2013, the CAR made international
headlines for the first time in a decade when the Séléka rebel alliance
took control of the capital and toppled the president. Séléka's ensuing
violent rule led to the creation of ad hoc Anti-Balaka militias, which
sought to protect their communities; however, the militias have also
gone on to commit violence against civilians. Numerous peacekeeping
missions have been deployed since the mid-1990s. Nonetheless, despite
accomplishing a number of military successes against rebel forces, they
have failed to rein in the violence between armed groups. When Séléka
leader Michel Djotodia lost control of his forces, he had to secede to
a transitional government in early 2014. Two years later, general
elections brought a democratic, peaceful change of power in government and Parliament. Nevertheless, security is again deteriorating as
fragmented Anti-Balaka and former Séléka forces spread and trigger
spiralling violence between communities. The ongoing conflict has
deepened social divides in the CAR and hundreds of thousands, predominantly Muslims, remain displaced.[30]

Somalia is often dubbed the clearest example of state failure.[31]
Mogadishu has changed hands countless times since 1990 and much
of the south central areas are still contested between the radical Islamist
Al-Shabaab and the government with its international and local allies.
Puntland, however, has fared somewhat better, while large areas of

---

[29] Good introductions into the recent crisis can be found in de Vries & Justin 2014;
     Rolandsen 2015a.
[30] On the recent developments in the CAR, see Glawion & de Vries 2018;
     Lombard 2016a; Marchal 2016.
[31] E.g. Spanger 2007: 86; Ottaway 2002: 1002.

Somaliland have been peaceful for fifteen years. It is for this reason that I chose Somaliland as a focus of this study. Somaliland shares a comparable history with South Sudan, as both experienced an armed struggle against an abusive central government which ultimately led to the declaration of independence. Despite Somaliland's 1991 declaration preceding South Sudan's by twenty years, it is yet to be formally recognized by other states. Scholars often describe it as a de facto state,[32] given it has attributes that resemble those of formal states, such as an administrative structure, a defined (albeit contested) territory, registered citizens, and status as a legitimate authority. Nevertheless, Somaliland today provides a peculiar model in which state and traditional institutions are heavily intermixed.[33]

New Comparative Insights on Local Security

With this book, I aim to contribute both empirically and theoretically to the field of comparative security studies. From an empirical perspective, the countries of interest here are broadly under-researched (specifically the CAR) and largely inaccessible due to conflict (especially South Sudan). The insights I gather here often stem from contested localities that are some distance from their capitals and have seldom been studied. The original data for this analysis was gathered between 2014 and 2017 and contributes to the debate on local security by incorporating empirical aspects from locations thus far rarely studied.

From this vast empirical data and the literature on arenas,[34] I derive the concept of the 'security arena'. Clarifying the conceptual lens of a security arena can aid our understanding of security dynamics and facilitate the comparison of local contexts. By looking through this conceptual lens – but not becoming limited by it – I aim to contribute broadly to the nexus between order-making[35] and security governance,[36] a relationship that thus far remains 'under-utilised and under-theorised'.[37] I critically engage with debates on state-building,[38]

[32] E.g. Caspersen 2012: 6; Balthasar 2013: 218.
[33] Good introductions into Somaliland politics can be found in Bradbury 2008; Renders 2012.
[34] See Chapter 1.   [35] E.g. Kalyvas *et al.* 2008; Meagher *et al.* 2014.
[36] E.g. Bagayoko *et al.* 2016; Baker 2010; Krahmann 2003; Van Munster 2007.
[37] Worrall 2017: 709. Cf. also Luckham 2017: 109.
[38] E.g. Call & Wyeth 2008; Fukuyama 2004; Lund 2016; Tilly 1990.

non-state security alternatives,[39] and international intervention.[40]
Many of these studies emphasize decisions international actors can
take to improve security;[41] in doing so, they limit local agency.[42]
Agency draws from sociocultural aspects to enable a group of individuals to act collectively[43] and in general is understated in security
studies, which often use institutional and functional approaches.[44]
I thus adopt an actor-focussed, process-oriented viewpoint on the
above-mentioned issues.[45] Using a bottom-up perspective and
a comparative lens, I aim to fill a gap in local security studies by
showing how physical security improves or deteriorates for inhabitants
on the ground.

   This analysis can also serve as a guideline for policymakers of all
types (e.g. revolutionaries, administrators, interveners) to understand
the respective security arenas they are engaged in. As will be laid out in
the following sections and throughout the book, actors tend to collaborate with those groups that use similar ways to order a security arena
and thereby neglect other aspects of the arena. With the help of the
varying ordering effects on security deciphered in this book, those
present on the ground can gauge the effects of their actions, particularly
towards those ordering forms and actors that are most different from
their own and from themselves.

Core Argument: Stable and Fluid Ordering in the Security Arena

A security arena is composed of actors that interact on the issue of
physical integrity around a preselected centre of study. Security is the
felt durability of physical integrity and insecurity is the felt threat of
physical harm. The centres of study are the main meeting points of the
small town chosen by the researcher. The actors of the arena have
different organizational characteristics, attributes, and resources. In
trying to order security arenas in ways that seem fit to them, actors

---

[39] E.g. Reno 1998; Jackson 2003; Mampilly 2011; Mkandawire 2002.
[40] E.g. Autesserre 2009; Kühn 2011; Stedman 1993.
[41] E.g. ICISS 2001; Krasner 2004; Paris 2010.
[42] E.g. Mac Ginty & Richmond 2013; Schroeder & Chappuis 2014: 141.
[43] For a more in-depth discussion of actors and their agency in modern society, see
    Meyer & Jepperson 2000.
[44] E.g. Daase & Friesendorf 2010; Kühn 2011.
[45] E.g. Collins 2008; Elwert 1999; Kalyvas 2006.

draw on varying strategies from a fluidity–stability ordering spectrum to relate to other actors, including supporting or threatening one another.

There is no 'better' side on the fluidity–stability ordering spectrum. Perceptions of security vary widely within and across cases, as well as over time. In Somaliland security is ordered with vast degrees of fluidity and people generally feel relatively secure. The South Sudanese government, on the other hand, tries to impose rigid structures; however, widespread conflict there makes the country's inhabitants some of the world's least secure. In the CAR, the state and international actors claim to order in a stable manner but this is matched by a large degree of real fluidity on the ground. Struggles over the forms used to order security arenas impact people's perceived levels of security.

Towards the stable end of the ordering spectrum, actors establish institutions, channels, and hierarchies by investing significant resources and thereby making themselves highly visible. As a result, a change in ordering becomes costlier.[46] Stable ordering can create continuous security, as well as constant insecurity. Fluid ordering, on the other hand, is less able to create continuous, predictable security but thus also avoids institutionalizing organized insecurity. Fluid ordering offers particular possibilities to change individual or group aims and to negotiate contrasting aims because it does not seek to rigidly impose certain modes or institutions on an arena. In sum, stable ordering generates more predictability, while fluid ordering creates more modifiability.

The key research interest lies in the relationship between ordering and security. In this book, I thus suggest that there is a spectrum from 'stable' to 'fluid' ways of ordering and that 'security' is the outcome. Actors seeking stability is therefore not the same thing as actors seeking security – an easily made mistake since 'stability' and 'security' are widely used in close connection or even interchangeably in the literature.[47] Within a security arena, however, the two are clearly differentiated: actors seeking stability use stable forms of ordering, including regularized hierarchies among actors. This is the process of

---

[46] Or as Roger MacGinty puts it, stabilization 'risks excluding creativity, innovation, dissent, resistance and pluralism' (2012: 27).

[47] Cf. Mac Ginty 2012. The OECD and many international policymakers use the term 'fragile and conflict-affected contexts', which suggests the two go together, while the opposite would be 'stability and peace'.

stable ordering. Although stable ordering processes can, as an outcome, generate security for the populace, they can also create
insecurity.

Different actors in an arena might pursue contrasting forms of
ordering depending on their particular interests. Actors who believe
that the current modes of ordering best suit their interests might seek to
(further) institutionalize them. Those threatened by the more stable
parts of the current security arena may seek to generate more leeway to
act independently. Actors can change what they pursue over time and
may seek to stabilize a particular part of the arena while keeping other
parts fluid. This analysis differs from other conflict studies, which focus
on the types of interests (e.g. economic, political, social, or rational/
irrational) that result in security or insecurity.[48] Here, I concentrate not
on a specific interest but rather on the trajectory – that is, the type of
ordering – via which actors believe they can best pursue their interests.

Neither side on the ordering spectrum is linked to more or less
insecurity per se. Security deteriorates when competition over ordering
turns violent. How ordering struggles impact people's perceptions of
security is shaped by where the struggles take place and who is
involved. There are four key relations in a security arena that explain
ordering variations and their impact on people's perceptions of security. First, negotiations between actors and inhabitants of the centre
and the periphery create higher levels of security for both
sides than does central actors' neglect of the periphery or pursuit of
submission. Second, at the local level the security arena is divided
between an inner circle dominated by stable forms of ordering and an
outer circle dominated by fluid forms of ordering. The more prominent
the division appears on the ground, the more strongly inhabitants
perceive that insecurity is emanating from the outer circle. Third, at
first sight state actors and internationals seem to tend towards stable
ordering, while non-state actors allegedly favour fluid ordering to
pursue security provision. However, all types of actors vary their
ordering along the full spectrum of the arena competing over who
and how should be in charge over security. Fourth, international actors
have to deal with the entire spectrum of ordering forms, actor types,
and arena parts in order to improve people's perceptions of security.
One-sided interventions unbalance arenas and create insecurity among

---

[48] See discussion in Chapter 2.

populaces. These four key dimensions explicate a large degree of ordering variation in security arenas and the impact thereof on security.

A common criticism of my research endeavour is that the explanations for security variations are much more obvious than reflections on security arenas might suggest. For example, colleagues have pointed out that the CAR is in conflict, while Somaliland is not. However, conflict leading to insecurity seems too tautological to hold analytic value. Pre-, in-, and post-conflict settings are not independent conditions or causes of the security arena.[49] The question must rather be why there is security in some arenas of Somaliland and insecurity in many of those in the CAR. One condition I found that could clarify why unarmed non-state actors can provide security is that they do not have to face external spoilers. This then raises the question of why spoilers are a problem in some local arenas in the CAR but not so much in those of Somaliland. The answer is not the absence of heavily armed groups in Somaliland's vicinity – there are potentially threatening actors in the Ogaden, in the rump of Somalia, and across the Gulf of Aden.[50] Rather, Somaliland's state security forces, unlike the CAR's, take protecting their borders very seriously. Without these outside spoilers, non-state actors in Somaliland are better able to take up security matters than their CAR or South Sudanese counterparts because they need only deal with internal matters. Nevertheless, all three Somaliland security arenas witness levels of internal social tensions comparable to those found in the CAR and South Sudan; though theirs have not escalated. In the CAR, international actors are often the ones that keep a lid on tensions as the impact of traditional authorities is limited, as is also the case in South Sudan. In Somaliland, on the other hand, traditional institutions and ordering forms play a key role in maintaining security, while the state often only takes on an enabling role; international actors are mostly absent from Somaliland. In short, rather than simply seeing conflict as a cause of insecurity, I aim to identify additional explanations of why there is conflict and insecurity in many of the CAR and South Sudan cases I observe and why Somaliland's inhabitants witness much less conflict and insecurity. I shall do this by examining their respective local security arenas.

[49] Cf. Richards 2005: 13ff.   [50] Cf. Hoehne 2015.

Book Structure

Everything seems to be connected to everything in the security arena: history to present, peripheries to centres, and state to non-state and international actors. I successively investigate varying aspects of ordering security arenas to uncover generalizable trends across my nine arenas of study. The book structures the rich underlying material from the broad to the detailed, from history to the present, and from theory to empirics. It is divided into three parts, the first of which establishes the theoretical and historical basis of my analysis (Introduction and Chapters 1 and 2). The second part focusses on the shape of the arenas and detects different spheres on an international, national, and local level (Chapters 3 and 4). In the third part, I use short succinct chapters to investigate ordering struggles in the security arenas by looking at why actors use stable ordering, fluid ordering, mix the two forms, or detach from the arena all together (Chapters 5, 6, 7, and 8). Finally, the Conclusion brings the successive aspects together.

In Chapter 1, I provide the research framing of this study. First, I discuss relevant academic works on arenas and combine them with my own empirical insights. I define 'security' and describe the two key dimensions of actors and their interactions. Second, descriptive commonalities and differences in ordering practices in the local security arena lead me to decipher analytical insights that call for more in-depth investigation – namely, the respective roles and interactions of state, non-state, and international actors; the dividing lines between inner and outer circles in the local arena; and different relations between peripheral local cases and their respective centres. In the methodological section, I explain why I chose these three countries and the local arenas within them, how I gathered data through an explorative mix of methods, and how I analysed the data through process tracing and the Comparative Area Studies approach.

In Chapter 2, I provide the historical and local background to my analysis. I describe political developments in the CAR, Somaliland, and South Sudan before, during, and after colonization. These changes shape the way these countries' respective political systems function today. I then move to the local level and provide a brief description of the key actors and issues at stake in each of the nine local security arenas. These case descriptions on the national and local level will form the basis of the analysis that follows.

In Chapter 3, I draw on the historical basis laid out in the prior chapter to establish how the current national security arenas of each country came about and what it means for the local cases under scrutiny here. Going beyond the national level, decisions made by peacekeeping headquarters and mission contributors inform the actions of international actors and form a sort of international security arena. The described historical legacies, narratives, and capacities of actors on the national and international levels shape the corridor in which different ordering practices can be negotiated at the local level.

In Chapter 4, I focus on the local level in order to examine the way different parts of arenas lend themselves to varying forms of ordering. Within an inner circle, actors engage more regularly, revealing themselves to one another and thereby creating pressure for a stable order. An outer circle is more illegible, diffuse, and widespread, which allows actors to use it as a refuge for fluid ordering. The shape of an arena is not a deterministic structure but rather one that actors deliberately mould to support the forms of ordering that benefit them most. I pursue this line of research by ascertaining (1) why, how, and where actors create the dividing line between an inner and outer circle (drawing the line); (2) why and how actors enter or leave an inner circle (crossing the line); and (3) what forms of interactions make a line obsolete between inner and outer circle actors (erasing the line).

Having discussed the shape of the arena both above and across the local level, I then turn to ordering struggles in security arenas. In Chapter 5, I first investigate more stable forms of ordering the security arena. They are characterized by clearly voiced claims, hierarchized actor relations, and structured processes of security provision. Such ordering is commonly expected by the state but state practices often fall short of its narratives of stable ordering. Other actors also turn to stable ordering, when they believe they are able to gain larger stakes in the arena. Actors can even resort to force, when they have the means to press their claims. Stable ordering can create predictable security but it can also create organized insecurity.

In Chapter 6, I show how actors turn to more fluid forms of ordering to adapt to movements and new issues in the security arena. Fluid ordering can compensate for minimal resources but can also reduce possible gains in the security arena. Non-state actors often attempt to mediate security issues as an alternative to absent state enforcement but often lack the influence to resolve conflict. State and international actors themselves recurrently choose to engage the arena through flexible conflict resolution. Fluid ordering that turns violent is particularly hard to grasp as perpetrators deliberately keep their actions and organization obscure. Ordering towards the fluid end of the spectrum can improve security by allowing for more modifiability but it also allows insecurity to arise as violence remains unchecked.

Neither of the two sides of the ordering spectrum should be seen by itself. In Chapter 7, I analyse how actors frequently mix forms of ordering within their actions and by collaborating with other actors. Mixing ordering can bridge the difference between centre and periphery as well as inner and outer circle by using appropriate forms for each – centres and inner circles lend themselves more to stable and peripheries and outer circles to fluid ordering. Actors also collaborate or compete among each other based on their different forms of ordering. When actors see the use of other forms of ordering than their own as threatening, security quickly deteriorates, while security improvements can be achieved through collaboration of differently ordering actors. Security is thus not the outcome of one form of ordering but of the complementarity of ordering within the security arena.

In Chapter 8, I scrutinize why actors should embed themselves in the arena in the first place and when they prefer detaching from everyday security. The question of embedding or detaching is particularly relevant to newly arriving peacekeepers but also poses itself to national militaries. Embedding into the arena forces an actor to engage in fluid ordering as everyday contact and spontaneous security events necessitate immediate reactions. Detachment, on the other hand, allows for more organized and directed engagement of the security arena through stable ordering. However, detachment can fuel rumours and allegations thereby deteriorating the overall security situation. Actors become torn between fulfilling local demands for robust intervention by accepting fluidity, on the one hand, and meeting international demands of stable ordering through detachment, on the other.

In the Conclusion, I sum up by establishing patterns of how actors order different parts of an arena and create security. I present the key findings along the four dimensions of the historical legacies of centre–periphery relations, distinctions between inner and outer circles, competition or complementation between stable and fluid ordering forms, and embedding or detaching interventions. My analysis contributes novel answers to questions about local security in conflict-affected countries and an original framework capable of facilitating future comparative analyses on the matter.

I aimed to keep this book as concise and accessible as the matter allows – that is, four years of research in nine localities across three countries in less than 250 pages. Nevertheless, for the reader with little time on her or his hands, I can recommend reading the theoretical Chapter 1 on the security arena, the key analytical Chapters 4 and 6 on the inner-outer circle and on fluid ordering, respectively, as well as the Conclusion, first. For all other readers, I promise to consecutively build a picture of the security arena in Africa from Chapter 1 to the Conclusion, wherein the reader will progressively become more familiar with the issues at hand, the people involved in dealing with them, and how this can deepen our understanding of local order-making.

1 | *Ordering the Security Arena*

In late November 2014, a South Sudanese military intelligence officer 'went missing' in the village of Garia, near Mundri town. Local security actors organized a joint visit to the village in early December. The situation was tense: what had the intelligence officer been doing in Garia? Was he keeping the peace by investigating the construction of a rebel training camp? Or was this yet another sign of the government's paranoid repression of the people of Mundri? I was sitting in the acting commissioner's office while state officials planned a trip to Garia to find out for themselves. They didn't expect me to understand Arabic and spoke quite freely. Two important things were happening: first, most of the discussions were about finding enough cars and fuel to even make the journey to Garia. Second, a National Security Services (NSS) officer repeatedly walked in and out of the office, fully engaged in the planning. When, on our request, the acting commissioner invited my colleague and me to join them on their trip, the National Security officer intervened: 'No, of course they cannot go.'[1]

The local government, chiefs, youths, police, wildlife forces, and national security thus left without us. Most significantly, the army, whose clarifications other stakeholders sought, did not appear as promised. My trip to Mundri was one of the first I undertook during this study and indeed these impressions raised many questions that would guide me throughout my years of research for this book. Who are all these actors in the local arena that come together for the trip to Garia? Who are the actors that are left out and why? Why are there so many complex steps involved in visiting a place that should, in principle, be under constant state authority? Why is the national government's role so contested in this local arena? And, most importantly, why is the situation so tense and security deteriorating? By travelling to eight further localities – thus a total of nine – I started developing arguments

---

[1] Notes on observations, Mundri, South Sudan, 6 December 2014.

along the difference between an inner and outer circle and of centre–periphery relations as well as the forms of ordering that hopefully can provide some answers to these questions.

Recent writings on public authority, areas of limited statehood, and oligopolies of violence have generated an awareness of the need to study security on a local level: they have put security at the heart of the analysis, taken crucial steps away from the country container bias and the state's monopoly of violence, and have engaged in comparative analysis. However, no studies within these strands have combined the three dimensions of security, at the local level, in comparison at the same time. While other concepts show great merit in their respective fields, I propose the security arena as a concept that can more adequately combine investigating the issue of security, within non-monopolized local contexts, and through a comparative lens. The security arena concept thus grants an entry point to pinning down the issue of security and the actors engaging in this issue.[2] Rather than looking simply at individuals and their actions, the security arena concept calls for the categorization of groups of individuals that comprise actors – such as a rebel group or a local police department – and the ways they relate to one another through myriad interactions, rather than merely in one-off encounters. This shall facilitate the analysis across a multitude of very different localities of how actors interact around the issue of security and, by doing so, engage in creating a political order. But, first, I turn to the merits and limits of existing strands of literature to draw lessons to be heeded for the security arena concept.

Authors who study areas of limited statehood conceptually differentiate statehood from governance.[3] This approach makes areas, rather than countries, the locus of interest. Areas of 'limited' statehood can be found even within established states and vice versa: so-called failed states, such as Somalia, can contain areas with some degree of statehood, e.g. Somaliland. Consequently, I will compare different localities across countries, rather than painting whole countries with one brush. The distinction between statehood and governance enables

---

[2] Cf. Kalyvas 2008: 397.
[3] Whereas governance describes the 'institutionalized modes of social coordination to produce and implement collectively binding rules, or to provide collective goods', statehood 'is defined by the monopoly over the use of violence or the ability to make and enforce central political decisions'; Risse 2011: 4, 9. See also Risse & Lehmkuhl 2007.

social scientists to analyse the provision of goods even when statehood is limited. In Somalia alone, examples of governance in areas of limited statehood range from indigenous justice provision[4] all the way to health services provided by external actors.[5] However, a differentiation of 'governance' from the struggle over a force monopoly – that is, statehood – only seems expedient for issues such as health and education. Who provides security and who holds the force monopoly, however, seem to be intricately linked.

Rather, another strand of literature more accurately describes these political struggles as the production of public authority:[6] some authors observe instances of bottom-up competitions for legitimacy between different power poles,[7] while others conceptualize hybrid orders between the modern state and indigenous customary actors and narratives.[8] Therefore, different actors and symbolic ideas form new institutions that are a mix of what can be called state or non-state and customary or modern.[9] This public authority is contested and re-evaluated in daily struggles over popular legitimacy that can be gained through public services provision and by invoking narratives of state and tradition. The level of security is explicated by the struggle over authority: security declines during processes of exclusion[10] and improves when attributions of public authority become accepted.[11] The public authority literature sets the bar of local knowledge very high, which has led to credibly grounded case studies. This study, however, sets its focus on gaining comparative insights from multiple cases.

The oligopolies of violence literature enables such comparison and still convincingly conceptualizes non-monopolistic settings. An oligopolistic setting is the antithesis to Max Weber's ideal-type state. First, it opens two of Weber's three dimensions to analytic debate: the territory and people of concern depend on the research question at hand. Second, rather than the prime dimension – the use of physical coercion – being monopolized, it is split between and competed over by different poles; it is oligopolized: 'Oligopolies of violence comprise a fluctuating number of partly competing, partly cooperating actors of violence of different quality.'[12] By assuming the rational choice both

---

[4] Simojoki 2011.   [5] Schäferhoff 2014.
[6] An overview of public authority literature is given in Hoffmann & Kirk 2013.
[7] Bierschenk & Olivier de Sardan 1997.   [8] Boege *et al.* 2009.
[9] See Lund 2006.   [10] Wimmer 2008, 2013.   [11] See Vandekerckhove 2011.
[12] Mehler *et al.* 2010: 10.

of beneficiaries and of providers, this model and comparable others then attempt to explain in which economic – fewer extractable resources means more security[13] – and market – the more monopolized the better[14] – contexts security improves or decreases.[15] Rational choice models have their limits, some of which the authors themselves admit. In the security market, paradoxically, more competition leads to less security[16] because the shares in the market diminish and become more competitive.[17] However, this is by far not always the case. More fragmented settings can also mean that no single group has the capability to engage in mass atrocities and the entrance of a strong peace-keeping force can at times halt violence quickly. While the market analogy thus grants a good entry point to analyse the inherently competitive nature of oligopolistic settings and the dangers of cartel formations,[18] the analysis would be hampered by seeing all actors as purely rational, security as a marketable good, and competition as having singular effects.

The underlying assumptions of these different strands only partly allow for the comparative analysis of local security in a non-monopolized political order. Theories of areas of limited statehood call for territorially differentiated intra-state comparison and a clear focus on the good that is provided. While this allows for the focussed comparison of certain goods, such as health, I do not find it expedient for the differentiation of security 'governance' from the struggle over the force monopoly that is statehood. Writers developing the concept of public authority propose in-depth evaluations of the social conditions and contexts influencing local struggles over order and security but thereby also make small- to mid-N comparison – that is, from two to around a dozen cases – difficult to achieve. The oligopolies of violence literature define parameters to investigate and compare different security markets but would reduce perceptions to surveys and comparative analysis to rational choice and market conceptions. Thus, while each strand of literature has particular merits, none of the four fulfils the specific three needs to conduct this analysis.

Drawing from the merits of each strand, the security arena provides a concept through which the researcher can (1) focus on perceived

---

[13] Branović & Chojnacki 2011: 562. [14] Lambach 2007; Mehler 2004: 545.
[15] Konrad & Skaperdas 2012. [16] Mehler *et al.* 2010: 10–11.
[17] See Branović & Chojnacki 2011: 560; Chojnacki & Branović 2011: 97.
[18] Lambach 2007: 7.

security (and not violence, conflict, or peace), (2) identify and analyse social and political aspects of local oligopolistic political orders, and (3) generalize gained insights on security provision through a comparative design.

Conceptualizing the Security Arena

I combine the issue of security with the actor-oriented concept of an arena[19] to facilitate a process analysis of the perceptions and agency of actors witnessed during my fieldwork. This concept enables each of the nine arenas in three different countries to be viewed in and of themselves, while at the same time granting common lines along which similarities can be unveiled.

Security as the core of the matter is an issue that naturally lends itself to the analysis of processes. A person can create security as well as undermine it. A person can feel secure or insecure as well as varying shades in between. Studying security is therefore inherently broader than studying conflict, as it opens avenues to people's perceptions,[20] and narrower than studying peace, which is heavily based on normative theory.[21]

The arena is a concept that brings together actors and their interactions around the spatial dimension of the locality under investigation. My comparison across the nine arenas builds on establishing similar knowledge of actors' characteristics and their interactions around the issue of security throughout the security arenas under scrutiny here. Based on the literature and insights from the field, *I define security as the felt durability of physical integrity and insecurity as the felt threat of physical harm.* I conclude that a security arena is composed of actors that interact on the issue of physical integrity around a predefined centre of study.

In 1995, Emma Rothschild published the article 'What Is Security?'.[22] In it, she traces the changing historical contexts of the contractual nature of security as the basis of politics and society and claims that, in the new liberal age, security concerns the conditions for personal liberty. In addition to her rich historical testimony, the article

---

[19] Cf. Long 1990.   [20] See Lind & Luckham 2017: 92.
[21] Cf. Galtung 1969; Lederach 1997, 2005; van Tongeren 2013.
[22] Rothschild 1995.

shows that security is a fluid concept that is hard to pin down. In fact, authors either define security vaguely[23] or narrow it down to the absence of physical threats to an individual or a societal group.[24] In both cases, many security studies investigate only insecurity and conflate this with the occurrence of conflict.[25] Defining one concept – security – by the absence of a second – conflict – begs the question as to why the author did not just analyse the latter concept from the start.

The ongoing debate on security in political science is driven by scholars who choose a deductive approach, including prominent contributions from the sub-discipline of international relations. Authors have analysed the creation of security communities,[26] the global privatization of security,[27] and the downward hybridization of state security.[28] Scholars of critical security studies problematize the political manipulation of the concept of security[29] and the discussion of human security proposes a widening of the term 'security' to domains beyond the physical.[30] David Baldwin proposed a guideline on developing security research. Two key questions – security for which values and for whom? – and five optional questions should specify the concept of security used for each respective study.[31]

While these recent studies have indeed questioned the state-centric viewpoint in security studies, they do not go far enough: security in the local arena needs to be judged from the bottom up, in and of itself, rather than as a deviation from state-centric norms.[32] In line with a recently proposed vernacular understanding of security,[33] I find that security has an experienced dimension and thus would ask: 'what makes you feel secure or insecure?'

I ask this question directly to interlocutors in the three countries to discover what matters in people's lives. A number of commonalities span individuals' responses across all three countries. First and foremost, statements on security and insecurity, in almost all instances, include the naming of actors: 'The presence of the army creates a lot of

---

[23] E.g. Abrahamsen & Williams 2008: 540; Baker 2010: 599; Hills 2014a: 166.
[24] E.g. Chojnacki & Branović 2011: 89; Mehler 2012: 50.
[25] E.g. Healy 2011; Joseph 2014; Mehler 2012.
[26] Adler & Greve 2009; Daase & Friesendorf 2010; Nathan 2006.
[27] Abrahamsen & Williams 2008, 2009; Krahmann 2008.
[28] Bagayoko *et al.* 2016.   [29] See Van Munster 2007.
[30] See Bajpai 2003; Owen 2004.   [31] Baldwin 1997.
[32] See Randeria 1999; Hönke & Müller 2012.   [33] Lind & Luckham 2017.

insecurity',[34] 'il y a un problème de sécurité qui se pose . . . des exactions de la part des hommes en armes',[35] and 'the peace in here is very well, sometimes youth makes problem, sometimes clan problems'.[36]

While respondents specifically name categories of actors, they are less clear in explaining how these actors impact security. In fact, many replies suggest something more than an immediate threat to physical integrity. Take this definition of security provided by the sub-prefect of Obo (CAR): 'La sécurité, c'est l'absence de troubles, d'actes qui font la confusion parmi la population; A fuir, à être inquiet de sa vie et sa famille. Vivre en paix, il n'y a rien de plus important que la paix.'[37] This absence of trouble is more than the absence of conflict proposed in the narrow definition of security from other studies. Aside from direct physical harm, trouble causes confusion, displacement, and worry. On the other side of the CAR, in Paoua, youth express themselves similarly: 'Depuis 2003 il n'y a pas de paix, il y a beaucoup de désordre.'[38] In South Sudan's Buseri, women describe their feeling of insecurity as 'people do not feel really secure, not even in the house. You have the feeling that anything can happen any time.'[39] A few thousand miles east, in Hargeisa's Daami quarter (Somaliland), youth frame their security worries almost identically, as: 'It can change at any time, any time people can fight and it can deteriorate, one moment it is good, another it is bad.'[40]

If insecurity is trouble, disorder, a feeling that anything can happen at any time, then the opposite can be found in Zeila, Somaliland: 'Security is very tight, it is different to other regions; if you go and your house is open and you go to Hargeisa or Boroma in the summer and come back it will still be left alone.'[41] In Somaliland's Baligubadle,

---

[34] Focus group discussion with Sultans, Raja, South Sudan, 27 November 2014.

[35] English translation: 'A question of security arises . . . exactions by men in arms', Interview with Catholic Abbot, Paoua, CAR, 24 February 2016.

[36] Focus group discussion with Women of Ilays women's group, Zeila, Somaliland, 16 May 2016.

[37] English translation: 'Security, it is the absence of trouble, of acts that create confusion among the population, to flee, to be worried about your life and family. To live in peace, there is nothing more important than peace', Interview with Sub-Prefect, Obo, CAR, 8 February 2016.

[38] English translation: 'Since 2003 there is no peace, there is a lot of disorder', Focus group discussion with Youth, Paoua, CAR, 28 February 2015.

[39] Focus group discussion with Women, Buseri, South Sudan, 25 November 2014.

[40] Focus group discussion with Women, Daami, Somaliland, 25 April 2016.

[41] Focus group discussion with Youths, Zeila, Somaliland, 18 May 2015.

people go one step further and call the security situation excellent, despite conflict being far from absent: 'Last year there was fighting between Arab and Ogadeen [clans]; … we collected diya [blood-money] for those persons … submitted [it] and the problem was solved.'[42] The acting commissioner of South Sudan's Mundri, in contrast, has the feeling that his security channels have broken down: 'Insecurity is caused by cattle keepers … When they came they were supposed to see the authorities … But they just sit wherever they want and give a hard time to our people … So people fear.'[43] People thus strongly relate security to how they perceive their security arena is ordered and feel insecure when the order breaks down, leaving malignant forces to cause 'trouble'.

Rather than proposing an objective standard, assessing security is based on subjective statements of respondents. Thus, *security is the felt durability of physical integrity and insecurity is the felt threat of physical harm*. In other words, subjective security is more than an immediate feeling; it involves an expectation of the future.[44] I positively define the term security (rather than conflating it with the absence of conflict), while not extending it beyond the realm of physical integrity, which would strain the argument. Physical integrity is not an easily quantifiable variable and thus the aspect of perception plays a crucial role. As indicated by the quotes above, perceptions of security are shaped by ascriptions to actors providing security or threatening harm and by the workings of the security arena between providing acceptable forms of ordering and promoting what people locally would perceive as disorder.[45] I will analyse this through the concept of the security arena.

Three theoretical and three empirical studies furnish the basis of the security arena concept: from the angle of theory, Nelson Kasfir's political arena; Stephen Hilgartner and Charles L. Bosk's public arena model; and, more recently, Tobias Hagmann and Didier Péclard's negotiating statehood.[46] On the empirical side, Thomas Bierschenk and Jean-Pierre Olivier de Sardan analysed the local political arena in

---

[42] Interview with Arab Sultan, Baligubadle, Somaliland, 30 May 2015.
[43] Interview with Acting Commissioner, Mundri, South Sudan, 8 December 2014.
[44] I thank an anonymous reviewer for this hint.
[45] Disorder exists when people feel there are no understandable avenues to seek security. This should not be confused with fluidity (or as many call it 'fragility'), which is a particular ordering form that leaves avenues of seeking security open to negotiation between involved actors and individuals.
[46] Kasfir 1976; Hilgartner & Bosk 1988; Hagmann & Péclard 2010.

the Central African Republic (CAR); Alice Hills, the Somali security arenas; and Manfred Öhm, local institutions and state-society relations in South Sudan.[47] All of these contain elements I want to draw on in this study.

While each study has a different emphasis, ranging from social problems[48] to activities,[49] all six studies centrally posit 'actors'. In fact, actors are the central constituents of the arena and therefore merit close attention.[50] Bierschenk and Olivier de Sardan place their analytic emphasis on three main power poles: the village chiefs, the farmers' organizations, and the churches.[51] Hagmann and Péclard prominently cited Bierschenk and Olivier de Sardan's empirical study of the CAR[52] when they developed their own negotiating statehood framework, in which they emphasize actors' resources and repertoires. Actors are varyingly described as 'personae', 'operatives', 'power brokers', 'power poles', and 'local institutions'.[53] Rather than suggesting that these studies all research the same issue under a different name, I argue that understanding differences between actors is in itself key to understanding how they impact security in the arena.

The image of an arena invokes ideas of action, struggles, and competition. Surprisingly, Kasfir's research on the political arena is the only study out of the six that grants an in-depth appreciation of actions by analysing how people enter and leave the political arena and how this affects political development.[54] In contrast to other conceptual terms, such as 'structure', 'setting', or 'order', the terms 'arena' and 'ordering' suggest a central emphasis on actions and processes. It is precisely through emphasizing actions that the security arena concept aims to appreciate human error, misunderstandings, and contradictory interpretations of one event. Through interactions, actors can form patterns that impact security processes in the arena. Actors engage and shape the security arena through varying forms of actions. Examples of this can be found in Öhm's case studies in Yambio and Thiet, in which he links war hierarchies

---

[47] Bierschenk & Olivier de Sardan 1997; Hills 2014a; Öhm 2014: chap. 4. Öhm's is the only study of the six that does not explicitly use the term 'arena'.

[48] Hilgartner & Bosk 1988.   [49] Kasfir 1976.   [50] Long 1990.

[51] Bierschenk & Olivier de Sardan 1997.   [52] Hagmann & Péclard 2010: 542.

[53] 'Personae' in Kasfir 1976. 'Operatives' in Hilgartner & Bosk 1988: 68–70. 'Power brokers' in Hills 2014a: 166. 'Power poles' in Bierschenk & Olivier de Sardan 1997: 443. 'Local institutions' in Öhm 2014: chap. 4.

[54] See Kasfir 1976.

and relations to the specific state-building trajectory of South Sudan, which ultimately led to what he calls the 'SPLA state', a political system in which the state and the Sudan People's Liberation Army (SPLA) armed group became inextricably linked.[55]

In sum, a security arena is composed of actors that interact on the issue of physical integrity around a predefined centre of study. The reduction of the security arena to two relational dimensions – actors and their interactions[56] – around a spatial dimension defining the research interest draws from existing works studying the arena while further specifying the concept. To situate comparative insights across arenas on how and why varying actors interact in different forms around the issue of security, I delve further into the characteristics and traits of actors and interactions. For the actors, these characteristics are their organization, attributions, and resource flows. Actors have interests that they pursue through varying strategies that can be observed as incidences of interaction in the arena.

Actors are the elementary units of the arena. In an area, geography takes precedence, while, in an arena, actors shape geography. Norman Long encouraged the actor-oriented viewpoint in order to move away from determinist interpretations of social change and to move towards identifying strategies and rationales.[57] What constitutes an actor in this study is based first and foremost on empirics: who are the people, groups, and institutions respondents talk about when discussing security? While respondents judge many actors as relevant to their security, some of these named actors do not officially concern themselves with matters of security but were described as relevant to respondents' perceived security. In their answers, respondents would list a variety of actors that span along a spectrum of very structured institutions, e.g. the US Army, to rather loose categorical descriptions, e.g. the youth or the farmers. While I include all mentioned actors, I attempt to distil from respondents' statements only those individuals and groups who are embedded with the power of agency.[58] Thus, while the 'youth' from the Daami quarter of Somaliland's capital might generally be categorized as threatening by some respondents, in analysing concrete

[55] Öhm 2014: 215. See also de Vries 2011.
[56] Individual actions of key security relevance are also investigated.
[57] Long 1990. [58] Meyer & Jepperson 2000. See also Förster 2015: 209–11.

incidences I can get closer to who is the driving force within this category – that is, where the agency lies. Actors endowed with agency can vary along characteristics of organizational structure, attributions, and resource flows (see Table 1.1).

Table 1.1 *Characteristics and examples of more stable and more fluidly ordering actors*

Institutionalized organization:	**Personalized organization:**
Members of the Somaliland army near Zeila are assigned there through national recruitment and deployment processes. No other person can become a member. Soldiers have designated roles, tasks, and rather regularized modes of interaction with other actors and individuals.	The Bongo chief of Buseri (South Sudan) holds strong personal authority. His role ranges from moral guidance to the integration of newcomers to conflict resolution. He deals with issues and actors as they come and as he sees fit.
Clear attributions:	**Diffuse attributions:**
The state judge of Bangassou (CAR) can thoroughly describe his official role as a provider of justice through deep knowledge of the country's penal code, all the while situating his official role within a deficient working context. Simultaneously, other respondents within the Bangassou arena would ascribe him a role similar to his self-depiction.	The vigilantes of the same town (Bangassou) are not able to clearly define their own role within the community – ranging from forceful action to engaging in intercommunity deliberation – and are highly contested within the arena: to some they are protectors, to others thugs.
Regularized resource flows:	**Ad hoc resource flows:**
The UN troops in the CAR and South Sudan have highly complex resource attribution systems from their contributing countries and the UN. They receive their salaries regularly, as well as food and lodging to sustain themselves. They are also fitted with weapons, vehicles, and technological infrastructure.	Elders of the Gabooye minority in Daami (Somaliland) receive only a token salary from the state. They depend on other business activities for their survival and have to negotiate with the (mostly poor) members of their community to collect contributions for the payment of compensation deals.

What respondents label an actor can range on the organizational spectrum from institutionalized, e.g. the US military in CAR's Obo, to personalized, e.g. quarter defence groups in CAR's Bangassou. On the one hand lie actors that assign membership, responsibilities, and codes of conduct according to rules and regulations. On the other end lie actors that assign membership and responsibilities according to individual leaders and personal decisions drive behaviour. Through the institutionalization of an actor, members ensure continuity even when composition fluctuates, while, within personalized actors, individual members have much more leeway for independent action.

When attributing characteristics to actors, different respondents at times used clear markers and recognized traits or would describe actors diffusely and in contradictory manners. I investigate how comprehensive self-attributions are and how such attributions are contested in the wider arena. Clear attributions from within and without are indicators of actor cohesiveness. Diffuse attributions, on the other hand, allow members to shape their actor as they see fit.

Actors seek both material and immaterial resources to pursue their agendas. Material resources in the security arena include arms, vehicles, and personnel. Immaterial resources include personal or institutional authority, laws, documents, and invoking the divine. Resource flows can range from regularized to ad hoc. Resources flow regularly depending on an actor's role (e.g. because someone is an officer of a certain rank) or due to ad hoc gains, such as leveraging fees at checkpoints, and often a mix of the two with different levels of importance.

Besides actors, inhabitants populate each arena. They are more than simple subjects to the activities of security actors. Inhabitants can become part of the actors through recruitment or by forming new actors themselves, they can grant and withdraw support and adherence to actors, and they debate which claims they perceive as legitimate.

The ways in which actors can relate to one another in the security arena are limitless. Respondents would voice discontent with another actor, threaten retaliation to an attack, describe a recent clash, speak of the possibility of dialogue or even a successful recent discussion, or mention the material goods they received from someone else or the support they are providing to others. In focus group discussions, participants could draw the arena as they saw it, with the aid of different shapes and colours of cardboard. I simplified the vast array of possible interactions to three broad forms of 'threaten', 'protect', and 'support' – very similar to the forms of interaction proposed by Ana Arjona.[59] In retrospect, respondents had difficulties distinguishing between 'protect' and 'support' and likewise, from a theoretical angle, the former can be subsumed as a sub-form of the latter. Broadly defined, threats include the (alleged) intent to engage in violence as well as the act itself.[60] Supportive acts are those in which an actor uses its own resources to further the aims of a second actor.[61] Both supportive and threatening acts always emanate from actors and deliberately or unintentionally target certain other actors and individuals of the arena. Nevertheless, both support and threats can be very diffuse and become more so the less people are able to attribute them to clearly defined actors, target groups, or the ability and willingness to follow through on them.

Actors can use multiple interactions along the spectrum, from supportive to threatening. An actor might use support towards certain actors and threats towards others or segments of the population. These interactions are the most visible forms of processes in the arena. They are visible expressions of the actors' larger strategies that they pursue to further underlying interests. However, the further one goes beyond observable actions, the less clearly a process can be pinned down. This study is empirical and therefore my emphasis lies on observable interactions based on (to me, mostly) unknown interests and strategies.

Take an auxiliary police officer who levies a fee by pointing a gun at a traveller. The threatening interaction can be observed but the strategy is less clear: by wearing a uniform, he might be signalling his continuing adherence to an actor and he might also want to retain this actor's influence (e.g. over travellers) in the arena. His underlying interest could be 'greed' because he wants more than he deserves – whoever defines this – or it could be 'grievance', such as when his salary is not paid or is insufficient to put food on the table and send his children to

---

[59] Arjona 2017.
[60] See the use of threats in the CAR: Lombard 2012 unpublished; Lombard 2016b.
[61] Numerous studies focus on why actors might choose to protect certain social groups in their bid to gain authority: Konrad & Skaperdas 2012; Mehlum 2002; Skaperdas 2001.

school.[62] Thus, while I speak of 'actors', my empirical data grants insights only into a collection of individual acts. However, through triangulation of multiple sources I distinguish truly one-off individual acts from those that are attributable to a larger actor – in other words, if the police officer did this once on his own terms or if the way the police established itself as an actor is what makes such acts of extraction possible and recurrent.

In sum, the security arena focusses on how actors of varying types interact through threatening and supportive actions. In a next step, when individual interactions are put together and seen in a broader picture, they can be analysed to discern the forms of ordering actors promote in the security arena on a spectrum ranging from fluid to stable ordering. When actors with different approaches to ordering meet in the arena, they can try to impose their form of ordering on the other or negotiate forms of cohabitation.

Stable to Fluid Ordering Spectrum

The varying settings of peace and conflict that countries experience are not just the outcomes of the decisions of actors but are part and parcel of the ways actors order their political system.[63] Too few scholarly contributions have searched for the order behind seemingly chaotic violence.[64] Those scholars who have investigated this have found varying but targeted aims behind even the most extreme forms of violence.[65] Kalyvas went as far as to pronounce 'order is necessary for managing violence as much as the threat of violence is crucial in cementing order'.[66] The ways actors create and undermine security can be seen as the directly observable building blocks of how actors order their larger political system. Thus, rather than looking at an established order, 'a set of predictable behaviours, structured by widely known and accepted rules which govern regular human interactions and behaviours',[67] I investigate the processes through which actors in the security arena try to bring about their desired order. In other words, I look at processes of ordering. Randall Collins, among other

---

[62] On greed and grievance: Berdal *et al.* 2000; Collier & Hoeffler 2004. And select critiques: Cramer 2006: 166–7; Nathan 2005; Wimmer *et al.* 2009: 317–20.
[63] Richards 2005.   [64] Worral 2017: 709.
[65] Mkandawire 2002; Kalyvas 2006; Valentino 2014.
[66] Kalyvas *et al.* 2008: 1.   [67] Worrall 2017.

Table 1.2 *Characteristics of the stable–fluid ordering spectrum*

	← Stable ordering	Fluid ordering→
Actor relations	Hierarchical and fixed	Horizontal and shifting
Depends on …	Regular, extensive resources	Occasional, minimal resources
Claim making	Seeking control	Staying elusive
Security impact	Predictability (structure)	Modifiability (agency)

sociologists, investigated at the micro level how individual and group interaction tend to escalate into violence and what factors most often inhibit situations from spiralling out of control.[68] The security arena concept remains micro-level enough to allow for the incorporation of individual and group-level spiralling processes,[69] while broad enough to compare varying cases.

Through the concept of the security arena, I propose a new process-driven concept to investigate how ordering impacts security (see Table 1.2). Stable ordering in the security arena becomes visible through hierarchical channels between actors and fixed distributions of responsibilities. Fluid ordering, on the other hand, is marked by horizontal actor relations with shifting distributions of responsibilities. To continuously enforce hierarchies and claim dominance over certain domains in the security arena, actors seeking to stably order the arena depend on regularized and, relative to other actors, strong resource flows. Actors that fluidly order the security arena can make do with occasional, lesser resources to navigate shifting horizontal relations without seeking dominance.

A key reason for choosing a type of ordering is the impact this has on security. While stable ordering lends more predictability, fluid ordering creates more modifiability. The debate on structure and agency is thus not only theoretical[70] but one that people live out on the ground. Some actors tend towards deliberately creating structures that will regulate methods to address issues of security in the arena: for instance, when the police are solely responsible for criminal cases, a person would have to challenge the order to seek justice for a murder with another

---

[68] Collins 2008; Collins 2012.   [69] See also Fearon & Laitin 1996.
[70] Cf. Giddens 1984.

influential actor he trusts. Other actors are more inclined to deliberately open flexible avenues for the pursuit of matters of security: in this case, a person could freely decide to report a thief to either the police, the gendarmerie, or an elder.

Most importantly, both forms of ordering coexist in an arena, either complementing one another or becoming the objects of violent struggles over the 'right' ordering forms.[71] Competition arises when an actor promoting stable ordering tries to extend its control into spheres of more fluidly ordering actors. Reciprocally, more fluidly ordering actors might feel threatened by the rising power of a dominant actor and seek to undermine its stabilizing claim. On the other hand, stable and fluid forms of ordering can cohabitate if the involved actors do not wish to take on the others' domains. They can even benefit each other, for instance when fluid ordering actors need a 'strong hand' or when stably ordering actors want to avoid the resource drain of all-encompassing control.

My analysis finds that neither side of the ordering spectrum provides more security per se. While stable ordering can provide predictable security, institutionalized, highly resourced, control-seeking actors can also create exactly the opposite – insecurity. Fluid ordering avoids predictable insecurity by opening modifiable pathways to seeking security. However, under constant flux, often with fewer resources, and the aim to stay elusive, fluid ordering actors cannot claim guarantees and therefore might enable the recurrence of insecurity. Security deteriorates when actors turn to violent activities in pursuit of their contending preferred forms of ordering. Security improves when actors agree on the ways in which (different parts of) the arena should be ordered. It is thus not fluid or stable ordering per se that explains variation of security among the nine cases but the struggles over contending forms of ordering. I investigate this hypothesis from the angle of the opportunities provided by the shape of the arena and from the angle of how actors order the arena in order to pursue their aims.

Actors and their interactions add relational dimensions to the arena that deliberately avoid confining analysis to predefined geographic containers. However, there is also a spatial aspect to the arena that remains hard to pin down. I argue that the arena is a scalable concept and the 'area' of the arena depends on deciding on a centre and a level

---

[71] Cf. Helmke & Levitsky 2004.

of analysis. My analysis principally revolves around 'local' arenas:[72] here, the midpoints are the administrative centres of the nine towns I selected for further studies. Who is and is not part of the arena are questions of ordering relevance. When I ask people downtown who matters to their security, all actors these people mention are considered, regardless of whether they are 100 metres or 100 kilometres away. The security arena is made up of actors that interact around a predefined core or, as I call it, an 'inner circle'. All areas beyond this inner circle are part of the outer circles.

The inner/outer distinction at the local level is mirrored by relations between centre and periphery on the national and international levels. While investigating local cases, there are certain decisions and pro-cesses that cannot be explained solely on the local level, because the arena in some instances is only a periphery to a higher-ranking centre of decision-making.[73] When travelling to the capital of each country, I analyse the national level arena and all actors and events become relevant that relate to politics of the nation – loosely, what happens within the countries' borders. When looking at the international level of the security arena, the centres become multiple: depending on the issue at hand, powerful neighbours, headquarters of international institutions, or transnational armed groups might draw the attention as varying centres of the arena.

Inner–Outer Circle

Scholars of borderland studies have put a strong emphasis on analysing local frontiers, linking local political trajectories to the ordering of international[74] and internal borders.[75] Igor Kopytoff, in particular, looks at the African frontier and depicts the distinct possibilities cre-ated by the relations between smaller centres and people moving to the frontier:[76] there, he argues, people can establish new political forma-tions aside the pre-existing, organized societies.[77] Achille Mbembe shows how a Cameroonian independence movement sought the possi-bilities of the 'maquis' to continue its agenda even during government repression. In the forests and bush, the revolutionary committees could

---

[72] A good example of a local arena study in the Ivory Coast is Heitz 2009.
[73] Cf. Mac Ginty & Richmond 2013: 773; Meagher 2012.
[74] De Vries 2012; Vaughan *et al.* 2013.   [75] Justin & de Vries 2019.
[76] Kopytoff 1987.   [77] Ibid.: 10f.

continue mobilizing the populace but, at the same time, disperse into the surroundings in the event of an attack by the much stronger colonial force.[78] The creation, handling, and erasure of dividing lines is thus a crucial object of study I wish to investigate through the concept of the security arena.

In the security arena, one possible delimitation can be drawn between an inner and an outer circle of the arena. This blurred line roughly relates to geographic indicators but goes beyond physical markers by focussing on the possibility of interaction. In Map 1.1,[79] we see an agglomeration of buildings at the bottom which is Baligubadle (the inner circle). To the south it borders Ethiopia (dashed line); towards the north the density of houses quickly thins. I have cropped the satellite image at the northern exit and show only a few hundred metres of the twenty-kilometre-wide plain of Gumburaha Banka (the outer circle) that one has to cross before reaching the top part of the image, Gumburaha village. Within the image I have marked the buildings of several key security institutions, the two market squares, and an exemplary temporary settlement in the grazing plains.

The inner circle is characterized by physical proximity, which creates the potential for daily interaction between inhabitants of different social groups, the interdependency of livelihoods, and the existence of numerous personal links between members of the different actors and social groups. Therefore, security in the inner circle is based on the necessity of continuous cohabitation.

The outer circle, on the other hand, is marked by irregular interaction or interaction based on particular social links (relatives) or activities (trade). Interviewees ascribe rumours, unclear intentions, and inconsistent labels to actors in the outer circle. Such rumours are facilitated by the scarcity of information in the countryside compared to the city and have played key roles since the French Revolution[80] to current spikes in violence.[81] Security in and from this surrounding sphere of the unknown is based on being able to face the irregular (rather than everyday security challenges).

While the dividing line between the two circles often has visible demarcations on the ground, such as rivers, forests, deserts, and population density, humans shape these natural boundaries to order the

---

[78] Mbembe 1996.   [79] Map data: Google, Digital Globe (2016).
[80] See Lefebvre 2014 [1932]: 157ff.   [81] Bhavnani *et al.* 2009.

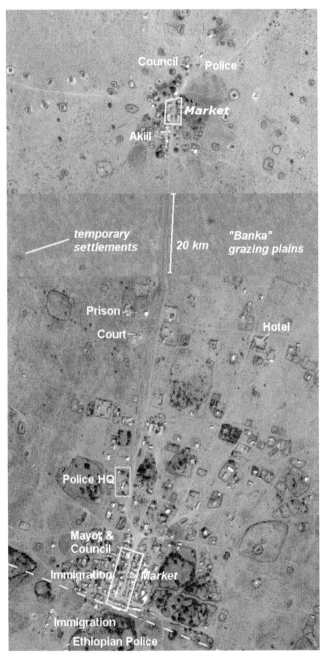

Map 1.1 Baligubadle town, Banka plains, and Gumburaha village, Somaliland

arena. I thus focus my analysis on the struggles revolving around the drawing, crossing, and at times erasing of the dividing line.

Centre–Periphery

Local arenas are not isolated contexts but relate to varying centres. Without a view beyond the local, some aspects of security would be impossible to understand,[82] such as why states send forces to the respective locality (or refrain from this), who deploys and funds peace-keepers, or how armed groups move in and out of local arenas in the changing national context of peace and conflict. I argue that there are two key elements to the relations between centre and periphery: the degree of a connection and the way of creating such a connection.

Jeffrey Herbst, in his landmark work, has shown that states do not necessarily seek to control their hinterlands, especially when popula-tion density is low and the security imperative for the regime is minimal.[83] It is thus more fruitful to investigate centre–periphery rela-tions that take into account the particulars of African state formation with a view both to the past and to the present. Kopytoff proposes looking at the extension of control and authority as frontiers. This grants a dual lens to the centre, which extends along frontiers, and to the frontiersmen and women who leave the centre for the particular opportunities of the frontier.[84] There are actors that deliberately seek to leave the range of the central state to avoid the potential violence and extraction emanating from it.[85]

Some actors engage multiple levels, in what Klaus Schlichte and Alex Veit called 'coupled arenas'.[86] Intervention forces and inter-national non-governmental organizations (NGOs) thus have to negotiate their actions where they have their headquarters, at the national level in the intervened country and on a local level, where they carry out their programmes. This often creates unintended side effects as the decisions made by stakeholders acting within the headquarter or national context are carried out in the local arena, which operates under different political logics. Some people use these different logics to their advantage. Actors can use the periph-eries to position themselves beyond the control of central powers to

---

[82] Luckham 2017: 114.   [83] Herbst 2000.   [84] Kopytoff 1987.
[85] Scott 2009.   [86] Schlichte & Veit 2007.

expropriate the populace and prepare for an assault on the capital.[87] 'The standard international legal practice almost always equates sovereign power with control of the capital city',[88] which makes it such a lucrative target in the first place but also distinguishes it from large areas with low population densities that central powers have difficulties in reining in.[89] Centrality and peripherality have to do with access and the closeness of people and actors.[90] Both sides have agency to interact with one another[91] and use the particularities of their sphere in the bargain. The same applies to the international sphere, where nations find themselves in more central or peripheral positions of economic chains and political decision-making.[92] Far from being the secondary choice of actors, James C. Scott has shown that leaving the centre to live in the peripheries can be a deliberate choice for people seeking to avoid the perils of control, such as taxes and conscription.[93] While the centre and periphery possess different characteristics, they are always in relation to one another and with some degree of friction, as the people in the periphery evading central control 'represent ... a constant temptation'.[94]

Central actors can choose to relate to the peripheries on a spectrum ranging from imposing their will – be it through governance or extraction – to meeting peripheral people for negotiation.[95] Mamdani argues more towards the former when he discussed how central powerbrokers impose themselves on rural subjects.[96] David K. Leonard more towards the latter end of the spectrum, when describing how urban African elites mediate their relations to the periphery through community-based social contracts.[97] In analysing the centre–periphery dimensions relevant to the local security arenas, I focus on the historical evolution of the state and its security apparatus. The relevance of the state and the structure of security authorities vary greatly among the three countries and in large part this variation can be traced back to long-held economic structures and sociopolitical settings – as Fernand Braudel calls them, the 'moyenne' and 'longue durée'.[98]

---

[87] Mkandawire 2002.   [88] Herbst 2004: 302.   [89] Herbst 2000: 145–6.
[90] Langholm 1971: 276.   [91] Kalyvas 2003: 486.   [92] Gidengil 1978.
[93] Scott 2009.   [94] Ibid.: 6.
[95] Cf. Doornbos 2010; Hagmann & Péclard 2010; Kasfir 1976: 161ff; Schomerus *et al.* 2013.
[96] Mamdani 1996.   [97] Leonard 2013.   [98] Braudel 1980.

The View of State, Non-State, and International Actors

Stable ordering, fluid ordering, and the struggle over their cohabitation can be assessed from multiple angles by looking through the lenses of state, non-state, and international actors. I make a distinction between actor types also because this was a key differentiation made by respondents on the ground. While such descriptions are not always clear and entirely distinct, I try to differentiate them for analysis. State actors are those that primarily claim to draw their means to order the security arena from the official state's laws and resources. Non-state actors are those that derive their means to order primarily directly from the people and from resources they extract without a detour over the state. International actors are those that primarily derive the resources and personnel to order the arena from outside the borders of the country they are involved in. While each can use aspects of other types – such as a state governor being a locally supported person or a traditional chief receiving a small state salary – assigning a type depends on what the actors themselves and other respondents perceive as the main source of making claims to ordering the security arena.

The African state has acquired a bad reputation. Jean-François Bayart and colleagues speak of its 'criminalization', in which state leaders mix political influence with economic stakes to gain a profit in illegal sectors.[99] Patrick Chabal and Jean-Pascal Daloz have famously concluded that 'Africa works' only for elites, who use 'disorder as political instrument'.[100] Especially in regard to the three states under scrutiny here, the devastating impact state actors can have on security becomes obvious. In the CAR, rulers have either neglected the peripheries or met them with extreme brutality. In South Sudan, where violence is used by multiple actors, state security forces are committing some of the most horrific atrocities of the ongoing civil war. Somaliland's declaration of independence in 1991 was a response to the Somali state's indiscriminate use of violence against Somaliland's people, including its bombing of Hargeisa in 1988. Whatever the alleged particularities of the African state, the state in its

---

[99] Bayart *et al.* 1999.
[100] Chabal & Daloz 1999. On why their theory does not hold up in the CAR, see de Vries & Mehler 2019.

bureaucratized form can also create violent open spaces in which state employees commit horrifying atrocities.[101] Some authors nevertheless call for a strengthening of the state as the best way to stabilize African states and recreate security.[102]

I propose that the state is neither, in itself, problematic nor helpful in creating security. Rather it acts as a powerful narrative around which actors position themselves and play out their struggles over ordering the arena.[103] State actors are defined, on the one hand, through the bureaucratic narrative of their position based in documents, laws, appointments, and officialized hierarchies – processes that tend towards the stable ordering end of the spectrum. On the other hand, state actors use their assigned roles to create fluidity to avoid the disintegration of their forces and for the ability to create a personal profit from an assigned position.[104]

State actors can create security through stable enforcement when they have the means and will to provide for predictable security. However, state actors undermine security when, through their enforcement, they weaken other actors that local inhabitants prefer entrusting with their security. Especially under the observed contexts of resource scarcity, state actors can also create security by facilitating flexible resolutions outside the official law.[105] This fluidity can also undermine security, however, when state actors use unaccountable violence against civilians.[106] Third, state actors and their officially stable ordering narrative coexist with other actors and forms of ordering in all nine cases, either competing or complementing one another. I thus also take a close look at the ordering forms of non-state actors.

Non-state actors that attempt to order the arena always have to relate in some way to the presence of state actors and their claims to a force monopoly. Within the distinct ways non-state actors impact the security arena, they often mix fluid and stable forms of ordering. State and customary institutions interact in 'processes of mutual

---

[101] See Baberowski 2015.
[102] E.g. Mengisteab & Daddieh 1999; Fukuyama 2004; Call & Wyeth 2008.
[103] Cf. Lund 2006: 686.
[104] For the example of Chad: Debos 2011; Debos 2016.
[105] I also heed the call of Niagalé Bagayoko *et al.* who lament a shortage of research on 'official security institutions, including the informal networks around them, and the complex ways they interface with non-state actors' (2016: 20).
[106] See, for example, Marielle Debos' and Joël Glasman's work on the fluidity of state security forces: Debos & Glasman 2012: 21.

diffusion'.[107] Hybrid governance scholars analyse such organizational arrangements[108] and Christian Lund labels the outcome 'Twilight Institutions'.[109] Bruce Baker investigated how state and non-state actors link up to the benefit of overall security provision.[110] Such linkages can mediate the fact that historical social contracts for most Africans are not between the state and individuals but between the state and communities[111] – non-state actors can thus act as intermediaries. But I heed Kate Meagher's words of caution: 'The condemnation of non-state order as institutionally destructive has been replaced by its celebration as a vehicle of embedded forms of order and authority.'[112] I therefore look at both sides of the coin of local non-state ordering: processes of improving and of reducing security.[113]

Different non-state actors should also be distinguished by whether or not they are armed. Most interview partners from non-state actors in this research were unarmed and situated in the inner circle. On the other hand, concerning armed actors, a lot of information was gained not *from* them directly but *about* them from other respondents in the arena – which is nevertheless very important as it says much about inhabitants' perceptions of security in the arena, which is the aim of this study. Armament grants non-state actors a very direct impact on the security arena as a means to impose authority on others and to use as stakes in negotiations. Armament, however, also makes actors a more visible target. Unarmed non-state actors have difficulties imposing their authority, which is often based on tradition or religion, when faced with armed actors. They thus have to rely on negotiation but also can have more freedom in doing so, as they can move about the arena and engage a wide variety of actors without being perceived as a threatening target. Non-state actors relating to state and international actors bring the need for cohabitation between fluid and stable modes of ordering to the fore. Actors can be at odds with one another when they attempt to force their way of ordering on the other but they can also complement each other when they use their different abilities of ordering to their mutual advantage.

---

[107] Boege *et al.* 2009: 17.   [108] Meagher *et al.* 2014; Albrecht & Moe 2015.
[109] Lund 2006.   [110] Baker 2010.   [111] Leonard 2013: 1.
[112] Meagher 2012: 1074.
[113] Cf. the relation between hybrid governance and security: Bagayoko *et al.* 2016; Luckham & Kirk 2013.

The literature describes particularities of non-state actors ranging from personalized rule to traditional institutions. On the personalized end of the spectrum, Mats Utas finds that 'Big Men are alternative governors of *peopled infrastructures*', who hold personal power, the ability to create a following, and the informal ability to assist people privately.[114] Conflicts are fought by Big Men over socioeconomic opportunities rather than politicized identities.[115] Similarly, William Reno describes how elites deliberately undermine state institutions to keep rivals off balance and channel resources through personal patron–client relations.[116] While these rivalries at times give rise to clashes of arms, fluid ordering lends particular possibilities to unarmed non-state actors as well. The literature on Somaliland's pathways of providing flexible security resolution apart from the state and its written laws is especially proliferate.[117] Roger MacGinty proposes traditional peace-building to be commonly based on moral authority, public elements, storytelling, relationships, and local resources[118] – in other words, aspects that are more on the fluid end of ordering the security arena.

Some non-state actors attempt to position themselves more stably in the arena. Paul Jackson describes how warlords present themselves as alternative governors when the state collapses[119] and other scholars scrutinize how rebels with initially personalized rule start erecting state-resembling institutions to generate sufficient legitimacy to stay in power.[120] However, 'conflating rebel governance with state order forces analysts to awkwardly transpose the state-formation framework onto an actor that actively resists the state's attempts to project order within its ascribed territory'.[121] Therefore, other scholars prefer ana-lysing rebel governance as a distinct form of finding ways to regulate social life.[122] The focus of the literature on (armed) rebel governance should not mask the fact that unarmed non-state actors can also create lasting, regularized institutions that can be a key avenue for inhabitants seeking predictable security aside the state.[123]

---

[114] Utas 2012: 6. Emphasis in original.   [115] See Utas 2012.
[116] See Reno 2002; Reno 1998.
[117] See Hoehne 2011; Renders 2012; Schlee 2013; Simojoki 2011.
[118] Mac Ginty 2010a: 349f.   [119] Jackson 2003.
[120] Mampilly 2011; Péclard & Mechuloan 2015.   [121] Mampilly 2011: 36.
[122] Arjona *et al.* 2015.
[123] Hobsbawm & Ranger 1983; Hoehne 2011; Logan 2013; Molomo 2009.

The discussion of the 'responsibility to protect' has given international actors strong leverage to intervene in states that are unwilling or unable to protect their own populace.[124] As all three countries are ranked at the bottom of fragility indexes and conflict is ongoing, interveners have entered each of them.[125] However, the impact on the local security arena can vary starkly from mission to mission and contingent to contingent. These intervening actors have to position themselves towards the actors already present on the ground, including stable and fluid ordering actors.

From a stable ordering perspective, security dilemmas between consolidated actors are key to understanding insecurity.[126] The logic of power-sharing draws from this international theory assumption by seeking the inclusion of all competing poles.[127] However, Denis Tull and Andreas Mehler point to the rather crude side effect that international enforcement of power-sharing agreements between warring parties creates incentives for would-be leaders to take up arms in order to obtain a position in government.[128] Severine Autessere warns that internationally enforced peace-building shows a disregard for local causes and dynamics of conflict.[129] International actors viewing struggles through stable ordering lenses can indeed miss out on other more fluid aspects of the security arena.

Roger MacGinty therefore calls for international actors to tackle fluid aspects of local security head-on.[130] Bottom-up peace-building cannot simply be enforced top-down but necessitates constant dialogue and the acceptance of alternative modes of ordering.[131] Jeni Whalan shows that peacekeepers need to seek local legitimacy to have a positive impact on the ground but this fluid embedding is counteracted by the institutionalized mode of peace operations.[132] The fluid embedding of peacekeepers in the local security arena remains under-researched and will thus form a main part of this book.

Unfortunately, international peacekeepers tend to undermine fluid ordering actors and contribute to a (mostly imagined) stable state. While internationals should engage the whole spectrum of actors and their ordering modes to engage security on the ground, they often revert

---

[124] ICISS 2001. [125] At least south-central Somalia, not Somaliland.
[126] Kühn 2011. [127] See Lijphart 1969; Wolff 2012.
[128] Tull & Mehler 2005; Mehler 2013.
[129] Autesserre 2010: 22–3. See also: Veit 2010. [130] Cf. Mac Ginty 2012.
[131] See Mac Ginty 2010b. [132] Whalan 2017.

to 'bunkerization' to protect their modes of ordering by separating themselves from the wider local arena.[133] Whether or not an intervention can have a positive effect on security on the ground depends on how they engage the entire spectrum of actors and ordering forms in the arena. Intervention forces can have an immediately positive impact on security when they forcefully engage a violent actor and push it from the arena. However, with limited local knowledge such enforcements can also have negative repercussions on social cohesion and lead to the creation of new violence. More fluid ordering by internationals can allow for adaptation to the local context. However, fluid intervention also provides foreign soldiers with opportunities to pursue ulterior motives, such as seeking personal profit or committing sexual abuse. Interventions are particular in that a new actor with distinct forms of ordering enters an arena with already established actors and modes of ordering. Interventions can have a positive impact on security when these new interveners are willing to engage the entirety of power dynamics in the arena, while they risk creating insecurity when they are biased towards certain actors of the arena.

Methodology

Although the social sciences, and especially political science, bear a long tradition of comparative studies, local security has seldom been the object of such research.[134] I attempt this through the analytic approach of intra-regional Comparative Area Studies (CAS).[135] The CAS approach is used by scholars who wish to combine profound area knowledge with comparison across cases. Theory-building based on contextual knowledge can be advanced by challenging European and North American inventions with comparative, empirical observations on the ground.[136] Qualitative field research on the security arena necessitates a degree of flexibility and CAS present a rather broad notion that can be filled with methods and analytical tools fitted to the research question at hand. This section will discuss the challenges of

---

[133] Duffield 2010; Fisher 2017.
[134] I thank Dominik Balthasar for this hint. Parts of this section were published at an earlier stage as a working paper: Glawion 2017.
[135] See Ahram 2011; Mehler & Hoffmann 2011; Ahram *et al.* 2018.
[136] Basedau & Köllner 2007: 113.

case selection, the gathering of qualitative data on the security arena, and its structured analysis.

Case Selection

This analysis has two levels of cases: three country contexts – the CAR, South Sudan, and Somaliland – as well as nine local case studies as seen in Map 1.2 from west to east: Paoua, Bangassou, and Obo; Raga, Buseri, and Mundri; Zeila, Baligubadle, and Daami. These cases are broadly under-researched. In Somaliland, Zeila had not featured in any renowned publication on the country, whereas Baligubadle and Daami are also seldom researched[137] compared to the more often studied areas in the east of Somaliland.[138] In South Sudan the cases of Mundri, Buseri, and Raja have been discussed in few publications in recent years.[139] Save for some rare publications, the CAR has not been the subject of any recent published academic analyses grounded in fieldwork.[140] Apart from reports on armed groups around Obo and Paoua,[141] the CAR localities examined in this book have not been the focal point of academic research.

While ideally case selection of small- to mid-N comparison – that is from two to around a dozen cases – should be non-random to enable representativeness and causal leverage,[142] studying security brings with it logistical and safety issues that set limits to theoretical considerations. The countries were selected according to alleged commonalities in the reduced role of the central state in the life of its people: all three countries have only minimal public services and an undiversified economy. Numerous indices rank all three cases as some of the most fragile in the world[143] and the Fragile States Index has even ranked them as the

---

[137] A sole exception on Daami is Vitturini 2017.
[138] See most prominently the writings by Markus Hoehne: Hoehne 2011; Hoehne 2015.
[139] See Blocq 2014; de Vries 2015.
[140] E.g. Carayannis & Lombard 2015; Lombard 2016a; Marchal 2016.
[141] Cakaj 2015; Spittaels & Hilgert 2009; Chauvin & Seignobos 2014.
[142] Gerring 2008: 645.
[143] See the Fragile States Index: Messner 2017; the indices of the Organisation for Economic Co-operation and Development (2015) 'States of Fragility 2015': www.keepeek.com/Digital-Asset-Management/oecd/development/states-of-fragility-2015_9789264227699-en#; And Monty G. Marshall (2017) 'State Fragility and Warfare in the Global System 2016': www.systemicpeace.org/warlist/warlist.htm.

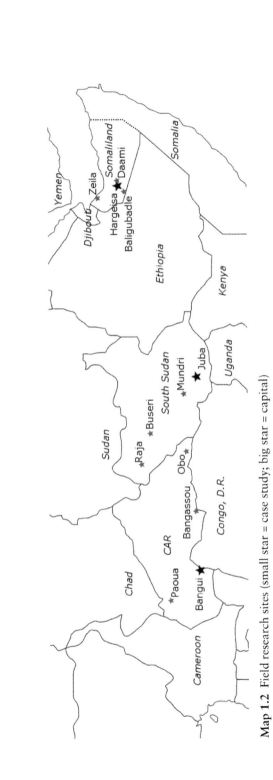

Map 1.2 Field research sites (small star = case study; big star = capital)

three most fragile states for four years in a row.[144] These rankings, however, are deceptive as the countries vary in sociodemographics, culture, resource potentials, and, most crucially, in political outlook.[145] The main comparison will not be of countries, however, but of local security arenas. I thereby heed the call for a move down from the national level and towards bottom-up local comparisons.[146]

Within each country, the cases were selected broadly along three theoretical considerations: first, variation on the sociospatial distance to the capital or a large administrative centre. A peripheral setting enables the investigation of local dynamics more clearly, as those holding power at the central national level do not view the locality as a key part of their rule.[147] When the willingness to provide state security (or other significant services) to the population is limited, alternative providers and constellations come forth more clearly. All selected cases can be considered peripheral: some more obviously through their enormous distances from the capitals – Obo and Raja lie more than 1,000 kilometres from their respective capitals. Others, such as Daami quarter in Somaliland's capital, were selected due to prior knowledge of the cases and their specific political and economic marginalization.[148] A second selection criterion was some limited variation on population size. This enabled talking to most of the relevant security stakeholders, whereas in large cities finding a manageable pool of respondents could create a selection bias. Third, the cases varied according to the presence or absence of different forms of security actors, most notably government institutions, alternative security actors, and international peacekeepers. Therefore, the varying relevance of each actor, its specific impact on security, and relational setting within the arena could be compared. And, finally, the cases were varied along their levels of security. Somaliland was added to the two original countries to include cases with rather successful

---

[144] Messner 2017. See online data centre for rankings on all measured years: http://fundforpeace.org/fsi/data/.

[145] See Glawion *et al.* 2019.

[146] E.g. Ansorg 2017; Mac Ginty & Richmond 2013; Mehler 2009a; Schroeder & Chappuis 2014.

[147] Heitz 2009: 112; Pouligny 2009: 5–9.

[148] As Jeremy Lind and Robin Luckham suggest, margins 'might exist in distant borderlands as well as the neighbourhoods of capital cities', depending on social and political factors (2017: 93).

security provision at a time when both South Sudan and the CAR had fallen back into heavy conflict.

The deliberately sought-out absence of a monopoly of force often coincided with contesting claims by various groups, creating security constraints for the researcher. Logistical issues, often linked to security threats such as roadblocks, further reduced the amount of possible research localities. Case selection confined by security and logistics had repercussions on the research design: avoiding cases with high levels of violence or latent instability could result in bias towards a rather optimistic look on non-state alternatives. Overcoming logistical constraints on the ground by aerial routes was often facilitated by large NGOs or international organizations, bringing with them a significant outside influence that again impacted statehood on the ground. In actual practice, cases were thus often selected according to, first, (subjectively) interesting security dynamics gathered on the respective locality on arrival in the capital and from talking to numerous locals and internationals. These cases were then narrowed down by the possibility to get there and the feasibility of safely conducting research. This selection calls the representativeness of cases into question and therefore the generalizability of the findings, which I discuss further in the 'Limitations' section.

Data Generation

I investigate each of the nine local arenas as a 'semi-autonomous' field that is bound by the ordering processes around the issue of security but is nevertheless related to other arenas and larger society.[149] Viewing a case as an 'arena' incorporates the social space principle, which states that political struggles are about making an explicit consensus out of individual thoughts[150] – hence the focus on actors and their actions in the arena. Field theory as 'an analytic approach, not a static formal system' informs this analysis of arena as a quest to make 'complex social phenomena intuitively accessible'.[151] A key lesson from field theory that also applies to gathering data in the security arena is to reflect on the positionality of the researcher himself.[152] Indeed, my position and mobility in the arena varied, which changed the type

---

[149] See Moore 1973: 722.   [150] See Bourdieu 1985a: 729; Bourdieu 1985b.
[151] Martin 2003: 24, 36.   [152] See Martin 2003: 25.

and breadth of data I received. With these lessons in mind, I collected information through interviews, focus groups, non-participatory observation, and monthly reports in each of the nine local arenas. This array of methods did justice to the explorative nature of this research endeavour due to access restraints, concerns for security, and the novelty of the research approach.[153]

Data was gathered during field research trips to each of the three countries and each of the nine localities: one pilot field trip of one month's length each and another research trip of two months each one year later (plus a short follow-up visit to the capitals of the CAR and Somaliland in the third year). After the first research stay, further research trips to South Sudan had to be cancelled due to an upsurge in conflict in all selected research sites and the capital. On average, I spent four months in each country and two to three weeks per locality. Considering this relatively brief period per case, I used site-intensive methods that aim at generating in-depth case knowledge, while avoiding the conceptual baggage and time constraints of ethnography.[154] Lotje de Vries and I conducted most of the field studies in the CAR and South Sudan together and Andreas Mehler briefly joined us for research in the CAR. Having a team of two during most field stays was an incommensurable benefit to data validation: combined interview questions could probe broader and deeper, complexities were immediately discussed thereafter, and the at times draining conflict environment was jointly navigated. Just as the benefits of co-conducting fieldwork surpassed my expectations, likewise did splitting each field study into multiple trips: interviewees were positively surprised by my kept promise to return. Discussions gained a whole new level of trust and I could refer back to issues that were too sensitive the previous year.

Interviews with members of security actors and the populace offered rapid, albeit subjective, insights into the issues at stake in the security arena and into broader security perceptions.[155] Interview partners were selected in a snowball fashion: official state authorities had to be visited first and they would recommend (and authorize) talking to further state forces, such as the police, army, and gendarmerie. Additional interview partners were selected according to the names and stories presented during interviews, group discussions, and as

[153] See Cramer *et al.* 2011; Malejacq & Mukhopadhyay 2016; Read *et al.* 2006.
[154] Kapiszewski *et al.* 2015.   [155] See Rathbun 2008.

suggested by local research assistants. More than 300 interviews were conducted. Each interview lasted between one and two hours, and, if permitted, interviews were audio-recorded. The interviews were not transcribed but notes were typed on the spot in near-exact wording (depending on the rapidity of the speaker). While I was fluent in two languages – English and French – and attempted to deepen my knowledge of further research languages – Arabic and Somali – many interviews had to be translated by local research assistants. I will thus use the information provided in the interviews only within the specific context it was given and not to interpret the specific usage of language.

Focus group discussions were the second most important method.[156] During the first trips, discussions with broadly defined societal groups (such as youth, women, elders) gave a sense of the contested security issues in the arena and provided the selection of further individual interview partners. During the second trip, participants were selected along certain key population groups (varying from arena to arena by ethnicity, age group, gender, or geographic categories) to enable the creation of comparable actor mappings. To do so, an attempt was made to select two groups of participants from different sides of the most salient sociopolitical divide and a third group of fairly neutral or mixed inhabitants: in Paoua (CAR), for example, youth from the ethnic Tali, a group of women from the ethnic Kaba, and a group of radio journalists. Such selection was not always straightforward. Research assistants would at times interpret selection criteria differently and some participants did not show up or left early. The discussion would proceed for close to two hours, during which the participants created a map of their perceived security arena with the aid of questions and flash cards along the following steps (see Figure 1.1): (1) introduction; (2) societal groups on oval shapes; (3) actors on rectangular shapes; (4) closeness of actors and groups; (5) and (6) interactions of threat, protection, and support on red, green, and blue arrows, respectively; (7) security incidence examples; and (8) perceptions of security. Continuously asking for real-life examples helped guide the abstract discussion. It was particularly insightful to have numerous focus groups discuss the same recent example of a key event – e.g. the arrest of an armed group leader – to gauge different people's interpretations.

---

[156] See Hennink 2007; Ryan *et al.* 2014.

Figure 1.1 Steps of actor mappings

A total of around fifty group discussions were conducted, that is, on average three actor mappings and three general group discussions per locality.

Monthly reports written by local research assistants recorded changes within each locality in small (monthly) increments. In these two-page reports, the assistant first filled out all changes in actor hierarchies, changes of key elites, the departure or arrival of new actors and populations, and some proxy indicators, such as fuel and sugar prices. Second, the report included security-relevant events of the month to build a continuous security event log for each locality. Some research assistants kept track of every slightest change in the locality, while others only mentioned large events. Also, the reports were often irregular due to a lack of internet or mobile phone connectivity and, in the cases of South Sudan, they were interrupted completely due to the resumption of war. At the very least, these reports aided in bridging the gap between the first and the second trips, facilitating the tracing of exact changes within the security arena. On top of that, they were often the sole source for triangulating perceived security with actual events in the locality, as international media seldom covered the cases studied here. In total, more than seventy-five monthly reports complemented information gathering during periods away from the field.

Participatory observation and primary documents of intercommunal meetings and security measures were used as a final measure to triangulate narratives with actions. Owing to the relatively short stay in each locality, the insights gained from observations are limited. Nevertheless, interviewees were always sought out in their office or home (area) to gain a glimpse of the context within which they act. Thus, I visited the prison in Baligubadle and can compare its well-constructed building with the padlocked shack at the commissariat in Obo. Among others, I also met mediation committees in the CAR and elders in Somaliland and was given written documents on their conflict resolution activities. In total, around fifty primary documents, of which the number per arena ranges widely, contribute to the analysis.

Nevertheless, some actors, such as armed contraband groups, refused an exchange and state forces denied access to certain areas and actors, making the gathered data biased towards actors and inhabitants on the safer side of the arena. I will therefore indicate every actor whose members did not have the opportunity to voice their viewpoint with an asterisk (*) in actor mappings as well as other tables and figures. This confinement overlaps with a theoretical distinction between the inner and outer circle, as outer-circle actors were often harder to reach.

Data Analysis

The three countries – CAR, Somalia, and South Sudan – are most similar in a key characteristic:[157] the state holds no legitimate monopoly on the use of force throughout its territory and over all its people. Comparable indicators on low state budgets, minimal public service provision, and dire economic outlooks further support seeing the three countries as most similar. At the same time, they vary strikingly along security outcomes, ranging from rather high security in some parts of Somaliland to very low security in large parts of South Sudan and the CAR.

The local arenas are often very dissimilar to one another,[158] varying in population size, distance to the capital, and variety of actors. Nevertheless, certain processes in the security arena share remarkable commonalities: state actors use similar references to claim a monopoly on authority, while non-state actors use similar processes to find pockets of self-government outside the state, and peacekeeping missions adapt in comparable manners to very different surroundings. Processes in the arena play out both in relation to the context they find themselves in[159] and to more generalizable trends seen across contexts.[160]

I analyse processes in the security arenas to find patterns that resemble each other across different security arenas.[161] Process tracing tests alternative explanations of the effect by tracing events in fine detail.[162] This method enables a refutation of symmetric causality – bidirectional relation between cause and effect – and an understanding of the cause–effect relationship. I deliberately abstain from formulating hypotheses and testing them because the data I gain through the very explorative nature of my research does not support such an endeavour. Rather than

---

[157] Cf. Brady 2008; Gerring 2008: 668–70; Mahoney 2000: 399–402.
[158] Cf. Basedau & Köllner 2007: 119; Gerring 2008: 650–67.
[159] See Ahram 2011.   [160] See Lund 2014.
[161] Cf. benefits of process tracing to covariation in comparative politics: Hall 2003.
[162] See Bennett 2008; Bennett & Checkel 2015.

comparing evidence for and against predefined theoretic assertions, I thus follow my broad sets of subjective data sources[163] to build a triangulated story that fits the overall picture found in and across arenas, to answer the question: *what are the effects of varying forms of ordering on perceptions of security in the local arena?*

As a key resource in drawing the broader picture of settings and processes in the security arena, I engage in focus group discussions to gain an impression of the arena. During my first trip to each arena, these discussions were rather open-ended, while, during my second trip, I guided participants to create comparable mappings of the arena. I try following up on all the actors respondents mention in these and other debates for interviews. However, the story always begins with the insights gained from inhabitants and actors of the inner circle and their perceptions of relevant actors and issues of security. From there, I move as far as possible (which frequently is not that far) towards the views of the actors in the outer circle that are often seen as spoilers. Unfortunately, the more insecure the investigated arena, the more my answers are biased towards perceptions in the inner circle. This is particularly the case for the level of security in the arena. I approximate security perceptions by asking people for their personal assessments and triangulate their perceptions with the unfolding events described to me in monthly security event logs written by research assistants, and descriptions provided in discussions and interviews (see also Box 1.1).

The output of this analysis will mostly take the form of written text, in part supported by graphs and tables. Thus some notes on the presentation of the written analysis are due: first, I use the present tense in the majority of the text for describing more general processes and perceptions in the security arena as I saw them during my visits, although these will have naturally evolved by the time of publication. I use the past tense, on the other hand, only when recounting specifi-cally dated events. In most instances, I confine myself to the events that happened during my fieldwork or to recent events that were recounted in detail by local respondents while I was there. I thus assess the wide array of data that I have gathered over time in the security arena to trace processes of ordering. I then compare these respective processes

---

[163] See Jacobs 2015.

Box 1.1 Triangulating the Ugandan military's role in Obo, CAR

In Obo, where security is perceived to be moderate in town and poor outside of it, the Ugandan military (the Uganda People's Defence Force, or UPDF) commander claims that 'I am the prefect'. While others did not use the label of 'prefect', the commander's statement indeed reverberates with the results of focus group discussions in Obo, in which respondents position the UPDF hierarchically above national state security forces (see Figure 1.2, box A), and with responses in a number of individual interviews with actors and inhabitants in the town. On the other hand, while the commander uses this label to describe a purely positive role on security in the arena, at times others mention devastating atrocities committed by this same actor, such as accusing Ugandan soldiers of gruesome rape and of supporting the LRA (see Figure 1.2, box B) rather than pursuing them, as was their mandate. In brief, through this triangulation of different data sources, the UPDF can be said to take on quite a dominant role in the security arena while it at times has negative impacts on people's perceived security.

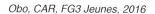

Obo, CAR, FG3 Jeunes, 2016

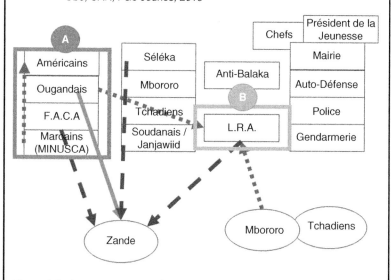

Figure 1.2 Actor mapping with youths from Obo, CAR, 16 February 2016

---

across arenas to find generalizable patterns of how and why actors order the arena and of the impact of ordering struggles on security.

Limitations

Nevertheless, there remain limitations to this research endeavour that could benefit from further investigations, such as the explorative nature of the research, the unbalanced data pool, the confinements of the actor lens, and the restricted generalization of my findings.

The first concern is the truly explorative nature of this research. While the empirical novelty of the data gathered provides an important contribution to the debate, it also means that few context conditions could be predefined. Volatile security circumstances at times demanded quick adaptations to case selection and research timing. Most constraining was my inability to return to the three South Sudanese cases due to the outbreak of open conflict in the locations I visited during my first and only trip in 2014. This brought much less breadth and depth to the data gathered here in the form of less-structured focus group discussions, no actor mappings, and fewer interviews. Owing to the scarcity of primary data gathered on South Sudan, I exceptionally extend my data through reports by research assistants and media sources on the events that followed shortly after my own trip.

Second, conflict was a key reason why data differs from case to case. In many local security arenas, I could not fully probe outer circles and their potential spoilers. My research in South Sudan was the most confined spatially, to the inner circle, and temporally, to one research trip. The CAR and Somaliland received the same time in the field – two main trips plus a short follow-up. However, the outer parts of local arenas were much more accessible in Somaliland than in the CAR, where armed actors were present. All in all, while my study does investigate the crucial importance of the outer parts of an arena to security, most of my findings relate to how people of arena centres perceive that outer circle, rather than first-hand observations of and interviews with people in the outer circle. Nevertheless, through the explorative mix, I also discovered a range of very fruitful methods to be employed. I found that dividing the research into two main trips each helped gain local respondents' trust even when total time per locality was limited. Conducting most of the field research in a team of two was a huge benefit to navigating the security arena more quickly, broadly, and safely. Local research assistants, despite their lack of formal training, were of particular value in gaining access, avoiding dangers, and keeping me informed between the two trips to each local arena or after the sole trip to South Sudan. Finally, the guided actor mappings were a fruitful tool to allow respondents to create comparable depictions of their security arenas across their different contexts. Overall, I thus gathered an abundance of data that by far outweighs the security constraints.

The third limitation concerns the confinement of the actor-driven security arena concept. While this made comparing characteristics of actors and processes of ordering security across arenas more straightforward, it also obscured most of the individual aspects of security in the local arena. Emotional, spontaneous, and unorganized aspects have thus remained underappreciated, although I did try to incorporate some of these aspects under the umbrella of fluid forms of ordering. The actor focus also overemphasized the role and perceptions of male individuals, because most of the security actors are led by men. I tried to explicitly seek out women's representatives and conduct group discussions with women to gain their perspectives but overall their representation in the respondent pool remains far below their proportion in the local population.

Finally, choosing three countries with varying historical backgrounds and, within these countries, three different local arenas granted me some degree of ability to decipher ordering patterns across variegated contexts. Because the primary level of comparison is the local level (except for the national comparison in Chapters 2 and 3) the results of this study are not directly transferrable to other parts of the respective countries. The tense relationship between the populace and the South Sudanese government found in the three arenas studied, for instance, would most likely be even worse in places such as Bentiu[164] but better in a town such as Aweil.[165] The aim of this study is thus not to make generalizations on the three countries per se but on processes of ordering security that can be related to one another in the local arenas under scrutiny. In a second step, these findings can be theorized to hold value as explanations for ordering processes – not outcomes – in other local security arenas.

---

[164] See atrocities committed by government army and government-allied militias: ICG 2015: 15–16.
[165] See the positive image of the SPLA in Aweil: Gorur *et al.* 2014.

Local security studies have thus far been conducted mostly through concepts of areas of limited statehood, public authority, and oligopolies of violence. While each has its merits for studying either perceived security or local non-monopolized contexts or to make a comparison, none combines all three aspects. I therefore build on the established literature and relate it to my empirical insights to specify the security arena concept.

Analysing nine local case studies across three countries calls for a concept that can frame data in a comparable manner. The security arena concept fulfils these requirements. The arena is made up of actors and their interactions. Actors range from more loosely described agglomerations, such as 'the youth', to highly structured institutions, such as the US army. An actor can broadly threaten or support another actor and mix actions to order the security arena on a spectrum ranging from fluid to stable ordering. The outcome of stable and fluid ordering can be security or insecurity for different parts of the arena's inhabitants. I measure security as a subjective variable, as *the felt durability of physical integrity*.

I analyse larger processes of ordering the arena and their impact on security on a spectrum from fluid to stable: on the fluid end, actors vary their interactions frequently, making flexible adaptations possible; on the stable end, actors fixate hierarchies, making a change of ordering costly. Security through stable ordering is continuous but so is insecurity. Fluid ordering can avoid the institutionalization of insecurity but is also less adept at creating continuous security. In sum, stable ordering lends more predictability, while fluid ordering creates more modifiability.

Stable and fluid ordering are not equally feasible in every part of the arena at any point in time. Actors divide the arena into different spheres both in speech and through specific actions such as the erection of barriers at town entrances. The open space of the outer circle lends itself more readily to fluid ordering, while the constant interaction in the inner circle demands greater degrees of stable ordering among actors. On a higher level, the difference between an inner and outer circle is recreated by the relations between centre and periphery.

I select cases within three countries that experience low degrees of state authority monopolization and a multitude of actors involved in security. Within each country, I choose three local arenas with varying attributes of sociospatial distance to the capital, population size, and the varying presence of security actor types. I gather data through an explorative mix of methods such as focus group discussions, interviews, monthly reports, and observations. With the help of the CAS approach, I then trace processes within each local arena through the triangulation of my data sources, and subsequently compare the cases to find generalizable patterns of how different ways of ordering the security arena impact security.

The nine local security arenas under scrutiny here cannot be seen in temporal and geographic isolation. The histories of how actors in those arenas relate to varying centres on the national and international level have vast repercussions on the way ordering plays out in the local arena. In the next chapter, I turn to this broader historical and geographic context to establish why such marked differences exist between the three countries and turn to the local arenas themselves in more detail.

2 | National and Local Histories of Security

Baligubadle is a small border town south of Somaliland's capital Hargeisa. The security arena of the town and its surroundings represents the Somaliland security model to the point. The chief justice of Hawd region, of which Baligubadle is the capital, invites me to share his woven mat on the dusty floor and listen to his tales of providing justice.[1] He is a very knowledgeable man who has only recently been appointed. Before taking up his current state position, he was a Sharia judge and says he now effortlessly combines both positions, as Somaliland's state law is based on Sharia.[2] Afterwards, I cross the market square and meet the mayor in his office. He proudly explains how he attained his post by tricking the less experienced council members to vote for him without knowing what they were doing.[3] At the same time, the mayor is an important caqil – a mid-ranking traditional leader – of the region's dominant Arab clan.[4]

Most clan members do not live in the town of Baligubadle but in the wide, open grasslands around it – the Gumburaha Banka, which is Somali for 'plains by the two hills'. As I talk to some of the more sedentary as well as the more nomadic herders – the former are mostly women and children herding goats and sheep, the latter young men travelling with camels – they all tell a very similar story: when there is trouble, we talk to the traditional elders. If it gets really bad, the police intervene. And how is security? Every time I travelled through Gumburaha to Baligubadle, I witnessed great tranquillity – a stark contrast to many of the other cases. In observations from inhabitants of Baligubadle, they themselves cannot yet explain why the Somaliland

---

[1] See Figure 2.1.
[2] Interview with Chief Justice, Baligubadle, Somaliland, 1 May 2016.
[3] Interview with Mayor, Baligubadle, Somaliland, 1 May 2016.
[4] Arab is a Somali clan name that is not to be confused with 'the Arabs', such as from Saudi Arabia.

Figure 2.1 Interviewing the Chief Justice (middle) of the state, Baligubadle, Somaliland, May 2016

model still works here, while in other arenas it is slowly falling apart, as in Zeila, and in some it never worked, like in Daami. Baligubadle's historical position in the struggle for independence and the support of its inhabitants for the newly independent state have to be accounted for in order to understand its continuing model character for the Somaliland way of providing security.

Tracing the origins of each state and comparing them from pre-colonial times to today unveils certain long-term trends and key breaking points that shape the relationships between centre and periphery. Fernand Braudel differentiates the impacts of underlying social and economic structures of the 'longue durée', developments of significant magnitude of the 'moyenne durée', and short-term 'événements' that shape a country's political trajectory.[5] Here, I analyse and contrast long-, medium-, and short-term developments, while not using Braudel's terms in the strictest sense of his definitions.

The nine cases under scrutiny bring with them a true myriad of actors, issues, and events. The comparative lens necessitates switching from one case to the next, thousands of kilometres away, at times

[5] Braudel 1980. See also Lind & Luckham 2017: 94.

within the same paragraph. I thus wish to provide the reader with an introduction into each country's history of the formation of their respective political orders. Afterwards, I provide an overview of the nine security arenas through a very brief summary of the respective socioeconomic composition, key security actors, and the main ongoing security issues and perceptions. These rather descriptive sections will form the basis for the ensuing analysis and will allow the reader to judge for themselves the credibility of the order-making argument.

Central African Republic

The CAR was and is situated at a crossroads and therefore became the most sociopolitically diverse of the three countries. People from four large language families[6] and numerous ethnic groups cohabit the country.[7] In recounting the impressions of European explorers in the late nineteenth century, Pierre Saulnier extracts three remarkable features of pre-colonial society in the CAR: the extreme diversity of groups, their physically detached living habits, and the absence of chiefs (except for sultans in the east).[8] Didier Bigo, in his research, did define three chiefly institutions situated in the chiefs of peace, chiefs of war, and secret societies. Nevertheless, their impact was constrained to certain social and political domains.[9] As compared to the other two cases, the degree of political hierarchy was lowest, counteracted by the separation of responsibilities among the institutions and by a large degree of individual, family, and village self-reliance.

French colonizers committed few resources to expanding authority in the Central African region. Instead, they sought protectorate treaties

---

[6] These are Nilo-Saharan, Adamawan, Bantu, Oubanguian. See Woodfork 2006: 5.
[7] The following trace their history in the CAR to the nineteenth century: Gbaya (33 per cent), Banda (27 per cent), Manza (Mandja, Mandjia) (13 per cent), Sara (10 per cent), Mboum (7 per cent), Yakoma (4 per cent), and Biaka (Baaka, Aka) (4 per cent). See Woodfork 2006: 8. Two quite distinct groups with a long history are Pygmies, the most ancient ethnic group in Africa, and the Peulh, nomadic cattle herders who trace their origins to the Niger basin.
[8] Saulnier 1998: 49ff.
[9] Chiefs of peace had little enforcement power aside from providing mediation, chiefs of war could not lead outside their realm of conflict, and secret societies formed a mystical, at times deliberately diffuse, form of authority. Bigo 1988: 19ff.

with the main sultans of the late nineteenth century.[10] Alliances
were struck to split groups and undermine the CAR's tradition of
indigenous self-reliance so as to rule them more easily. During the
scramble for Africa, sultanates received weapons to pursue their
conquests in exchange for slaves and ivory to powerful nations,
such as France, Egypt, and Britain.[11] The most fierce slave raids
were led by Muslim sultanates both in and near to today's CAR,
which remains a vivid memory for non-Muslim Central Africans
and lays a basis for current prejudices against Muslims, especially
of Chadian and Sudanese origin.[12] The French installed a concessionary system to encourage private companies to seize control of
the land so as to extract profits and taxes for the colonial authorities.[13] What these concessionary companies lacked in numbers
and legitimacy they made up for in brutality – burning down
villages and taking women and children as hostages for unpaid
taxes became commonplace.[14] Slave trading, forced labour, and
epidemics brought in by foreigners led to massive displacements
and countless deaths that lowered the population in the Central
African colony from more than four million in the nineteenth
century to less than a million by the early twentieth century.[15]
Resentment towards the colonizers triggered a number of popular
resistance movements.[16] These recurrent rebellions aimed at defending their region's self-government against a colonial centre that
wanted to extract the periphery's resources and abuse its people
but was unwilling to connect with them in a peaceful and meaningful manner.

Barthélemy Boganda founded the CAR's first party, the Mouvement
pour l'Évolution Sociale de l'Afrique, in 1952, and developed the

---

[10] Bandia and Zande Sultans of Bangassou, Rafai, and Zémio, and Sultan Senoussi
      in the north-east. See Kalck 2005: xxvi.
[11] Saulnier 1998: 63ff; Woodfork 2006: 11–12.
[12] These were the Sultanate Darfur, Dar-al-Kouti, and the influential Egyptian
      Sultan Sabah. See Woodfork 2006: 33.
[13] Hardin 2011. The concession paradigm also underlies politics today: Marchal
      2015a: 68.
[14] Saulnier 1998: 81ff; Woodfork 2006: 12.
[15] Saulnier 1998: 49–50; Smith 2015: 19.
[16] Such as the 1916 Zande insurrection, the 1918 rebellion in Bougbou and
      Mobaye, and the 1928–31 Baya uprising, also known as the Kongo-Wara
      insurrection. Kalck 2005: xxviii; Saulnier 1998: 92ff.

national motto: unity, dignity, work.[17] As a leading and visionary figure in Central African politics, he combined the idea of African unity with the African pursuit of the ideas of European civilization. However, the colonial period ended with a traumatic shock when Boganda died in a plane crash on the eve of independence. Politics in the new state began with a power struggle between Boganda's successor in spirit, Abel Goumba, and his nephew, David Dacko.[18] Dacko took the upper hand through a crooked deal: in exchange for the deputies of the assembly electing him president, he offered to extend their mandates for another five years.[19] Rather than breaking with colonial neglect, the new ruler showed that politics would continue to be centred in the capital without peripheral involvement.

Army chief of staff Jean-Bédel Bokassa took power on New Year's Eve of 1965 through a military coup. Today, people often ascribe a spike in the CAR's state-led development to his rule.[20] Despite this image of his reign, however, it was during this period that the rule of thumb 'the country ends at Kilometre twelve' was established: development projects and state administration rarely go beyond the twelve kilometre point from the centre of the capital Bangui.[21] Bokassa increasingly centralized power not only in the capital and his home village Berengo but also in his own hands, symbolized by proclaiming himself president for life in 1972 and emperor in 1976.[22] Bokassa co-opted his contenders by making Ange-Félix Patassé prime minister and former president Dacko a personal advisor in 1976 and thus solidified the closed elite circle tradition of the CAR that is centred on the capital.[23] While the state in general neglected its peripheries, it also engaged in selective punitive missions to assert specific resource and power claims when it felt challenged.[24]

While on a visit to Libya in September 1979, French troops took control of the Bangui airport, barred Bokassa from returning, and reinstalled Dacko to the presidency.[25] Dacko surprisingly won the presidential elections of 1981 in the first round with 50.23 per cent to

---

[17] Unity of the different ethnicities becoming one nation, dignity as an appeal to the colonizers that every human is a human (Sango: 'zo kwe zo'), and work to promote Africans taking control of their economy. See Saulnier 1998: 101.
[18] Bigo 1988: 42.   [19] Saulnier 1998: 102–3.
[20] Unrecorded discussions with people in Bangui in early 2015 and early 2016.
[21] Saulnier 1998: 107.   [22] Bigo 1988: 121.   [23] See Kalck 2005: 11.
[24] Cf. Bigo 1988: 101–3.   [25] Kalck 2005: xxxv–xxxvi.

Patassé with 38.11 per cent and then proclaimed martial law. However, General André Kolingba took over power and installed a military council. The French cut their budgetary aid in the early 1980s leading the CAR government to lay off more than 3,000 civil servants. Kolingba created a single-party system and had himself elected president for a further six years in 1986. He also promoted a personality cult around himself to solidify his power. However, recurrent student strikes questioned his policies and rule and, by 1991, strikes throughout public and private sectors brought the country to a standstill. Kolingba conceded, reinstalled multi-partyism, and set presidential elections for 1993. The 1993 elections were carried out relatively freely and fairly and brought Patassé a narrow victory over Goumba.[26] The honeymoon period of the new democratic regime was brought to a violent end in 1996, when soldiers staged a mutiny in the capital due to salary arrears and a dreaded deployment to the peripheries.[27] With his focus on holding on to central power, Patassé neglected the country's peripheries and allowed armed groups to proliferate – most infamously the zaraguinas (road cutters) in the north-west.[28]

François Bozizé seized power from Patassé in 2003, with the help of Chadian mercenaries, euphemistically labelled 'liberators'. He was at first greeted with enthusiasm and subsequently won the 2005 presidential elections.[29] However, he soon surpassed Patassé's level of clientelistic rule by centring power on himself and his close associates. Numerous rebellions sprung up in the north-west, driven both by Patassé loyalists aiming for a return to power and by local grievances against the continuing threats posed by road cutters and armed Chadian cattle keepers who seasonally migrated southwards.[30] In the mid-2000s, Bozizé fought back rebellions through desperately violent means and therefore followed in Bokassa's footsteps of compensating for a lack of state capacity with an abundance of cruelty. Bozizé's nephew, Eugène Ngaïkosset, combatted the rebellion of the Armée Populaire pour la Restauration de la République et la Démocratie (APRD) in the north-west through such repressive means that he was infamously nicknamed the 'butcher of Paoua'.[31] Bozizé's repression of the rebellions in the north-east was no less violent and was supported

[26] Ibid.: xlvii.   [27] ICG 2007: 10.   [28] See Chauvin & Seignobos 2014.
[29] The International Crisis Group (ICG) went as far as judging the electoral success 'fair and square': ICG 2007: 16.
[30] Chauvin & Seignobos 2014.   [31] ICG 2007: 23, footnote 117.

by French air and ground attacks.[32] The growing rebellions in the north-centre and north-east, ironically, were joined by numerous (now former) 'liberators',[33] who felt they had not received their fair share for bringing Bozizé to power.[34] Power struggles and violence in CAR were centred in the capital and thus were increasingly challenged by armed resistance from the peripheries.

CAR's presidents gained from dominating the diamond and gold trade and President Bozizé took such self-enrichment to new heights.[35] In 2008, he appointed his relatives and loyalists to eastern diamond buying offices that had previously been held by allies of rebel groups.[36] This move provided an economic incentive for those rebel groups to join forces in order to regain their economic stakes. In addition, the rapprochement of Chad and Sudan over the Darfur crisis in 2010 brought a change in the political environment of the north-east: up until that point, Sudan had armed Chadian opposition rebels who had taken up camp in the CAR's north-eastern province Vakaga, while Chad supported their competitors.[37] These former adversaries came together as the Séléka alliance in 2012. The Séléka swept across the country, conquering two of the case studies in this analysis (Bangassou and Paoua) in early 2013 and taking the capital in March. Their short-lived rule was devastatingly violent,[38] leading to two reactions: rising resistance by local auto-defence groups, collectively called the Anti-Balaka,[39] and the deployment of an international peacekeeping force.[40] The Séléka president was forced to step down in early 2014. A transitional government and international peacekeepers were left to try and build bridges between deeply divided social groups after the war.[41]

The political debates during my visits in early 2015, early 2016, and August 2017 revolved around a national dialogue forum in Bangui,[42] the change from a transitional to an elected government, the full deployment of a UN mission, and high levels of violence in the peripheries.[43] Citizens were consulted during the drafting of a new national constitution, national and international organizations prepared (relatively) free and fair elections, and election results brought forth a

---

[32]   Ibid.: 23–7.   [33]   Debos 2008.   [34]   Smith 2015: 39.
[35]   See Southward *et al.* 2014: 5–6.   [36]   ICG 2010: 6.
[37]   See de Vries & Glawion 2015: chap. 2.   [38]   See Lombard 2016a: 47–8.
[39]   See Weyns *et al.* 2014.   [40]   See de Vries & Glawion 2015.
[41]   See Marchal 2016.   [42]   See Mogby & Moukadas 2015; Marchal 2015c.
[43]   See Glawion & de Vries 2018.

change towards a new civilian national leadership under President Faustin-Archange Touadéra. However, continuing violence in numerous peripheries called the short-term impact of changes in the centre into question. The Séléka fractioned into multiple groups, now labelled collectively as Ex-Séléka, which often fought among each other or with a myriad of local Anti-Balaka groups that pursued a mix of defensive and racketeering aims. The United Nations Integrated Multidimensional Mission in the Central African Republic (MINUSCA) tried to rein in violence from the vast array of armed groups but found itself caught up in scandals of excessive violence and sexual abuse.

Somaliland

The Somali people base their heritage on the myth that descendants of the Prophet's near relatives embarked across the Gulf of Aden onto the northern shores of the Horn of Africa in the late ninth century. Each Somali clan family traces its roots to a separate ancestor.[44] In fact, trade connections between Arab regions and the Horn of Africa can be traced back to Roman times and the linguistic origins of the Somali people can be traced to population movements from East Africa even before that.[45] Soon after the founding of Islam, Muslims and their descendants spread southwards along the Horn, intermixing with local populations all the way to present-day north-eastern Kenya.[46] The people who call themselves Somalis share a common language and livelihoods centred mostly on nomadism.[47] Aside from a few city-state sultanates (e.g. between Harer and Zeila), historically Somalis have not created centralized political structures of control.[48] Small units of up to 100 families (the *diya* group) organize most aspects of social life. Somalis share a particular mode of interaction through contracts (*xeer*) and compensation that traces back centuries and has enabled continuous cohabitation, even after violent incidents.[49] From a territorial and political perspective, members of Somali society have always been accustomed to self-rule and negotiated

---

[44] Birnbaum 2002: 32.   [45] Bradbury 2008: 9–10.   [46] Ibid.: 10–11.
[47] See Lewis 1961.   [48] Cf. Bradbury 2008: 15–16; Lewis 1961.
[49] See Leonard & Samantar 2011; Lewis 2008.

relations. Anthropologist Ion M. Lewis famously labelled this sociopolitical system a 'pastoral democracy'.[50]

Somalis were a largely nomadic society that colonizers had difficulties controlling. The ethnic group of Somalis spanned the entire Horn of Africa by the time colonial powers arrived in the late nineteenth century. The competing colonizers – French, British, Italian, and Ethiopian – divided the Horn into five separate colonies with borders that cut through Somali communities. The Somali flag's five-pointed star symbolizes this division and is used as a political statement of the desire to reunite the five Somali inhabited territories under one nation. Somaliland, which became a British colony, was for the British merely a peripheral colony.[51] While Italy sent thousands of settlers to its Somali colony (today's east and south Somalia), no British settlers went to Somaliland. The British did not engage in missionary activities and the first public school was not opened until 1938. British interest was directed towards the commercial and geopolitical issue of protecting the trade route through the Gulf of Aden rather than towards the territory itself.[52] Somaliland was put under Indian government control and organized purely as a coastal colony assured through protectorate treaties with the clans of the Ciise, Gadabuursi, and Isaaq and by integrating clan leaders into administration.[53] The colonizers, however, were forced to assume some measure of control of the Somaliland hinterlands, where they were confronted by rebellion: a religious leader from the eastern region, Sayyid Muhammad Abdille Hassan, mobilized against the British colonizers and against Somalis of a different religious tradition in the so-called Dervish Wars of 1900–20. The British, in turn, armed opposing militias leading to rising levels of armament in the area.[54]

Somalia and Somaliland gained their independence from Italy and Britain, respectively, in 1960 and decided to unify into one Somalia. The colonial legacies differed drastically, however: the British had committed hardly any effort to install an administrative structure, whereas in the Italian colony efforts were made, albeit with limited impact, to weaken the traditional system and create an educated, cosmopolitan class.[55] Mogadishu became the capital and politics centred in the south and centre far from Somaliland. From 1960 to

---

[50] Lewis 1961.   [51] Samatar 1989: 41.   [52] Ibid.: 30.
[53] Bradbury 2008: 25.   [54] Ibid.: 27.   [55] Lewis 2008.

1969, Somalia's political system was based on colonial centralized rule with democratic processes hastily implemented in the final years before independence.[56] The Somali Youth League's one-party rule was highly corrupt, autocratic, and opposed by large parts of Somali society.[57] As a result, when Colonel Siad Barre toppled the government in a coup in 1969, he was at first greeted with enthusiasm.

After Somaliland and Somalia integrated just days after their independence, northerners felt marginalized by successive central governments and Siad Barre's coup in 1969 also did not turn matters in their favour. Droughts in the mid-1970s hit the north particularly hard, causing many to be resettled to state farms and fishing settlements in the south.[58] President Barre's government in Mogadishu promoted 'scientific socialism',[59] through which it officially sought to abandon traditional structures, which were especially strong in the north, due to the weak footprint of the British colonial administration. In reality, the president engaged in 'clan clientelism' by basing his rule on three Darood sub-clans of his near kin and by arming loyal clans to encourage division among the remaining clans.[60] After being the 'peripheral' colony of the British, Somaliland now found itself the peripheral region of the independent Somali state.

Numerous rebel groups formed in the 1980s to resist President Barre's clientelistic and dictatorial rule. In the north, the Isaaq Somali National Movement (SNM) started operating out of Ethiopia in 1982 but gained strong clan backing only in 1988, when President Barre carpet-bombed Hargeisa and Burco.[61] President Barre armed non-Isaaq clans in the north – the Gadabuursi, Ciise, Dhulbahante, and Warsengeli – to fight the SNM.[62] By 1991, a southern rebel group had driven Barre out of Mogadishu and another had taken control of Puntland,[63] while the SNM took hold of Hargeisa. The SNM engaged in dialogue with its former enemies in the north rather than continuing the war after Barre's defeat. On 18 May 1991, delegates at the Burco conference dissolved the union with Somalia and proclaimed the

---

[56] Bradbury 2008: 32–3. [57] Adam 1995: 69. [58] Lewis 2008: 63.
[59] The initially popular reformist agenda included abolishing traditional clan institutions, a national cult around the president, and crash programmes on literacy and rural development.
[60] Lewis 2008: 76. [61] Bradbury 2008: 68–9; Renders 2012: 77–9.
[62] Adam 1995: 76–7; Renders 2012: 83–4.
[63] Adam 1995: 77ff; Johnson & Smaker 2014.

independence of Somaliland within its former colonial borders –[64] at the same time, conflict escalated in rump Somalia.[65] A series of conferences followed in Somaliland with participants pursuing two aims: resolving issues of conflict and creating political institutions.[66] Even though the mid-1990s saw this process off to a rocky start with SNM infighting and breaks with other actors,[67] the Republic of Somaliland was successfully established and started spreading throughout the former British colonial territory.

Somaliland's stakeholders tried resolving their deadly leadership struggles of the mid-1990s through conferences and by moving to a more democratic selection process. Presidential elections took place in 2002 and were followed by elections for a lower house of parliament to serve alongside the unelected house of elders in 2005.[68] The second presidential elections in 2010 somewhat stabilized the governmental system, showing that a peaceful change of power was possible.[69] However, the evolution also showed that the Somaliland state in Hargeisa was unable to present itself as a viable centre to its most distant peripheries in the eastern areas bordering Puntland. People in this area remained sceptical of the minimal government services – which remain low even for the minimal standards the poor Somaliland government is able to provide – and the heavy-handed means through which the state tries to impose itself on these defiant areas.[70]

While the CAR and South Sudan have been drawn into deep and prolonged conflict, security did not deteriorate in Somaliland, even though neither development nor political consolidation significantly progressed. Parts of the population in the east continue to feel marginalized and periodically take up arms to voice their claims.[71] Somaliland's political integration seemed to plateau by 2010. International recognition is far from probable and draws ever further away as the internationally backed government in Mogadishu makes its first steps towards consolidation of power.[72] The cohabitational system seems to very gradually shift towards more governmental authority and diminishing clan influence, while both sides avoid a clear break with the past. Without international recognition and

[64] Bradbury 2008: 80–3.   [65] See Menkhaus 2007.
[66] Bradbury 2008: 95–6; Walls 2009.   [67] See Balthasar 2013.
[68] Bradbury 2008: 184ff; Hansen & Bradbury 2007.
[69] See Walls & Kibble 2011.   [70] See Hoehne 2015.   [71] See Ibid.
[72] Hammond 2013.

economic development, people continue to depend on remittances and unemployment remains at devastating levels.

During the time of my visits to Somaliland in the spring of 2015 and of 2016 as well as in November 2017, contestation over the overall workings of the political system was boiling but had not yet reached a breaking point. The unelected nature of the 'traditional' house, the House of Elders, in which many current members had inherited the seats of their deceased ancestors, was called into question. Elections for the House of Representatives were postponed (by 2017, deputies had served twelve years without facing re-election) and presidential elections were continuously rescheduled before finally taking place in November 2017.[73] The presidential elections on 13 November 2017 were largely peaceful and resulted in the ruling party regaining the presidency but with a new candidate.[74] While security continues to be relatively high in most regions of the country and there are no active

Figure 2.2 A voting booth during the presidential elections, Lughaya, Somaliland, November 2017

[73] I served as short-term observer in the election observation mission. See Figure 2.2.
[74] Pegg & Walls 2018.

open rebellions, frustration about economic underdevelopment and the lack of progress on international recognition persists.

South Sudan

Similar to both other countries, South Sudan was historically a remote and lightly populated area. It had only the Nile River granting an important access route. Unlike Somalis' shared language and organizational structure, South Sudan featured a much larger diversity of groups, structures, and livelihoods.[75] The Azande and Shilluk kingdoms as well as the neighbouring Darfuri Sultanate were well-established pre-colonial political orders. The pastoralist Dinka and Nuer communities were more itinerant in their livelihoods and flexible in their sociopolitical structures, where conflict over cattle was a constant part of group interaction.[76] Of the agricultural communities, many lived independently from each other with minimal hierarchical institutions and were more quickly impacted by colonial rule than the nomadic cattle keepers.[77] South Sudan thus had few centralized rulers that a later colonial administration could co-opt into its rank, a reason why traditional chiefs were later imposed in those areas that did not have them.[78]

The region that now comprises South Sudan was abused as a slave reservoir similar to the CAR. Slave raids were led by some of the same centralized powers, such as the Darfur Sultanate.[79] Revolving around the slave and later ivory trade, South Sudan faced successive, nominal colonizers: the Ottomans established the rule of the Turkiyya, the Mahdist revolution transferred power into northern Sudanese hands, and the British dominated the Anglo-Egyptian conglomerate, bringing the region into the reins of Europeans.[80] However, all of these successive regimes shared a minimal interest in governing the whole territory. Governmental interest was so minimal that, even by the 1920s, there were only 700 pupils in school – that is, in primary schools run by missions rather than the state.[81] Aside from colonial control of the Nile River, interaction was based on the desire to extract resources and

---

[75] See Rolandsen & Daly 2016: chap. 1.   [76] See Leonardi 2013: 103.
[77] See Ibid.: 31.   [78] See Ibid.: 32, 181.   [79] See Johnson 2011: 2.
[80] See Johnson 2011: 3ff; Rolandsen & Daly 2016: chap. 2.
[81] Rolandsen & Daly 2016: 47.

manpower, in exchange for a questionable 'pacification' of conflict between tribes.[82] As this exchange was obviously flawed, local groups strategically positioned themselves to either tip the balance in their own internal feuds or openly resist the colonizers. Agriculturalists more readily collaborated with the European colonizers in hopes of protection against the better-armed pastoralists, which also led to the early dominance of sedentary Equatorians – southern agricultural communities – in colonial administration and security forces.[83] Pastoralist resistance, especially by the Dinka and Nuer, was particularly ferocious and struck devastating blows to the Egyptian and British colonizers in the late nineteenth and early twentieth centuries.[84]

Sudan gained independence in 1956, at a time when administrative structures and educational levels were still entirely lopsided in favour of the north. Southerners were largely left out of the process towards independence and the establishment of the state's ensuing structures.[85] Therefore, for southerners, 'independence' seemed like just another change of hats from the Turkiyya, Mahdists, British-Egyptian conglomerate, and now to the northern Sudanese oppressors.[86] In the year prior to independence, a mutiny in Torit triggered heavy government oppression, which in turn strengthened defiance by southerners, who, by 1963, had mounted the Anya-Nya rebellion. Fighting soon reached a stalemate because the Khartoum government was unwilling to invest sufficient resources to suppress the rebellion and instead retracted to garrison towns, making only occasional punitive missions into the peripheries. At the same time, the rebellion was too poorly armed and coordinated to take over the garrisons. In the late 1960s, two events turned the tide: vast Israeli support for southern rebels in revenge for Sudan's participation in the 1967 Six Day War and, following his military coup in 1969, the new leader Nimeiri's need to strengthen his weak support base by appeasing the south.

[82] Cf. Johnson 2011: 11; Rolandsen & Daly 2016: 35ff.
[83] See Rolandsen & Daly 2016: 36.
[84] See Leonardi 2013; Rolandsen & Daly 2016: 41ff.   [85] Johnson 2011: 22ff.
[86] Rolandsen & Daly 2016: 65.

While Somalia began drifting apart in the 1970s, hopes for peace grew in Sudan. Southern Sudan was first established as a political unit after the 1972 Addis Ababa Peace Agreement which brought the southern regions their first united administration within Sudan. The national president nominated a regional president who ruled from the new capital Juba with a High Executive Council that was checked, at least in theory, by a regional assembly.[87] The fragile entente was flawed in multiple ways. The integration of the Anya-Nya into the national army was not pursued thoroughly and generated southern suspicions. Integrated units resisted forced relocations by staging recurrent mutinies throughout the 1970s.[88] The agreement was also fraught by the lack of checks against the powers of the Sudanese president, who could and frequently did force the resignation of the regional president and the assembly.[89] In the early 1980s, the introduction of Sharia law for all of Sudan and the redivision of the south into three regions further alienated southern politicians and military leaders.[90] Most of the Anya-Nya veterans had deserted and fled to Ethiopia by 1983 but the establishment of the idea of Southern Sudan as a political entity had taken root.

In 1983, political tensions in Sudan between north and south mounted and a mutiny in Bor was met with heavy government repression, triggering the start of a second civil war.[91] The Sudan People's Liberation Army (SPLA) formed out of defected battalions from the Sudanese army and some former Anya-Nya veterans.[92] The SPLA was more powerful militarily and more savvy on the political front than former rebel groups. The government in Khartoum responded with a divide-and-rule strategy, arming local groups along ethnic and regional lines against the SPLA:[93] most notably, several groups in Equatoria, William Chol's Anya-Nya2 group in the Upper Nile, and Fertit protection groups in Bahr al-Ghazal.[94] In the SPLA and the political party Sudan People's Liberation Movement (SPLM), politics were funnelled predominantly through the barrel of the gun. In 1991, the SPLA split and

---

[87] Johnson 2011: 39ff.   [88] Rolandsen & Daly 2016: 102–3.   [89] Ibid.: 101–2.
[90] Johnson 2011: 53–4; Schomerus & Aalen 2016: 11.
[91] Rolandsen & Daly 2016: 105; de Vries & Schomerus 2017a: 32–3.
[92] Rolandsen & Daly 2016: 108.   [93] Johnson 2011: 91ff.
[94] Rolandsen & Daly 2016: 106.

fighting escalated even further as the government sought to take advantage of internal tensions – many of these divisions would re-emerge in the most recent civil war.[95] Towns switched hands between different southern rebel factions and the government and back again during the 1990s. The Khartoum government's encouragement of Islamic revolution in neighbouring states gave it the image of a 'rogue state' and shifted international support towards the SPLA.[96] The war lasted until 2005 and brought forth a massive militarization of Southern Sudanese society. Atrocities committed by all sides put a devastating toll on civilian life, with up to half of the population becoming displaced.

South Sudan's path to independence provides striking resemblances to the Somaliland case: a different colonial heritage to the main Sudanese state (British versus Egyptian), heavy repression and marginalization by the centre, and a violent struggle for independence. However, marginalization in South Sudan was much more pronounced, the struggles for independence lasted longer and cost multiple times as many lives, and its independence came twenty years later than Somaliland's – however, then it did come with full international recognition.[97] South Sudan's war was halted – albeit briefly – during negotiations and the ensuing ceasefire in 2002. That year, Riek Machar rejoined the SPLA, ending the split that had weakened the movement since 1991. The USA, UK, and Norway formed a 'troika' that put its weight behind the peace process led by the Intergovernmental Authority on Development (IGAD). The Comprehensive Peace Agreement (CPA) was struck in 2005 and set cornerstones for wealth-sharing, border demarcation, elections, and a referendum on secession.[98] However, the process was fraught with dangers. Northern opposition groups felt abandoned in their own struggles against the Khartoum government. Conflict flared up in Darfur starting in 2003 and tensions rose in the contested border areas of Abyei, Southern Kordofan, and Blue Nile.[99] In 2011, an overwhelming majority of the population voted for independence. The southern government that took control in first 'Southern' and then, as of 2011, in 'South' Sudan turned out

---

[95] de Vries & Schomerus 2017a: 33.   [96] Rolandsen 2015a: 130.
[97] See Le Riche & Arnold 2012.   [98] See Young 2012.   [99] See Ibid.: 12–13.

to be inefficient and corrupt, while the multiple, parallel security forces brought further insecurity for many civilians.

Hopes were high that South Sudan would come together. These hopes were dashed. After independence in July 2011, pressing issues remained with rump Sudan concerning oil revenues and border demarcation.[100] At the same time, the fragile internal coherence faltered. Since 2002, the movement had been kept together mostly by the common enemy in Khartoum and the common goal of self-determination. Following independence, leadership struggles in the SPLM re-emerged and tore the army apart.[101] In December 2013, President Salva Kiir accused his former Vice President Riek Machar of planning a coup and tried to arrest him – he fled and formed the SPLA-in-Opposition (SPLA-IO).[102] While the conflict between the two factions became the main public narrative, in fact, a number of hotspots formed where actors held their own local and regional agendas – many of which were based on resistance to the increasingly repressive central government.

During my visit to South Sudan in late 2014, the debate shifted from the binary conflict between the SPLA and the SPLA-IO to the issue of spreading violence in other regions.[103] In Equatoria and Western Bahr al-Ghazal (where the three cases under scrutiny are located), people accused the government of using repressive means and sending armed cattle keepers to chase local farmers from their lands. Peace negotiations did not include such local issues and were confined to forums hosted in foreign countries.[104] The government showed no leniency for voiced opposition and repressed dissent violently. Throughout the country, violence spread, combined with internal disputes, local resistance, and the SPLA-IO vying for national power. The toll on civilians was devastating: a 2018 estimate put the toll of violent deaths since the start of the crisis at 190,000[105] and UNHCR estimates more than four million people to have fled their homes.[106]

---

[100] See Jok 2013: 14; Spittaels & Weyns 2014.
[101] See de Vries & Justin 2014; de Waal 2014.
[102] Johnson 2014; Rolandsen 2015a.   [103] See ICG 2016; HSBA 2016.
[104] See de Vries & Schomerus 2017b.   [105] Checchi *et al.* 2018.
[106] UNHCR (31 January 2019) 'South Sudan Situation': https://data2.unhcr.org/en/documents/download/68226.

Forming the State

In pre-colonial times, there was an absence in all three countries of all-encompassing, centralized political systems that could be merged into a national state within today's boundaries. Somalis lived as nomads and organized themselves in conflicting clan lineages, while South Sudan was inhabited by a diverse range of ethnic groups with vastly differing organizational structures. The CAR was similarly diverse but groups interacted less frequently.

The three countries were of marginal importance to their colonizers, receiving only minimal attention and limited development but experiencing heavy repression. The colonial and slave-raiding onslaught in the CAR depleted and divided its population. South Sudan experienced particularly heavy forms of resistance to changing colonizers. Somalis saw themselves divided among five different nations by competing powers grabbing their lands. Nonetheless, Somaliland remained a weakly controlled protectorate that mostly experienced 'benign neglect',[107] contrasted with colonizers using 'divide and rule' in the CAR and violent 'indirect rule' in South Sudan.[108]

Out of these different colonial experiences also came varying paths towards independence that would shape post-independence issues of security. While in the CAR people resisted only locally after independence, the levels of violence and organization in South Sudan and Somaliland were far greater. And while Somaliland had mostly ended its violent struggles by the 1990s, armed conflict was taking off even further in South Sudan.

South Sudan, Somalia, and the CAR are often described as 'fragile', which suggests instability even though many of the characteristics of these states were consolidated twenty or thirty years ago. The countries have developed security-relevant characteristics that they trace back over decades and are faced by new issues. The CAR's deliberately weakened state contrasts with the militarized state of South Sudan and the inherent mix of state and non-state actors in Somaliland. These long trends are met by new events of armed group proliferation in the CAR and South Sudan and the questionable viability of the Somaliland state. As none of the states fully controls its entire territory, local political order can vary strongly from one place to the next.

---

[107] Prunier 1998: 225. As cited in Bradbury 2008: 32.
[108] Rolandsen & Daly 2016: 49ff.

Nine Local Security Arenas

Nine localities will form the locus of this study: Paoua, Bangassou, and Obo in the CAR; Raga, Buseri, and Mundri in South Sudan; Zeila, Baligubadle, and Daami in Somaliland (see Chapter 1, Map 1.2). Here, I wish to provide some very brief insights on each locality separately to provide the reader with crucial background information. Some brief data is summarized in Table 2.1 and the contents are discussed in the local case descriptions.

Paoua lies in the north-west of the Central African Republic and, with its approximately 30,000 to 40,000 residents, is an important town in Ouham-Pendé and part of the second most populous prefecture,[109] with more than 500,000 inhabitants. Until the recent civil war came to Paoua in 2013, the region was considered the breadbasket of the country and exported considerable amounts of cotton. Paoua is situated at a strategic point of commerce to and from neighbouring Chad and Cameroon. Society is composed of numerous ethnicities – one focus group mentioned fifteen – of which the Kaba and Tali are by far the largest.[110] In 2013, the Séléka alliance conquered Paoua, looting, killing, and ransacking in town. Founded out of the remnants of a former regional rebel group,[111] the Révolution et Justice (RJ) was formed to defend locals against Séléka atrocities. Two competing mediation boards attempted to engage the Séléka to pacify their activities but, by 2016, only one mediation board was still active – the Comité d'Appui Spirituel aux Autorités Locales (CASAL). In late 2013, the French Sangaris operation was briefly deployed to drive the Séléka out by force. Sangaris also struck a deal with the RJ for the latter not to enter Paoua town after the Sangaris operation took place. Nonetheless, in the wake of the Séléka retreat locals pillaged Muslim quarters and forced thousands to flee – almost none of whom had returned more than two years later. As the RJ are mostly ethnic Kaba, disenchanted Tali militants formed the small, loosely organized armed groups of the

---

[109] A prefecture is the highest-level administrative subunit in the CAR. The equivalent in Somaliland is called region, and in South Sudan state. The next level administrative units are called sub-prefecture in the CAR, district in Somaliland and county in South Sudan. Lower-level administrative subunits are called municipality or village in the CAR as well as in Somaliland, and Payam and Boma in South Sudan.

[110] Focus group discussion with Tali women, Paoua, CAR, 1 March 2016.

[111] The APRD. See Chauvin & Seignobos 2014; Spittaels & Hilgert 2009: 7–10.

Table 2.1 Key indicators on the nine local cases

	CAR			Somaliland			South Sudan		
	Paoua	Bangassou	Obo	Daami	Baligubadle	Zeila	Mundri	Buseri	Raja
Distance to capital (km)	480	740	1225	0	60	350	180	650	1,000
Approx. population	32,000	36,000	10,000	25,000	10,000	10,000	35,000	7,000	10,000
Key security actors	MINUSCA Gendarme Police Mayor Chiefs RJ GP MPC Cattle keepers* Committee	MINUSCA Gendarme Police Tribunal Auto-Defence Mayor Chiefs Committee Peulhs LRA Séléka	UPDF US Army MINUSCA FACA Mayor LRA Police Gendarme Committee Committee Poachers	Elders Gabooye youth Isaaq youth Gangs* Police Village committee	Police Governor* Mayor Court Elders Eth. local gov* Eth. police* ONLF*	Police Governor Mayor Court Ciise elders Sam. elders Ciise youth Sam. youth Village chief Council	SPLA Herders Police Rebels NSS Local gov Chief	Herders SPLA Police (UNMISS) Chief	SPLA Defectors Rebels Darfuri (UNMISS) Police NSS Local gov Chiefs
Perceived security	Medium/Very bad	Good/Bad	Medium/Bad	Medium/Good	Very good/Good	Very good/Good	(Bad/Very bad)	(Good/Bad)	(Medium/Bad)
Field visits	February and March 2015, January to March 2016, August 2017, July and August 2018, January 2019, June 2019			April to June 2015, May and June 2016, November 2017			November and December 2014		

Approximate population numbers are collated from data provided in (often dated) statistical accounts and interviews and then roughly estimated. Actors marked with an * were not interviewed during this study. Actors in brackets were not permanently present or recently left the local arena. Perceived security is based on focus group discussions (see also Chapter 4).

Group des Patriots (GP), variably also labelled Anti-Balaka or 'bandits'. Recently, an ex-Séléka group, the Mouvement Patriotique Centrafricain (MPC), returned to Paoua and has become the most powerful non-state armed group in the prefecture.[112] A small Cameroonian peacekeeping contingent has been based in Paoua since 2008[113] under different mandates. In September 2014, it was transferred to UN tutelage and grew to around 200 soldiers. By early 2016, a dozen support staff (police trainers, military observers, and political and civil affairs officers) joined the local UN mission base. State institutions are little more than a token presence. Debates on security revolve around a myriad of issues, including the presence of numerous armed groups, the threat they pose on overland routes and in town, the real or alleged ethnic division of the arena, the displacement of large parts of the Muslim community, and the contested presence of Cameroonian peacekeepers. Paoua's arena is described as one of the most insecure of all the nine cases, both within town and especially in the wider region.[114]

Bangassou has around 35,000 residents and is the capital of the Mbomou Prefecture, which has around 180,000 inhabitants. The town's Catholic school is considered one of the nation's best education institution outside the capital. Bangassou's society is composed predominantly of three ethnicities of comparable size – Yakoma, Nzakara, and Zande – and mostly Muslim minorities. The town connects the east of the country to its centre and to Bangui and borders the Democratic Republic of the Congo (DRC) across the Mbomou River. Séléka rebels briefly controlled the town in 2013 and pillaged all moveable goods. African Union (AU) peacekeepers dislodged them in late 2013 and installed a permanent presence in the arena. In the wake of the Séléka departure, locals displaced thousands of Muslim inhabitants and pillaged the administrative quarter and the markets. Since late 2015, state

---

[112]   The group now has its own independent structure from the MPC and goes under the name Mouvement national pour la libération de la Centrafrique (MNLC).

[113]   In the peacekeepers' camp, the soldiers had erected murals remembering all the contingents that had ever been placed in Paoua. The earliest notice of Cameroonian soldiers I could find dated back to May 2008 under a Force Multinationale en Centrafrique (FOMUC) mandate. Most contingents mentioned on the walls were Cameroonian, followed by those of Gabon, Chad, and both Congos.

[114]   Based on focus group discussions. See more details in Chapter 4.

personnel are slowly returning to Bangassou and reactivating former security and justice institutions (gendarmerie, police, and the tribunal). MINUSCA has a strong presence in the arena: around 200 soldiers, multiple patrols per day and at night, armoured vehicles, and barriers or controls on all four entrances to town. Non-state security actors organize, on the one hand, in a peace mediation committee and, on the other hand, in multiple vigilante groups. The roads north-west to Bambari and south to the DRC border are difficult to travel due to an Ex-Séléka presence but can be passed with a fixed, predictable fee. When talking about security concerns, respondents mention the presence of Anti-Balaka and former Séléka groups barring access to the overland routes leaving town, rumours of attacks by the Lord's Resistance Army (LRA), and tensions between local ethnic and religious groups. Most recently, the town was attacked by an auto-defence group in May 2017, resulting in the deaths of more than 100 local inhabitants. The Security Arena in Bangassou is divided between a comparatively high level of security within town – this was measured before the May attack – and continued insecurity in the wider Mbomou prefecture.

Obo lies in the CAR's far eastern corner at the border triangle with South Sudan and the DRC and within the lightly populated prefecture of Haut-Mbomou with around 80,000 inhabitants. The approximately 10,000 town residents are mostly Zande – a tribe that spans an area encompassing all three countries in the border triangle and with a rich history of political order and organized forces. The Zande inhabitants engage mostly in farming, fishing, and small services. Muslims form a diverse minority in Obo: Chadian Muslims are mostly traders and Peulh cattle keepers live in Obo and its vicinity. Traders depend on the connection to the east, which crosses the border to South Sudan after around 100 kilometres, at Bambouti. The Ugandan army (UPDF) was stationed in Obo from 2009 to 2017 in pursuit of the LRA, a rebel group led by Joseph Kony that originated in Uganda in the 1980s. As of 2011, the several hundred Ugandan soldiers in Obo were assisted by around 100 American military advisers, who operated their own base with offices and an airstrip. Both of these militaries withdrew from the CAR in mid-2017 (after my second field trip). Since early 2016, MINUSCA has also deployed a small contingent of around fifty soldiers to Obo. State actors have absolutely minimal resources – e.g. there is one sole police officer for the entire prefecture. The biggest security concerns for locals are the alleged presence of the LRA, the alleged abuses of Ugandan troops stationed in the village, and, more recently, the arrival of splinter groups of the Séléka and Anti-Balaka in the region. Security in Obo is perceived to be quite poor but this differs within town and in the wider region.

Baligubadle, as the first Somaliland case, lies at the border to Ethiopia and is inhabited by around 4,000 people. Another several hundred families live in the surrounding nomadic Gumburaha Banka (Somali for 'the plains by the hills') and the population swells during the rainy season.[115] The largest population group by far is the Isaaq/Arab[116] clan, which has multiple sub-clan divisions and members living on both sides of the international border. From 1988 to 1990, the town served as the headquarters of the Somali National Movement that liberated the country from Siad Barre and formed the Somaliland state.[117] To this day, the strong cooperation of security actors in the small regional capital and its nomadic outskirts perfectly exemplify the Somaliland model. Many individuals embody multiple actor roles: the mayor is at the same time a key local elder, an 'caqil' (pronounced 'aakil'),[118] of a local sub-clan. The state judge is simultaneously a respected Sharia judge. While the police commander is from another region, large shares of the rank and file are locals who are regularly paid by the central state in Hargeisa. The biggest security issues stem from the pressures on the traditional communally held grazing lands that are being privatized by state actors for agricultural development and personal property, the recurrent droughts depleting locals' livestock in the plains, and a particularly strenuous relationship towards Ethiopian security actors across the border. Inhabitants perceive security to be very good in town and still good in the wider arena.[119]

---

[115] Interview with Arab Sultan, Baligubadle, Somaliland, 7 May 2016.
[116] Clans are written as clan/sub-clan.
[117] Focus group discussion with Arab Elders, Baligubadle, Somaliland, 30 April 2016.
[118] Pronunciation guide for Somali words: c as guttural a, Arabic letter (ع); dh as guttural d mixed with r sound, Arabic letter (ض); q as guttural k, Arabic letter (ق); kh similar to 'ch'-sound in German 'Dach', Arabic letter (خ); x as strong h, Arabic letter (ح); ' as glottal stop, Arabic letter (ء); other letters similar to English pronunciation.
[119] See also the research brief Observatory of Conflict and Violence Prevention 2015. 'Baligubadle. District Conflict and Security Assessment Report': http://ocvp.org/docs/2015/Wave5/Baligubadle%20DCSA%202015.pdf.

Zeila borders a desert to the south and the Gulf of Aden to the north and has around 4,000 inhabitants of diverse origins. It lies only around twenty-five kilometres from the border to Djibouti. The two main groups in competition in the wider arena are the Ciise and the Gadabuursi. Ancient ruins remind of the town's Ottoman and pre-Ottoman glory but the port of Zeila has been surpassed by modern competitors in Somaliland's Berbera and in Djibouti, leading to economic decline and a focus on smuggling to Yemen. Security in town is considered very good due to the presence of around twenty-five policemen and the fact that the town is so small that it would be difficult for a potential thief or perpetrator to hide. Within town, clan structures have become mostly irrelevant and the Imams play only a spiritual role. The surrounding towns and villages are inhabited by the Ciise clan, which continues to rely primarily on traditional structures, and its leaders span the area between Somaliland, Djibouti, and Ethiopia. The rural population seems to handle problems using traditional structures and go to the police only when absolutely necessary. In fact, the neighbouring Ciise people feel that the government is expropriating them and that all the non-traditional positions in Zeila (business, security forces, administration) are predominantly occupied by non-Ciise. Between the rural surroundings and the administrative town of Zeila lies Tokhoshi, where many people engage in vast artisanal salt mining activities. Here, state, clan, and economic actors and narratives meet and at times clash with one another. Key security issues in the arena concern the contested political representation of different clans, tensions between the said clans in Tokhoshi over salt mining activities, and illicit cross-border movements to Yemen and Djibouti. Within the two towns of Zeila and Tokhoshi, respondents said security was very good, whereas they found it still good in the wider area.[120]

Daami quarter in Hargeisa hosts around 25,000 people. Non-pastoralist minorities, collectively labelled the Gabooye, were originally pushed from the town's centre to the outskirts in the 1950s.[121] Owing to Hargeisa's massive growth, the quarter now seems to lie quite centrally in the capital. In addition to the Gabooye, Daami also hosts many Oromo migrants from Ethiopia and borders a quarter inhabited

---

[120] See also the research brief Observatory of Conflict and Violence Prevention 2016. 'Zeila. District Conflict and Security Assessment Report': http://ocvp.o rg/docs/2015/Wave6/Zeila%202016.pdf.

[121] Vitturini 2017: 199–203.

by the politically influential Isaaq/Issa Musse clan. Gabooye elders play an important role and a village committee interacts with external donors. The police have only a minimal presence with half a dozen officers but reinforcements can be called from the nearby national headquarters. The youth are to a large degree without formal employment. One estimate put youth unemployment in Hargeisa at 80 per cent.[122] Young people pass the time chewing qat, meeting up, or playing football. Conflicts often arise over the use of football fields or results of the matches. Daami is also infamous for being host to criminal gangs that roam at night, creating insecurity within the quarter and throughout the capital. The main security concerns for inhabitants are state marginalization, at times even felt state repression, the presence of gangs, and the latent tensions between Gabooye and Isaaq/Issa Musse that frequently erupt into violent clashes. Security within the quarter is perceived between good and bad, while the wider capital's security is described as rather good.

Mundri town in South Sudan, with about 35,000 inhabitants, connects the capital, Juba, with the western part of the country. The predominantly Moro inhabitants mostly rely on a mixture of farming and forest-related activities, as well as some animal keeping, for their livelihood. Police and wildlife forces are present in Mundri with mostly locally recruited rank and file. The national army, SPLA, has a large contingent of around 200 troops stationed in the vicinity of Mundri. The National Security Services has a handful of officers in the area. During my field visit in late 2014, the commissioner was on 'sick leave' – he had left town after having been accused of accepting bribes from cattle keepers – and thus an acting commissioner had taken charge. Dinka cattle keepers had moved into Mundri West county from Jonglei and Lakes after the outbreak of renewed war in South Sudan in late 2013. Local chiefs and youth leaders suggested that the cattle keepers were sent by the national government with the agenda of taking the Moro's land. Rumours spread that the Moro are forming their own rebel training camp. Tensions culminated in the killing of Mundri's director of National Security Services in Mundri West by unknown assailants

---

[122] Document 2: Paragraph on employment in Somaliland, written by expert group on Security Sector Assessment, dated 31 October 2012, received May 2015.

in late December 2014.[123] Clashes between armed cattle keepers and local Moro farmers are the main security concern of Mundri's inhabitants. Security is perceived as very bad in the bush, where the cattle keepers pose a threat, and still bad in Mundri, as the government is said to pursue a violent agenda against local inhabitants.

Buseri is a calm village of around 7,000 people and lies just twenty kilometres outside South Sudan's second largest city of Wau. The inhabitants are mostly from the Bongo tribe but new tribes arrived in the 1960s and 1980s due to insecurity in other areas.[124] Inhabitants engage mostly in farming and a gravel site presents a key economic activity for the youth. Social communities of youth, elders, and farmers, each of which has a chairperson to handle internal problems, are gaining in prominence.[125] Locally, the Bongo chief exerts the strongest authority. New ethnic groups are integrated into society by recognizing the authority of the chief. The Catholic Church previously operated a renowned secondary school in Buseri in the mid-twentieth century and the ruins of its magnificent former buildings remain scattered throughout the forest. There is an SPLA camp close to the village for temporary stationing before reinforcements are sent to Raja. There are only five police officers for the entire administrative unit (the boma) and they have no means of transport. The large town of Wau lies north of Buseri and hosts key security actors, such as a large SPLA division, a contested state government, and a large UN intervention force. Here, a conflict over locals' marginalization and a felt Dinka domination in state institutions led to violent conflict in 2012.[126] Back in Buseri, people have two main concerns regarding security: first, armed cattle keepers enter the area on a seasonal basis and there are numerous reports of the destruction of crops and of threats against local farmers. Second, inhabitants are concerned about the misbehaviour of the special police forces or SPLA occasionally stationed in the village. Inhabitants feel rather safe within their village but feel threatened by cattle keepers when tending to their fields.

---

[123] Eye Radio (29 December 2014) 'National Security official shot dead': www.eyeradio.org/national-security-official-shot-dead/.
[124] Focus Group with elders, Buseri, South Sudan, 22 November 2014.
[125] Focus Group with youth, Buseri, South Sudan, 24 November 2014.
[126] Interview with Balanda Elder, Wau, South Sudan, 22 November 2014.

Raja town is the administrative centre of South Sudan's most expansive and least densely populated county.[127] Around 60,000 people live in the county,[128] of which around 10,000 reside in Raja town. The county shares a contested border with Sudan in the north and an unpoliced border with the CAR to the east. There are fifteen tribes which are about equally distributed among Muslims and non-Muslims.[129] Raja's inhabitants largely depend on goods from Sudan, even though the border was officially closed during my visit in late 2014. The road to the south-east, in the direction of Wau, is cut off for about half the year during the rainy season. The small, lightly populated, weakly connected town seems to be at the centre of national and regional politics: tensions of the sovereignty over the Kafia Kingi border region to the north have led both Sudan and South Sudan to station vast numbers of troops in or near Raja county.[130] The South Sudanese government hosts Darfuri rebels – locally dubbed the Tora Bora – near Raja town as a token in its struggle against the Khartoum government and as an ally against the southern opposition. The Tora Bora have been estimated to number up to 10,000. Local actors – the county commissioner, police, and elders – have no influence on their presence in their county. Even the United Nations Mission in South Sudan (UNMISS) is barred from investigating the area where the Darfuris took up camp. Owing to a change in strategy, UNMISS closed its Raja base in late 2014. While the Tora Bora seem to be generally well behaved towards the populace, their presence causes two serious security concerns for local inhabitants: first, the Sudan Armed Forces retaliated against this safe haven for their enemy by bombing the town in late 2014; second, the government represses any dissent against the Darfuris' presence, leading to widespread paranoia and fear. In late 2014, attacks on the commissioner's convoy and other ambushes by 'unknown' assailants pointed to rising resistance against the national government. Security is perceived as decent in town and very bad in the surroundings.

[127] During the time of visit. In October 2015, President Kiir redivided the ten states into twenty-eight, making Raja the capital of the much smaller Lol state. The implications are analysed in Schomerus & Aalen 2016.
[128] International Organization for Migration (2013) 'Village Assessment Survey. County Atlas. Raja County. Western Bahr el Ghazal State': http://iomsouthsu dan.org/tracking/sites/default/publicfiles/documents/WBeG_Raja_Atlas.pdf.
[129] Focus group discussion with Sultans, Raja, South Sudan, 27 November 2014.
[130] See Spittaels & Weyns 2014: 77–81.

Each of these local arenas provides for such a multitude of processes around the issue of security that each would merit individual analysis, from the geopolitical front line running through Raja to the historical legacy of the Gabooye's marginalization in Daami quarter.[131] However, the aim of this research is to look beyond single cases and find patterns. As a very first step in analysing the security arenas, I look for broad similarities as regards the type of strongest actors, their differentiation into an inner and outer circle, and the peripheral setting of the arena.

State penetration is comparatively deep in Somaliland and South Sudan, where multiple government institutions coexist, such as local administration and police, as well as nationally linked administrators and national army bases. In South Sudan, the national state presence is particularly high in Mundri and Raja, where large military contingents are based. The small Buseri village is left mostly to its own devices but lies only twenty kilometres from the second largest town in the country, Wau. The situation in Somaliland is similar: Zeila and Baligubadle have high state security deployments, due mostly to their locations bordering the Gulf of Aden and Ethiopia, respectively. Daami quarter, on the other hand, features only a minimal police presence but, as a part of the capital, police and army headquarters are not far away. The cases in CAR, in comparison, experience much lower state penetration, as administrations are underfunded (at times not funded at all) and state security effectives are a fraction of those in the other two countries, even when controlling for population levels. Only Bangassou saw some state redeployment during my visit in 2016 (see Table 2.2).

In addition to state actors, people also turn towards non-state actors to varying degrees. In Somaliland, strong traditional institutions take on many key security responsibilities. Their importance is particularly high in the nomadic area around Baligubadle but less so in the commercial port town of Zeila and the capital quarter of Daami. In South Sudan and the CAR, traditional leaders hold a weaker standing, their institutions having in many cases been invented by colonial authorities, but armed non-state actors are more proliferate. In South Sudan, traditional leaders and local government are often caught up amid competing government and rebel demands for loyalty.[132] Only in Buseri does the leadership of a traditional chief play a leading role in

---

[131] Vitturini 2017.   [132] See, historically, Leonardi 2013.

Table 2.2 *Local cases sorted by relative importance of actor types, degree of remoteness, and level of security*

	More	Average	Less
Strong state actors (CAR)		Bangassou	Obo, Paoua
(Somaliland)	Baligubadle, Zeila	Daami	
(South Sudan)	Mundri, Raja	Buseri	
Strong non-state actors	Paoua	Bangassou	Obo
	Baligubadle	Zeila	Daami
	Raja	Mundri, Buseri	
Strong international actors	Bangassou, Paoua, Obo		
			Baligubadle, Daami, Zeila
		Buseri, Raja	Mundri
Peripheral	Obo	Bangassou, Paoua	
	Zeila		Baligubadle, Daami
	Raja	Buseri	Mundri
Perceived security high		Bangassou, Obo	Paoua
	Baligubadle, Zeila	Daami	
		Buseri	Mundri, Raja

the security arena but, compared to non-state actors in other arenas, he has very limited means for ordering the security arena. In Mundri, civil leaders, and even armed groups, play a significant role in opposing the state. While in Raja most peaceful voices have been silenced by state repression, there is a heavy presence of Darfuri rebels and signs of oppositional forces outside of town. In the CAR, the disconnection from the central state has by default put many responsibilities in local institutions, despite their own weak authority and means of enforcement. Armed groups proliferate and are strong around Paoua. The vicinity of Bangassou also contains some armed groups and has quite an influential mediation board, as also seen in Paoua. Obo's non-state actors are relatively weak in comparison to the other arenas.

The CAR has a comparatively large intervention force in all three cases studied and has even had multiple deployments in Obo. South Sudan has hosted international interveners for many years but their presence is a rather marginal phenomenon in all three arenas studied: in Raja they closed down their base, in Buseri they are only in nearby Wau town, and in Mundri there is no international presence at all. None of the Somaliland cases has experienced an intervention, although officially the country is still part of Somalia, which hosts the world's second largest international peacekeeping mission.

In each country there is one case very distant to the capital: Raja, Obo, and Zeila. Buseri is itself a small village but, due to its proximity to the large South Sudanese administrative centre of Wau, not very peripheral. In the CAR, Paoua and Bangassou are hundreds of kilometres from the capital but are themselves important administrative centres. Baligubadle is about three hours from Somaliland's capital, while Daami quarter is even part of the capital and thus very centrally positioned. Mundri in South Sudan is also quite close to its capital and an important economic transit centre.

Finally, respondents describe security as the highest in two Somaliland cases, Zeila and Baligubadle, and the lowest in two South Sudanese, Mundri and Raja, and one CAR case, Paoua. The other cases fall roughly somewhere between these extremes. While these commonalities present some important descriptive findings on the cases, I argue that the crux is to be found in the ways actors order the arena. In other words, the nine local cases at the heart of this comparative study face different issues of security ranging from overlapping intrastate and interstate warfare in South Sudan's Raja to mostly non-lethal debates on land and grazing rights in Somaliland's Baligubadle. By embedding the findings comparatively into the security arena concept over the next chapters, I unveil crucial ordering patterns that span across these variegated security arenas.

3 | *Creating Centres and Peripheries in the National Arena*

There was a restaurant and bar serving decent pizza right next to my hotel in South Sudan's capital. It was a quiet place where I took out my laptop to get some work done. When I got back to the hotel in the late afternoon, a friend urgently counselled me not to go back to that place at night. In the evenings, she said, it was roaming with men in arms getting drunk. Many of these armed men are not simply from the neighbourhood. They used to be part of militia groups roaming through peripheral areas of the country. Today, they are members of official state forces and their behaviour is rarely checked. In fact, Juba hosts a large number of armed men that do not originate from the town itself. These former militia men hold power up to the highest echelons of administration – a feat that recurrently causes frictions with those populaces who see themselves as the autochthones of the area around Juba.[1]

Actors of centres and peripheries relate to one another in different manners. Broadly speaking, the CAR has mostly been characterized by peripheral neglect, South Sudan by central imposition, and Somaliland by negotiation between the two. The trajectories evolved from similar starting points after independence, when none of the three had a viable state or nation. The CAR was an agglomeration of vastly different groups that had little contact to one another. Conflict was kept comparatively low by the perpetuation of neglect, against which people in the peripheries did not feel the need to resist collectively until the Séléka rebellion in 2012. In Somaliland, independence came with high hopes of realizing the narrative of reunifying Somalis who had been divided by colonization. In the pursuit of this, however, the national government in Mogadishu turned to ever more violent means, to which peripheral actors reacted with resistance: some by toppling and taking over the government, and others (Somaliland and Puntland) by seeking

---

[1] See also Kindersley 2019.

88

independence or autonomy. Southern Sudan sought a similar path to Somaliland but with the difference that there never had been a strong local drive for a unified Sudan and that the centre was still too powerful for Southern Sudan to successfully break away.

Today, South Sudan is ruled by the SPLM/A, most of the leaders of which have backgrounds in the military struggle for independence afar from the capital. Militaries and their mind-sets continue to dominate the politics of South Sudan,[2] leading to hardened fronts between centre and periphery: the central government tries to impose its authority and faces resistance by peripheral contenders. CAR governments have long combined neglect of the peripheries with select punitive missions. But only since the mid-2000s have peripheral actors begun resisting the centre to change this, rather than just to create space for peripheral self-rule. In the early 1990s, Somaliland created a combined system of clan and political rule in which the centre continuously negotiates with the peripheries. Democratic and socioeconomic changes are slowly tipping the balance of power towards the state but the general combination persists. Somaliland's state authority is accepted by most but continuously defied by some peripheral actors in the east. In the three countries, relations between centre and periphery continue to be renegotiated.

Before comparing the local security arenas, I wish to delve into questions that cannot simply be answered on the local level. Through a cross-country comparison of historical trajectories and current characteristics of the national and international security arenas, I aim to trace changing relations between centre and peripheries. I investigate the national security arena to retrace the formation of the three respective states with three highly divergent security apparatuses and varying relations between national centres and their peripheries. Then, I look at the international arena to examine how security in the nine cases is shaped by international interventions as well as by more unofficial regional power plays. I conclude by briefly comparing how the three countries' struggles between centre and periphery have shaped today's national security arenas.

[2] Cf. Öhm 2014: 217.

National Security Arenas

In the CAR, rulers interpreted state forces as a potential threat, as they had either themselves come to power through a coup d'état or seen others attempt to do so. Each successive ruler attempted to pre-empt the threat by reducing the overall strength of state security and recruiting parallel forces mostly from his ethno-regional origin.[3] While in the CAR self-enriching leaders ruled an officially bureaucratic state, Somaliland transformed a clan-based reality into a state. The rebel group SNM stood at the origins of independent Somaliland. Its forces were converted into the state security forces and made up the bulk of the country's fighters.[4] These former SNM combatants were mostly recruited from Isaaq clan militias. Other clans and militias continue to be underrepresented, although even 'enemy' armed groups during the civil war of the 1980s were partly recruited into the official forces. In South Sudan, similarly, the new state created its forces by integrating militias. Under a 'big tent' policy, all armed groups in South Sudan – those fighting for independence, allies of Khartoum, and local armed groups – were expected to put on the uniforms of the new state.[5] In comparison, South Sudan's roughly 300,000 state security personnel[6] vastly eclipse Somaliland's approximately 20,000[7] and the CAR's around 5,000 operational state forces.[8]

The security apparatus of the CAR, the weakest of the three, is the outcome of a deliberate reduction of the state army. Ruling presidents were regularly challenged from within, by members of the small elite circle in the capital oftentimes, just when an elite risked falling from grace. In other words, as Lotje de Vries and Andreas Mehler demonstrate, the disorder rulers created in the CAR has also made them

---

[3] See Bigo 1988: 80f; Herbert *et al.* 2013: 4–5; Mehler 2012: 54–5.
[4] Renders 2012: 93–6.   [5] Pinaud 2014; de Waal 2014.
[6] This includes all armed state forces as estimated before the recent civil war in de Waal 2014: 355.
[7] Cf. Caspersen 2012; Hills 2014b: 174.
[8] The Inspector General of the army spoke of 7,000 currently enrolled army members but of these he could not guarantee more than around 2,000 to be operational. The gendarmerie, he said, officially has 4,000 officers and the police should be even smaller than that. Based on reports from former and current real effectives, I would estimate that, optimistically speaking, the police and gendarmerie have 1,500 operational officers each. Berman & Lombard 2008: 13ff; ICG 2007; Vircoulon 2017. Interview with Inspector General of the Armed Forces, Bangui, 20 August 2017.

unable to stabilize their claims to power.[9] The army became a tool to voice a challenge to the ruling regime. A cursory glance throughout history demonstrates this recurring trend: Jean-Bédel Bokassa set the precedent only five years into independence, on New Year's Eve 1965. Then president Dacko started doubting then commander-in-chief Bokassa's loyalty and threatened to dismiss him[10] – Bokassa pre-empted this step by taking over the capital with his army of just 500 soldiers. After Bokassa was toppled by the French in 1979, the French reinstalled Dacko, who was soon ousted by army general Kolingba in 1981. Half a year later, two other army generals, Bozizé and Mbaikoua, together with civilian party leader Patassé, tried unsuccessfully to stage a coup against Kolingba. Patassé then won the 1993 elections but faced army mutinies by 1996, which he could only withstand with the support of an international peacekeeping mission. In 2001, General Kolingba attempted to take back power but was unsuccessful. Afterwards, it was again General Bozizé's turn for first an aborted putsch in 2002 and then a successful attempt in 2003. Bigo interjects that due to the government's minimal effectiveness and authority we cannot speak of a 'coup d'état' since there was no state of which to speak.[11] In more theoretic terms, CAR's presidents did not need a large security force because they did not aim to control the peripheries, while the actors in the peripheries rarely resisted and, if so, only for peripheral self-governance (until the Séléka rebellion).[12] State security forces were thus more of a threat to regime survival than they were a safeguard.[13] The absence of the army in two of the three local security arenas studied and only a minimal presence of police and gendarmerie in all arenas are the present legacy of this history.

South Sudan could not differ more drastically. A whole array of state security actors with large effectives is present in all three of the studied local security arenas. After the SPLM signed a peace agreement with Khartoum in 2005, they became the de facto government of then Southern Sudan. From a position of strength, SPLM leader Salva Kiir integrated a vast array of formerly conflicting groups into the SPLA fold under his 'big tent' strategy.[14] While the SPLA's territorial reach thus grew on paper, in reality the 'integrated' forces retained their command structures and stayed in their original areas. Militia leaders

---

[9] De Vries & Mehler 2019. [10] Bigo 1988: 54–5. [11] Ibid.: 51.
[12] Cf. Lombard 2015. [13] Mehler 2009b. [14] Pinaud 2014; de Waal 2014.

frequently resorted to conflict in their bids to claim a better share in national or local politics – such as David Yau Yau[15] or Peter Gadet.[16] The need to appease resistance through integration meant that, rather than demobilizing security forces, the army grew from 40,000 in 2004 to 240,000 in 2011.[17] The failure to integrate the varying forces enabled the rapid and violent rift after the December 2013 fallout at the highest level of government, between President Kiir and his recently dismissed Vice President Machar.[18] In August 2015, a new peace agreement was struck with an overbearing presence of armed actors – perpetuating the impression that access to central power is best gained through violence. The dangerous bargain to bring both government and opposition forces into the capital failed: in July 2016, the two forces – most likely instigated by the government – fought each other in the capital and caused further splits to the nation's security apparatus.[19] Such splits can also be witnessed in the studied local security arenas, where suspicious government forces are fighting rebel groups that include defected soldiers.

In Somaliland, the SNM rebellion started similarly but evolved differently. It only fully got underway in 1988, when President Barre ordered his air force to bomb Hargeisa. Appalled by the immense civilian casualties, a multitude of Isaaq clan militias joined the rebellion, massively expanding the movement.[20] War ended in 1991, leaving only minimal time for the new forces to integrate. After independence, sub-clan divisions remained apparent in the new state forces and led to heavy infighting in 1996 and 1997 over control of the two most strategic assets, the Hargeisa airport and the Berbera port. After conferences in Hargeisa, Somaliland's political leaders decided they needed to integrate the forces to create a viable, democratic state.[21] In the late 1980s and early 1990s, almost all weapons and armed forces were embedded in clan militias. To reduce clan armament, the government required recruits to bring their own weapons upon joining the security forces where they would in return receive employment. This was highly successful in transferring manpower and weaponry to the weak Somaliland state, thereby tilting the balance: while the state had thus far depended on clans for enforcement, clan leaders now had to rely on

[15] Schomerus & de Vries 2014. [16] See HSBA 2013. [17] de Waal 2014: 355.
[18] Rolandsen 2015a. [19] See UNMISS 2016. [20] Bradbury 2008: 68–9.
[21] Renders 2012: 154–9.

the police and army to enforce their traditional contracts. Mutual security interdependency between traditional peripheral and central state institutions is therefore a deliberate and inherent part of Somaliland's political system. The local security arenas host state forces that are made up of former militia forces and recruits from Somaliland's dominant clans. This creates a good rapport with clan leaders of those same clans, while fuelling suspicion from leaders of other clans.

The integration of non-Isaaq forces was indeed contested, as many of the remaining clans had fought the SNM on the side of Barre during the civil war. Members of the Warsengeli and Dulbahante clans in the east were sceptical of integration and many preferred keeping the weapons in their community and area. The bring-your-own-gun approach to disarmament discriminated against members of the Gabooye minority, who rarely owned guns or had the means to purchase one.[22] Full disarmament and integration into the state were thus confined to Isaaq areas in the centre, followed by Gadabuursi and Ciise in the west, and the least by peripheries inhabited by the Dulbahante and Warsengeli in the east. Government hierarchies in the security domain are strongly linked to the Ministry of Interior, which supervises the governors, the police, and even the traditional elders. Traditional structures also find themselves represented both in the peripheries, where usually lower-ranking elders live and take office in rural institutions, and in the capital where the higher-ranking sultans reside and are integrated in the House of Elders and the board of the nine clans.[23] This variety also means that aspirant elites can draw on multiple sources of legitimacy, including state, tradition, religion, business, and education.[24] Baligubadle, as a former SNM stronghold, unsurprisingly features a positive rapport between local and central actors.[25] Zeila's Ciise inhabitants prefer handling issues outside state channels, while Daami's Gabooye feel they never were given the chance to partake in state security institutions.

Even more so than Somaliland's security apparatus that gradually loses authority towards the country's fringes, the CAR's security forces were always heavily concentrated in the capital. Contact to its

---

[22] Interview with Police Trainer, Hargeisa, Somaliland, 25 April 2016.
[23] In fact, Alice Hills finds clan-based relations between centre and periphery to be the main connecting factor: Hills 2016: 1077.
[24] Glawion *et al.* 2019: 287. [25] Cf. Figure 3.1.

Figure 3.1 House painted in colours of the Somaliland flag, Baligubadle, Somaliland, May 2015

peripheries was confined to short punitive missions. In 2006, Bozizé used state forces to punish the population in and around Paoua for (alleged) support of the APRD rebellion and to seize the diamond collecting offices in the centre and north-east and place them in the hands of his loyalists – a move that fed into the rise of the Séléka rebellion. State officials often refuse to take up posts in the periphery and, when they do, they lack allocated budgets, staff, and the equipment to do their jobs.[26] Prefects and their subordinates thus manage administration in an ad hoc manner, based on their personal traits and interpretations with minimal supervision (or help) from the centre. Army forces are sent to the country's margins without equipment and with accumulated decades of salary arrears. Police forces hold only a token presence outside the capital, with few tools of enforcement and minimal oversight by central institutions. The state security apparatus is not only weak but also largely disconnected between centre and periphery. Although chiefs – Chef de Quartier, de Village, et de Groupe – play a key but low-ranking role in state administration, they have no say at the national level. Civil society organizations are

---

[26] See on the education sector in rebel-held Ndélé: Le Noan & Glawion 2018.

widespread but, aside from youth and women's organizations in numerous localities, their national headquarters do not consolidate issues at the centre.[27] Political parties and candidates visit the peripheries almost exclusively during election time. The Catholic Church is an exception with its almost nationwide and hierarchical structures. These examples show how the disconnect spans across most parts of state and society. Recurring conflict in the CAR erupts in the peripheries – such as through Bozizé's liberators or the Séléka alliance – and then moves towards the capital, as the government is neither able to impose itself against peripheral violence nor willing to negotiate over underlying grievances. After the Séléka's unsuccessful bid to hold on to power from the capital, armed groups have again retracted to the peripheries.

In South Sudan, officially, state security forces are present throughout the country and in large numbers.[28] However, the national army was never truly consolidated and the recent rift between 'the government' and 'the opposition' was a dangerous simplification.[29] This binary view forced other actors to ally themselves with one of the two sides to gain a voice in the political arena. President Kiir even decreed the redivision of the peripheries into twenty-eight states (from a previous ten) as a political tool to reorganize political entities in a way more suitable to the centre, to divide oppositional strongholds, and to reward loyalists with state positions.[30] Many divisions between today's warring factions can be traced back to pre-independence militia groups. The remaining state army is dominated by members of the Dinka clan. The army, together with the NSS, acts as the extended arm of the central government in all three studied local security arenas. Other actors, such as police, administration, and traditional leaders, seem to be more embedded locally and at times even dare to resist central orders. Chiefs play a crucial role for people's everyday security concerns but the manipulation of this institution by competing centres, both historically and today, undermines their legitimacy.[31] Churches form some of the very few – possibly the only – non-state institutions

---

[27] For instance, while the Organisation des Femmes Centrafricaines (OFCA) women's organizations were active in three peripheral localities visited in early 2016, the national headquarter was closed and inactive.

[28] See the varying actual presence of state officials and the impact on security: De Juan & Pierskalla 2015.

[29] ICG 2016; de Vries 2015.   [30] Schomerus & Aalen 2016.

[31] See Leonardi 2013: 167ff.

with a role on multiple levels and a significant impact on security. For instance, the church-led Wunlit conference still is portrayed as a model for conflict resolution.[32]

Somaliland's security-related actors, such as state administrators, the police and army, and traditional elders, attempt to span the national arena from centre to periphery, seeking strong connections in both directions. Continuous negotiations over relative roles mean that claims to authority remain in flux:[33] the centre might seek to expand its domain (e.g. on land rights) but peripheral actors might defend their claims even through violence. South Sudan's centre seems to leave little room for negotiation with the peripheries. Rather, through centrally controlled actors such as its NSS and SPLA, it seeks to impose its will on the peripheries. These attempts are not often met with success, as peripheral actors stage violent resistance and centrally linked actors might defect to stage their own claims to a better position at the centre – in other words, a 'state' actor does not necessarily represent the central government. In the CAR, competition in and over the state has been centred on a small, closed elite circle in the capital being rotated in and out of government jobs.[34] Elites who take up positions at the centre quickly lose touch with their region's home base.[35] Central neglect and peripheral self-rule mean that few actors hold both central and peripheral roles.

The story becomes even more complex, because several security actors and incidences in the peripheral cases do not relate solely to the national centre. International entanglements of peacekeepers and transnational groups create decision centres outside the countries' national capitals.

International Security Arena

As national centres relate to their peripheries, other centres in the international arena similarly relate to the three countries as their own peripheries. This goes for international peacekeeping missions, for neighbouring states that seek regional dominance, and for transnational actors that look for opportunities beyond their country of origin. Somaliland remains mostly isolated from international forums as

---

[32] See Öhm 2014: 145, 174–7.   [33] Cf. Renders & Terlinden 2010.
[34] See Carayannis & Lombard 2015: 6–7.   [35] See Mehler 2011.

international actors and interventions focus on dealing with the rump Somalia state centred in Mogadishu. Somaliland thereby both evades the pitfalls and eschews the benefits of international integration. South Sudan is most contested in the international arena as multiple governments from within the region and afar play out their power struggles in the country. Despite heavy interferences and a large peacekeeping mission, foreign powers have proven incapable of halting the ongoing civil war. The CAR has only recently become the locus of official and heavy international intervention. Mostly it plays a marginal international role and is particularly hard hit by foreign armed groups crossing the CAR's porous borders for illicit extractions.

Rather than being subjects of international cooperation, all three countries are most often objects of foreign intervention. Regional organizations have played decisive roles in establishing peacekeeping missions and negotiating peace agreements. The IGAD is involved in the peace processes of its members Somalia and South Sudan. The CAR borders countries of the IGAD community and is member to the overlapping regional organizations of the Communauté Économique des États de l'Afrique Centrale (CEEAC) and Communauté Économique et Monétaire de l'Afrique Centrale (CEMAC).[36] Both organizations and its members played decisive roles in peacekeeping missions and the protection or unseating of CAR's governments.[37] While Somaliland is not officially recognized by any international organization, its relative stability has allowed several organizations to open coordinating offices for all of Somalia in Hargeisa.

On the non-military intervention side, the peace processes in all three countries have been greatly influenced by foreign powers. The CAR's recent transitory period (2014–2016) was dominated by international actors, first and foremost the UN, which provided security for the transitional president, as well as led most of the steps along the way from a national forum and constitution drafting to national elections.[38] The CAR's successive disarmament, demobilization, and reintegration (DDR) and security sector reform (SSR) programmes were marked by 'near complete dependence on donors' assistance',[39] primarily the UNDP, the World Bank, France, and the EU. In Sudan, international mediators pushed for an agreement that set the groundwork for

---

[36] See Gatsi 2016.   [37] See Meyer 2009; Welz 2014.   [38] See Marchal 2016.
[39] N'Diaye 2009: 56.

a southern referendum on independence. South Sudan's CPA of 2005 was ironically anything but comprehensive: it reduced the multiple conflicts in the Sudans to the north–south dimension.[40] Notable was the backing of the USA, Norway, and the UK, although the process officially remained under the guise of IGAD.[41] Aside from South Sudan, IGAD has also been involved in the peace process of Somalia.[42] Here, IGAD took up the task of re-establishing a federal government in Somalia in 2000 and has successively supported the centralized leaders' claim to power to the detriment of other actors in the country. Somaliland has not witnessed direct interference but rather limited international assistance in building up its security forces, mostly through training and equipment for the coastguard by the EU, for the overall security and justice sector by DFID and UNDP, and allegedly by private companies for the Oil Protection Unit.

As a response to violent civil wars in South Sudan, Somalia, and the CAR, international organizations have deployed large peacekeeping missions (see Table 3.1): the AU heads a mission of 22,000 in Somalia and had a mission of 6,000 peacekeepers in the CAR from 2013 to 2014. The UN took over the short-lived AU mission in the CAR in 2014 and now has around 12,000 soldiers and police officers on the ground, as well as a mission of 13,500 in South Sudan. Somaliland, on the other hand, has not seen any intervention force on its territory since independence.

The United Nations Mission in Sudan (UNMIS) was established following the peace agreement between north and south in 2005 to monitor the agreement, assist in resolving remaining issues of contention, and to support state-building efforts. Following independence in 2011, the mission transitioned by adding an S for 'South' to its acronym (UNMISS) but made minimal adaptions to its mandate. It was thus unfit to manage the tensions that were increasing within the south rather than with the north. When an inner-party dispute of the ruling SPLM led to the outbreak of civil war in December 2013, the UN was unable to protect civilians, and could not even stop atrocities from being committed (mostly by government soldiers) against humanitarians.[43] Civilians sought refuge from the fighting by fleeing

---

[40] ICG 2014b: 3.   [41] Young 2012.   [42] See Healy 2011.
[43] Cf. attack by government soldiers on humanitarians in the Terrain Hotel in July 2016: Simon Little (7 August 2017) 'South Sudan: Time for Humanitarians

Table 3.1 *International interventions and contributors*

	CAR	South Sudan	Somalia
Current mission	MINUSCA	UNMISS	AMISOM
Starting year	2014	2011	2008
Total personnel	11,850	13,500	22,000
Largest contributors	Rwanda, 1,300	India, 2,300	Uganda, 6,200
	Burundi, 1,100	Nepal, 1,900	Burundi, 5,400
	Pakistan, 1,100	Ethiopia, 1,250	Ethiopia, 4,400
	Cameroon, 1,050	Kenya, 1,050	Kenya, 3,650
	Egypt, 1,000	China, 1,050	Djibouti 950
Select other missions	EUTM-RCA, 2016–	RPF, 2017–	IGASOM, 2005–7
	RCI-LRA, 2009–17	UNISFA, 2011–	UNOSOM II, 1993–5
	Sangaris, 2013–16	UNMIS, 2005–11	UNOSOM I, 1992
	EUFOR-RCA, 2014–15		
	MISCA, 2013–14		

Total personnel and largest contributors in March 2016 for CAR and South Sudan and in April 2017 for Somalia.

to UN military bases. The mission became entirely preoccupied with protecting the more than 200,000 internally displaced people who had come on base. The mission thus neglected its wider duties and closed multiple smaller bases, such as that in Raja, and was wholly unable to enforce a ceasefire between the warring parties. IGAD sent a Regional Protection Force (RPF) to Juba to monitor and enforce a peace agreement signed between the opposition and government in August 2015. The first few hundred troops only arrived in mid-2017 – that is, one year after the peace agreement had failed spectacularly.[44]

While the intervention in South Sudan counts few successes, intervention in Somalia has been just as arduous. Ethiopian troops and a US-backed alliance of warlords toppled Somalia's Union of Islamic Courts in December 2006. As the Ethiopians were seen as invaders, this

---

to Get Tough', *Irinnews*: www.irinnews.org/opinion/2017/08/07/south-sudan -time-humanitarians-get-tough.

[44] UNMISS (8 August 2017) 'Press Conference on Arrival of Regional Protection Forces into Juba, South Sudan': https://unmiss.unmissions.org/press-conference -arrival-regional-protection-forces-juba-south-sudan.

intervention strengthened resistance movements such as Al-Shabaab.[45] The Ethiopians were soon replaced, first by an IGAD mission (IGASOM) that was then quickly succeeded by the African Union Mission in Somalia (AMISOM), which is active to this day. This mission originally excluded neighbouring states from participating, as both Kenya and Ethiopia, with their own large Somali minorities, would not be seen as neutral peacekeepers. In 2011 and 2012, however, Kenya and Ethiopia crossed into Somali territory to protect their borders from within Somalia. They officialized their interventions by paying lip service to the AMISOM command but continued to act autonomously.[46] These combined effectives make AMISOM one of the largest peacekeeping missions in the world. While Somaliland has not experienced any military intervention, it is important to keep in mind the immensity of the Somali intervention when investigating relations with its neighbours: as four key regional powers (Djibouti, Ethiopia, Kenya, and Uganda) have invested so much in Somalia, the mission has become too big to fail. Recognizing Somaliland could be interpreted as the failure of their foreign policy towards Somalia.

Following army mutinies in 1996, the first official peacekeeping mission deployed to the CAR. Since then, numerous missions have followed. They all had in common strong contributions by neighbouring and regional states as well as the deep involvement of France. The first missions were quite small in number and geographic distribution.[47] The African Union Mission in the CAR (MISCA) was the first large peacekeeping mission to deploy and it arrived in late 2013 after the Séléka had toppled Bozizé from power. A UN peacekeeping mission, the MINUSCA,[48] replaced MISCA in 2014 but initially kept most MISCA contingents on board. More than just a re-hatting exercise, MINUSCA increased its strength to more than 10,000 troops, almost 2,000 police, and nearly 1,000 civilian personnel. Unlike former missions, it deployed throughout all sixteen prefectures. While MINUSCA is now the dominant international security actor, it initially competed with other missions. A French force of 2,000 (Operation Sangaris) took the leading military role in dislodging the Séléka from 2013 until mid-2015, and fully withdrew in 2016, and a 1,000-strong

---

[45] See Elmi 2010: chap. 4; Hansen 2013: 57ff; Verhoeven 2009: 416.
[46] See Williams 2016.   [47] See Meyer 2009; Welz 2016: 578.
[48] UNSC (10 April 2014), 'Resolution 2149 (2014)', S/RES/2149: www
.globalr2p.org/media/files/unsc-resolution-2149.pdf.

EU force (EUFOR-RCA) deployed in 2015 to secure the capital. Both missions have re-enlisted members into the ongoing EU training mission (EUTM-RCA),[49] which attempts to reform the Forces Armées Centrafricaines (FACA) parallel to (or in competition with) UN disarmament and reform efforts.[50] Uganda was engaged with around 1,500 troops in the south-east and supported by around 100 American advisors in the Regional Cooperation Initiative against the LRA (RCI-LRA).[51] Up until they left in mid-2017, they had successfully kept the Séléka and Anti-Balaka conflict out of their area of operation, which includes Obo.

Heavy international interventions in all three countries have not brought forth the desired ameliorations in security, development, or state-building. Successive disarmament programmes and peacekeeping interventions in the CAR since the early 2000s could not prevent the 2012 rebellion, the legacy of which fuels violence to this day. Popular resentment towards MINUSCA is increasing, as it is unable to reinstate security, and inhabitants accuse it of having ulterior motives for its

Figure 3.2 Billboard advertising the EU training mission, Bangui, CAR, August 2017

[49] See Figure 3.2. [50] See Vircoulon 2017.
[51] See Titeca & Costeur 2015; Brubacher *et al.* 2017.

interventions. UNMISS and its predecessor UNMIS have not been able to halt South Sudan's trajectory towards further militarization since the peace agreement and independence. AMISOM's ten-year deployment has recently led to military gains against the Al-Shabaab Islamist insurgents but the failure to promote an internally legitimized political order could lead to the destabilization of currently secure political orders, such as Somaliland and Puntland. International intervention thus has no linear impact on stabilizing a state but rather presents opportunities for all involved actors to reposition themselves in the arena. And none of the interventions can be understood without the regional power players driving them.

Driving intervention and negotiations is one way of making a claim for regional dominance. Key powers also play indirect roles in the security arenas of all three countries. The interventions of regional organizations are often facades, behind which nations seek to obscure their power struggles. Chad attempts to influence the Central African scene through CEMAC[52] and IGAD is a platform for competition between Ethiopia, Kenya, and Uganda.[53] Ethiopia and Kenya are involved in interventions and negotiations in both South Sudan and Somalia. Uganda is even more ambitious: it was one of the first and main contributors to AMISOM, directly interfered to protect the South Sudanese government against the opposition, and sent a large anti-LRA force of 1,500 soldiers to the CAR.

With fighting between factions in South Sudan ongoing, latent tensions with Sudan have remained unaddressed. Parts of the border between north and South Sudan have yet to be demarcated. Sudan is benefitting from the turmoil in the south by creating facts on the ground in the oil-rich border areas, such as by trying to change borderlines around Abyei.[54] Uganda has long used South Sudan as a playing field for its struggles with its historical enemy Sudan, which among other things supported the Ugandan rebel movement LRA. However, tensions have eased since 2008 and it is no longer quite as simple to trace Uganda's current interests in upholding the Kiir government.[55] Historically, Ethiopian relations oscillated from strong support for the SPLA rebellion against Khartoum in the 1980s to chasing the rebels from their safe haven in Ethiopia after the Derg regime fell in 1991.

---

[52] Cf. Meyer 2009.   [53] Cf. Healy 2011: 116.   [54] ICG 2015: 20.
[55] Cf. Schomerus 2012.

Today, Ethiopia is largely driven by the aim to reduce spillover fighting in its own border territories and to claim regional dominance. Kenya and Ethiopia compete for the role of the dominant regional player in part through their influential roles in UNMISS and AMISOM.

The dominant issue of external interference in the CAR is the continued French influence following independence. After the CAR's independence from France in 1960, the former colonizer remained highly influential through a continuous military presence, high-level positions in the state administration, and by dominating the economy.[56] Three presidents, Bokassa, Patassé, and Bozizé, tried breaking this unilateral grip on power by using competition between France and Chad against Libya to their own advantage. However, while Bokassa was on a visit to Libya in September 1979, French troops took control of the Bangui airport, barred Bokassa from returning, and reinstalled former president David Dacko to the presidency.[57] Kolingba, who took over power in 1982, was also firmly in the grasp of French influence throughout the 1980s. Patassé won popular elections both in 1993 and in 1999, running, among other things, on an anti-French platform. While the president displayed a weak internal ability to hold on to power, external forces aligned to get rid of him: France tacitly endorsed coup-plotter Bozizé's return to the CAR;[58] the president of Chad, Idriss Déby, provided troops; DR Congo's president, Joseph Kabila, arms; Congo's president, Denis Sassou-Nguesso, funds; while Gabon's president, Omar Bongo, accepted the move.[59] Chad became heavily influential in the country as the 'bras fort' of the French.[60] Bozizé tried breaking the Chadian-French grip by seeking South African support. Chad then tacitly endorsed (if not supported) the Séléka rebellion to topple him, while regional as well as French troops in the country did nothing to save Bozizé.[61] The ensuing peacekeeping mission, MISCA, was composed of around two-thirds armed forces from neighbouring states (Chad: 860; Cameroon: 1,300; Congo,

---

[56] See Baxter 2011.   [57] Kalck 2005: xxxv–xxxvi.
[58] Andreas Mehler suggests that 'most successful coups are ... considered to have been tacitly endorsed by Paris before they actually happened' (2012: 52).
[59] ICG 2007: 15–16.   [60] See Käihkö & Utas 2014: 72–3.
[61] Gerold & Merino 2014; de Vries & Glawion 2015.

Rep.: 990; Congo, DR: 980).[62] As Roland Marchal succinctly put it, the CAR's regions form but the peripheries of its neighbouring states.[63]

The pan-Somali struggle shaped Somalia's post-independence era: the Shifta wars in north-east Kenya from 1963 to 1969, the Ogaden uprising in 1963, and the continued colonization of Djibouti by France all drove heated debates in Somali politics. During the 1970s, Barre supported the Ogaden National Liberation Front (ONLF) in Ethiopia and even went to war against the government directly. He lost and Ethiopia repaid him by hosting rebellious groups that were fighting Barre such as the SNM, which later founded independent Somaliland, and the SSDF, which created autonomous Puntland.[64] Barre armed Ogadeen clan members to fight against the mostly Isaaq SNM, leading to lasting animosities between the two groups, visible today in inter-clan tensions around Baligubadle. Although regional and international actors today view relations with Somaliland as secondary to those with the government in Mogadishu, the Somaliland alternative provides them with some strategic opportunities. Ethiopia's greatest worry is a strong Somali nationalist state that will again assert claims to Ethiopia's own Somali territories or support that region's rebellion against the Ethiopian government. Kenya similarly wants to stave off negative repercussions from bordering Somalia – especially since Somali terrorists attacked tourists on Kenyan ground in 2011 – and prevent their own Somali territories and minorities from becoming enflamed by jihadi-nationalist rhetoric out of Somalia. Kenya and Ethiopia play a dangerous balancing act between supporting a central government in Mogadishu with minimal internal legitimacy in its fight against the terrorist threat from Al-Shabaab and keeping the country divided to prevent an overall nationalist agenda.

---

[62] African Union Mission in the Central African Republic (2 September 2014) 'Troop and Police Numbers': http://misca.peaceau.org/en/page/116-troop-and-police-contributing-countries-1. The Chadian contingent was pressured to withdraw from the mission in April 2014 after killing numerous civilians at a demonstration in the capital. African Union Peace and Security Council (9 April 2014) 'Information Note of the AU Commission on the Incident that Took Place in Bangui on 29 March 2014 and the Withdrawal by the Republic of Chad of its Contingent from MISCA': www.peaceau.org/uploads/auc-info-note -427psc-car-8-4-2014.pdf.

[63] Marchal 2009: 5.   [64] See Lewis 2008.

Involvement by foreign governments and more clandestine actors in the three countries is facilitated by the porosity of their borders: the CAR's borders are the most uncontrolled, South Sudan's the most contested, and Somaliland's rather well secured apart from the east. The contested border towards rump Somalia creates overlapping claims in Somaliland's eastern areas.[65] While Somaliland defines its borders along the former British Somaliland territory, Puntland formed as an autonomous region in 1998 on the basis of clan loyalty of the Darood/Harti that extend into eastern Somaliland.[66] The outcome is parallel administrative institutions, the uncontrolled flow of arms, and frequent confrontations between pro-Puntland or secessionist groups and the Somaliland army. A very porous but less contested border lies towards Djibouti, where the Somali Ciise hold the presidency and thus draw dual loyalties of Somaliland's western population of the Ciise towards Djibouti. In South Sudan, following independence in 2011, the SPLA was split into groups that found themselves in 'their' new state, while those that remained in Sudan became the SPLA north. Sudan has largely occupied the border areas that officially still await demarcation to either of the two Sudans, leading to a massive military build-up in the border areas.[67] South Sudan, on the other hand, continues to hold ties with oppositional groups within Sudan, such as the SPLA-North and Darfuri rebel groups.[68] Compared to the militarized borders of South Sudan, the CAR's borders continue to be a non-entity: the state does not staff any of its significant border checkpoints, except for on the main trade route to Cameroon. At best, control of the borders is in the hands of its neighbouring states, leaving the flow of goods, arms, and people to external powers.

Far beyond international competition during the Cold War, regional power struggles continue to put pressure on the national security arena. Bozizé would not have gained power without regional backing – and, had he not fallen out of grace with Chad, he would not have faced the large rebellion that went on to topple him alone. South Sudan's

---

[65] De facto, the former British Somaliland and former Italian Somalia spent sixty of the last 100 years divided: the British defeated the Italians in 1941 and unified the territories but the Italian territories were returned under a UN trusteeship from 1950 until independence in 1960. A few days after independence, the two countries unified but Somaliland dismantled the union in 1991.

[66] See Doornbos 2002: 101–3.   [67] See Spittaels & Weyns 2014.

[68] ICG 2015.

president, Salva Kiir, received strong support from the Ugandan military to halt a powerful oppositional advance to the capital in early 2014.[69] Without this help, the civil war would have taken a very different turn (however, it is impossible to make assumptions as to whether it would have been any less violent). Somalia's federal government continues to claim authority over Somaliland but the Mogadishu government would not exist without the backing of diplomatic actors and the protection of 14,000 troops (almost three-quarters of the mission) from Ethiopia, Kenya, and Uganda. It is not internal developments but international strategy that continues to bar Somaliland from gaining recognition of its independence.

The Legacy of Centre–Periphery Relations

In Somaliland, the state regained its independence in 1991 from a position of strength, on the one hand – the rebel liberation movement SNM had won the civil war against the dictator Siad Barre and his local allies. On the other hand, the new state was extremely weak and leaders were divided. Consolidation of the state through enforcement would not have proven an easy answer after the enemy that kept the alliance together (Barre) had been defeated. Central actors of the SNM and other key clan leaders thus turned towards negotiation to create a feasible political order in Somaliland. The openness to dialogue sidelined some violent actors and allowed central actors to focus limited means of imposition on the few remaining hostile ones. The negotiated stance of Somaliland also made this peripheral country a dialogue partner for international centres, even when it failed to gain recognition of its independence. The constant possibility for peaceful negotiation between centre and periphery thus enables an environment where actors in the local arena have a larger say on matters of security than in the other two countries. This relationship continues to shape the local security arenas: Baligubadle, as the former SNM headquarter, sees trust among state and non-state actors; Zeila, as a historically contested and peripheral zone, has actors that are more suspicious of one another; and, while Daami quarter is part of the capital, it lacks the

---

[69]   Red Pepper (1 February 2014) 'Machar: UPDF Denied Us Juba Victory': www .redpepper.co.ug/machar-updf-denied-us-juba-victory/.

historically accepted clan institutions the Somaliland model demands and thus is marked at times by violent tension.

In South Sudan, centre–periphery relations were marked by a vastly different trajectory: shaped throughout the past century by much higher levels of violence, claims to power had become heavily militarized. Many peripheral actors in the studied local security arenas pursued more leeway to govern themselves but increasingly felt that even this self-reliance was hampered by a central power that sought to take away their land, which pushed many to take up arms. The international arena saw neighbouring states competing over regional hegemony even within the South Sudanese territory. The UN peacekeeping intervention was far too weak to oppose the government and was reluctant to use the minimal means it had to protect civilians and civil actors during the war. The relations between centre and periphery in South Sudan thus pit actors on both sides into direct confrontation over rigid claims that seem irreconcilable, while not allowing for negotiation over fluid cohabitation, as seen in Somaliland. All three local security arenas in South Sudan feature struggles between those that describe themselves as the first inhabitants of the land – the 'autochthones' – and those they perceive as violently encroaching on their arena with support from the centre.

The CAR is a particular case because centre–periphery relations are mostly interrupted, as actors on both sides rarely attempt to make a claim towards the other. The narrative of neglect has raised discontent in the peripheries. Peripheral grievances and transnational armed groups were brought into the centre and the capital by the recent Séléka rebellion. This rebellion triggered a massive international intervention force that tries to compensate for the state's failure to project itself onto the entirety of its territory. After the failure of the peripheral rebellion to install itself at the centre permanently, the country has returned to its former disconnected context but with heightened levels of insecurity in the peripheries. The new centre remains too weak to even occasionally impose itself on the peripheries, while peripheral actors no longer seem to seek power in the capital, all the while controlling vast parts of the remaining country, its people, and resources. All three local security arenas experience this historical legacy through strong international intervention forces, the near absence of the state, and the presence of armed non-state actors.

Table 3.2 *Strategies through which central actors relate to their peripheries*

I would argue that the centre can relate to its peripheries anywhere within the following matrix (see Table 3.2). To simplify the argument, I divide the graph into a two-by-two matrix. The first axis, left to right, shows the *degree* of the relation from connected to detached. By detaching from their peripheries, central actors allow for fluid self-governing in the peripheries; by connecting to them, the relationship between the two becomes regularized. The second axis, top to bottom, describes *how* central actors relate to their peripheries. Imposition describes a one-sided hierarchical ordering, whereas in negotiation ways of ordering are found through eye-level dialogue with peripheral actors. Each axis is a spectrum with infinite degrees in between the two extremes. Peripheries play an equal role in the relationship between centre and periphery. When central actors want to impose a connection to the peripheries or to neglect them, peripheral actors can stage resistance, either in pursuit of inclusion – e.g. through a violent take-over of power – or in pursuit of self-government. Peripheral actors' negotiations with the government can also either have the aim of inclusion in central projects (such as development and security), or of creating a sphere of self-government.

The interplay of central and peripheral actors defines the degree and approach towards connection or neglect. In centre–periphery relations, the ordering struggles from stable to fluid run diagonally to the proposed matrix: more stable ordering is brought about through a strong connection and centrally imposed hierarchies and fluid ordering through larger degrees of peripheral leeway and negotiation between actors, while the two ordering forms mix in between. Centre–periphery relations can be seen as a cascade from the local arena to the national arena and, eventually, to the regional and international arena.[70] Some players, such as peacekeepers, become active in multiple coupled

[70] Cf. Hönke & Müller 2012.

arenas. They act locally without responding to local demands, only in a limited fashion within national centres and mostly answer high up the chain to their headquarters in foreign countries.[71] Take, for example, the adaptations of MINUSCA in the CAR after cases of sexual abuse by peacekeepers in Bangassou surfaced: no local actor had any say in the eventual decision from UN Headquarters in New York to exclude the Congolese contingent from the mission. To the contrary, international outrage at the allegations was not mirrored on a local level, where people nevertheless preferred the Congolese contingent to stay.

In filling the matrix, some broad conclusions follow from the analysis in this chapter and Chapter 2 (see Table 3.3): in South Sudan's current political landscape, the national government at the centre violently imposes its claim to authority on increasingly defiant peripheries by seeking *Connection through imposition*.[72] *Detached through imposition* is seen in the CAR's national security arena, where historically no actor has been willing to take on the costly duty of creating enforced control against opposing actors in the peripheries. And, rather than tackling grievances voiced from the peripheries, presidents conducted punitive operations to detach peripheral protests from issues of central power. The situation was similar in Sudan before 2005. Somaliland *detached* its peripheries *through negotiation* in the past, when different clans or herders constantly negotiated their relative access to grazing lands and water holes without larger political entities trying to impose a centralized system on weaker ones. *Connected through negotiation* shapes Somaliland's present as central actors will not, or cannot, impose their will on the peripheries without taking into

Table 3.3 *Strategies through which centres relate to their peripheries in past and present*

↓Approach; Relation →	Connected	Detached
Imposition	1: South Sudan's present	2: CAR's past and present; Sudan's past
Negotiation	4: Somaliland's present	3: Somaliland's past

[71] See Schlichte & Veit 2007.
[72] Although Samson S. Wassara claims that the government is losing its hold over the country's territory and sovereignty: Wassara 2015.

account the (at times violently expressed) demands of peripheral actors.

When comparing the nine local security arenas, the centre–peripheral relations are a means of negotiation in Somaliland, a bone of contention in South Sudan, and weakest in the CAR. The choice of strategy of central actors has triggered reactions from actors in the peripheries: central actors in Somaliland choose to negotiate the degree of connectedness and the way the national arena should be ordered with peripheral actors through relatively peaceful dialogue. South Sudan's central imposition has caused peripheral actors to answer with resistance in order to keep independent spaces. In the CAR, the centre's neglect of the peripheries has resulted in some peripheral actors relying on themselves, while others have attacked the capital to implement a connection to the centre. While such relations might also stem in part from the different sizes of the countries, as Franzisca Zanker and colleagues put it, 'size does not matter nearly as much as historical patterns of state control'.[73]

These historical trajectories impact the main field of this study – that is, the security sector. In forming their respective states, central actors created drastically different security apparatuses. The security apparatus of CAR remained relatively weak as centres neglected their peripheries. The new South Sudanese state maintained and even increased the heavy militarization of former governments centred in the north. Leaders in Somaliland, in contrast, after massive militarization in the struggle against President Barre, opened negotiation channels between centre and periphery and integrated most militias in an appeasing way into the new state. These varying relations between centre and periphery on national and international levels explain elements of the security dynamics found in the nine local research arenas I now turn to. While the nine security arenas form peripheries to varying centres, they simultaneously form the core of their own peripheries. By delving into the ways through which the arenas are differentiated into inner and outer circles, I test the possibilities and limits of the new security arena concept on the local level.

---

[73] Zanker *et al.* 2015: 91.

4 | *Inner and Outer Circles of the Arena*

'Si vous voulez le tuer il faut le faire en brousse, pas ici',[1] said a chief in Paoua, CAR, to young men from his ethnic group, after they brought a goat thief to his house and said they wanted him dead. This response has many aspects to it that lend insights into the workings of the security arena for the people involved. The chief – though officially a state employee – did not tell the youths to take the culprit to the police. He also did not offer to take care of the thief himself, even though the youths had come to him with the matter, which could have been a sign of their respect for his authority. The chief heard what the youths wanted to do with the thief – kill him – and, while he did not refuse, he also did not acquiesce. He upheld this paradox in the arena – not refusing and not accepting the heated youths' demand – by making a distinction: you cannot do it here but you can do it there. He thus drew a line within the security arena, on each side of which different rules applied. Here, at his house, where his authority was respected, the youths could not do such a thing as kill a thief. But, in the bush, beyond the chief's and others' view, they could kill the thief. And, in drawing this line, he also built on aspects of the arena. In other words, he did not say take the thief to another populated area but rather from the town centre towards an unpopulated area of brush. Thus, while actors shape the arena, they are also shaped by the different parts and forms of the arena.[2] In other words, he marked a difference between a regulated inner and an obscure outer circle within the arena.

Such a distinction was invoked by a wide array of respondents in all of the localities I visited. To delve into the matter in a more structured manner, I asked the participants of focus group discussions two broad questions: on a scale from very good, good, bad, to very bad (hereafter

---

[1] English translation: 'If you want to kill him, you will have to do it in the bush, not here.' Focus group discussion with Group Chiefs, Paoua, CAR, 2 March 2015.
[2] Cf. Giddens 1984.

abbreviated as the number of answers for very good/good/bad/very bad), how good or bad do you view security as being within the town and, second, within the wider region?[3] The outcome, of course, is anything but a representative assessment of security in that locality. Rather, it is a deliberated reflection. I raised the question towards the end of two-hour group discussions and gave participants the opportunity to discuss their own assessment. Thereby, I gained a greater understanding of not just how but why they judged security in a certain way. With only one exception during seventeen focus groups in six different localities, the wider region was described as more insecure than the inner town (see Table 4.1).[4] The most striking difference was expressed in the CAR's Bangassou: almost all respondents found security to be very good or good within the town (5/7/0/0), whereas almost all respondents found security to be bad or very bad in the wider area (1/1/6/4). However, the difference between the inner and outer parts of the arena was not so substantial in every case. Take Somaliland's Baligubadle, where respondents described security as mostly very good in town (13/2/0/0) and still largely good in the wider area (5/7/1/0). Within this chapter, I aim to explain these variations by analysing how the inner and outer parts of the security arena shape both opportunities for the security actors involved and the perceptions of inhabitants of the varying parts of the arena. The two circles are the outcome of varying actors pursuing different strategies on the spectrum of fluid to stable ordering. I argue that the inner circle is more commonly used to further stable ordering, while the outer circle is seen and used as a sphere of fluid ordering.

Drawing the line between an inner and outer circle is a three-fold inquiry of methods, empirics, and theory. In a methodological sense, the differentiation underlies my research in the field. Owing to insecurity around Paoua, for example, I could not (or would not) travel beyond the UN barrier and talk to people outside of town during my

---

[3] I decided to pose this question in a structured manner only after my first trips to each study location. Unfortunately, due to my inability to conduct a second field trip in South Sudan, I only have incidental information on the possible responses for this case.

[4] The exception was a focus group with Issa Musse Youth in the majority Gabooye quarter of Daami. This outlier is in fact indicative of security variations in a reverse sense, as these youths viewed Daami as an outer area of the capital Hargeisa (and not so much as its own inner circle). Another focus group in Daami did not want to answer these particular questions.

Table 4.1 *Perceived security in inner and outer circles per local arena and number of responses for very good/good/bad/very bad*

	Bangassou, CAR	Paoua, CAR	Obo, CAR	Daami, SL	Zeila, SL	Baligubadle, SL
Perceived security of inner and outer circles	Good; Bad	Medium; Very bad	Medium; Bad	Medium; Good	Very good; Good	Very good; Good
Responses	Town: 5/7/0/0; wider area: 1/1/6/4	Town: 0/10/5/4; wider area: 0/0/4/15	Town: 2/9/0/7; wider area: 0/5/4/9	Town: 1/7/7/0; wider area: 4/3/2/0	Town: 13/11/0/0; wider area: 7/15/2/0	Town: 13/2/0/0; wider area: 5/7/1/0

first trip in 2015. During my second trip in 2016, I negotiated with the UN officials to cross the barrier in their convoys and talked to armed actors in neighbouring villages only within the setting of UN- and IOM-led negotiations. My analysis is thus based predominantly on the perceptions of people in the inner circle and only in a very limited way on spoilers' perspectives in the outer circle. In Somaliland, on the other hand, I was able to move quite freely – albeit accompanied by a mandatory personal guard – in and out of my case localities, which allowed for numerous visits to the respective outer circles. Thus, how obscure the outer circle seems in relation to the inner circle also depends on my own research constraints.

The restrictions of some outer circles that I imposed on my own research also drive the actions of many people on the ground: UNMISS staff are not allowed to leave town without a signed Movement of Personnel document; state security actors dare not confront violent actors beyond towns in the CAR; and Somaliland's police feel safer arresting a culprit outside of town when accompanied by his clan elder. The division, which at first glance only seems to limit research, is thus itself an object of ordering that calls for analysis. It influences how and where people live and interact. The line between the two circles reverberates in observable factors on the ground: UN forces in the CAR erect roadblocks at the entrances to Paoua and Bangassou; Somaliland's police checkpoints bar unquestioned entrance to Baligubadle and Zeila; various security forces set up barriers on the roads to South Sudan's Mundri, Wau, and Raja.

With the methodological restrictions in mind, such empirical observations can be analysed in more theoretical terms: physical proximity
creates the potential for daily interaction and furthers the interdependency of livelihoods between inhabitants. Therefore, security in the
inner circle is based on the necessity of continuous cohabitation. The
inner circle generates particular possibilities for forms of ordering on
the stable side of the spectrum, such as institutionalized channels of
interaction, hierarchies among security agents, and defined divisions of
respective responsibilities. Without efforts at stable ordering, the constant interaction as a feature of the inner circle would bring about
frictions over overlapping claims. Unclear hierarchies would constantly
be brought to the fore. The possibilities for avoiding one another in the
outer circle, on the other hand, bring about irregular interaction among
people. The outer circle thus provides particular opportunities for
security actors engaging in ordering further towards the fluid end of
the spectrum. Interviewees would ascribe rumours, unclear intentions,
and inconsistent descriptions and labels to actors in the outer circle.[5]
Rumours of alleged threats emanating from the outer circle can be
factually unfounded, while the limited interaction with people from
that outer circle allows false information to spread without the ability
of inhabitants to verify their accuracy.[6] The open space also allows for
unresolved overlaps in competencies to endure. Actors can eschew the
continuous control of hierarchical or clearly regulated relations by
moving about.[7] The outer circle can thereby serve as a reservoir,
a safe haven for actors who have been pushed out of the inner circle
by more powerful actors. These are my conceptual assumptions based
on my inductive research design and in line with some of the literature
mentioned in Chapter 1.[8] I will deepen and expand the argument by
drawing on rich insights from visits to the terrain, interviews, and focus
group discussions.

   In this chapter, I wish to answer three questions that arise when
thinking of the division between an inner and an outer circle in the
security arena: who draws this line and for what benefit? Why do actors
enter or leave the inner circle? How do inner-circle and outer-circle
actors interact to strengthen or blur the dividing line? I first delve into

---

[5] See historically and more recently on the relation between centre, peripheries, and
the spread of rumours that breed violence Lefebvre 2014 [1932]; Kirsch 2002.
[6] Cf. Bhavnani *et al.* 2009: 878.   [7] Cf. Olson 1993.
[8] See most prominently: Kopytoff 1987.

how actors draw the line between an inner and an outer circle. I examine how actors erect visible barriers and invoke vague narratives of such a division and the benefits that different ways of line drawing generate. In a second step, I analyse how and why actors cross the line to strategically make use of the different ordering opportunities in the inner and outer circles. Finally, I question the salience of the dividing line itself. I analyse who makes the division more prominent and why and how the line is at times almost erased.

Drawing the Line

The degree to which respondents perceive a difference between security in the inner circle and security in the outer circle overlaps with the rigidity with which the line between the two circles is drawn. Part of the line is drawn by specific actors setting up visible measures of differentiation. Bangassou, for instance, is cut off from the outside by armed UN checkpoints on all three roads into town. When a traveller is allowed to pass, a rope that spans the road is lowered to the ground, drawing a visible line in the sand between the inner and outer circles.[9] The checkpoint at Baligubadle's northern entrance, on the other hand, is staffed most of the time only by a sleeping plain-clothes police officer. In part, the line is also based on less influenceable geographic and demographic factors. The Zeila arena presents a particularly indicative example, as the town is cut off to the north and east by the sea and the west and south by the desert. Actors explicitly build on these natural boundaries by erecting their barriers at a town's entrance and on the main entry roads.

Security actors can choose to draw (parts of) the line more rigidly or more fluidly. The demarcation creates an inner circle in which an actor can assume responsibility for enforcing rules and an outer sphere where an actor shows more leniency vis-à-vis rule-breaking. When the line is drawn more rigidly through visible measures such as official checkpoints with explicit rules for passing through, it is made clear where an actor claims to hold authority and where it does not. Less distinct differentiations through unspecified talk of 'town' and 'the bush' can give an actor more flexibility for extending or withdrawing security responsibilities and can avoid the risk of defending an explicit

---

[9] Similarly, de Vries 2013.

claim – as well as reducing the resources required to do so. I will now turn to the drawing of this line through more stable, visible barriers and then to the more fluid and less clearly defined differentiations.

UN compounds in the CAR and South Sudan create an extreme form of division around their bases: high walls or mounts with barbed wire, iron barriers manned by armed soldiers, and lighting and clearings work together to differentiate between an inner space that is highly secure and an outer space that peacekeepers have to navigate with cars, uniforms, and even armed convoys.[10] The UN can control who enters and exits the compound. It can stop security threats from entering the base or tensions being created by its own forces leaving the compound.

Such highly visible barriers are not impermeable but actors go to great lengths to regulate them. In South Sudan, the UN peacekeeping mission took in more than 200,000 civilians at their military bases to protect them from the violence that erupted in late December 2013. In Wau, in 2014, I spoke to international UN police, whose sole responsibility had become monitoring the inflow and outflow of approximately 250 civilians on that UN base.[11] While it is laudable that these measures saved lives during the ongoing conflict, the taking in of these civilians and the mission's security responsibility for them at 'Protection of Civilians' sites also meant that UNMISS reduced its responsibility for the security of civilians outside its bases. The main reason put forth for this retraction was the limited personnel to simultaneously protect people within and outside the bases.[12] Matters of life and death are thus decided by the location a civilian finds themselves in within the security arena. If they are on the base, UNMISS takes responsibility for their security but not, however, if they are outside. The decision to adapt a mission mandate to protect civilians in such a limited way furthermore depends on choices made beyond the locality, at the mission headquarters and beyond. The erecting of UN compound barriers and the distinction of different spheres of responsibility thus fit on the side of stable ordering, due to both the regulated practices and the hierarchical origin of the differentiation.

While the compounds that individual actors create are indicative of a visible barrier in the security arena, more relevant to ordering security

[10]   See Duffield 2010; Fisher 2017.
[11]   Interview with UNPOL officer, Wau, South Sudan, 13 November 2014.
[12]   Closed discussion round with high-ranking UNMISS representative, Berlin, 2015.

are the ways that actors strategically differentiate more widely between an inner and an outer circle. When visibly differentiated, the character-istics of the two circles – control versus obscurity – also represent strategic opportunities. The South Sudanese government prohibited UNMISS from travelling outside of Raja town in late 2014, allegedly for security reasons.[13] North of town, Darfuri rebel groups allied with the South Sudanese government had taken up camp to fight against the South Sudanese opposition. In exchange, the Darfuri rebel groups received a safe haven and, most likely, material goods for their own struggle against northern Sudan. This fuelled tension with the Sudanese government, which was fighting these Darfuri rebels on Sudanese territory. In November 2014, the Sudanese government bombed the northern part of Raja and killed approximately thirty-five people.[14] UNMISS was barred from carrying out its own investigations in this outer circle. The obscurity created through the differentiation between an inner and an outer circle, and the government's ability to decide who could cross the border, enabled violent action and reprisals in the outer circle beyond the scrutiny of other relevant security actors from the inner circle.

Barriers are used to delineate responsibilities between a tightly con-trolled inner circle and a loose outer circle. The UN missions in Bangassou and Paoua staff armed barriers at all entrances to town. Within this perimeter they patrol multiple times daily; outside of it, only with occasional armed convoys. In Bangassou, a leading MINUSCA member described how they disarm actors within the town[15] and, in Paoua, MINUSCA bars actors from entering the town armed.[16] However, beyond the barriers, armed actors are left largely to their own devices. Their extractive practices, such as erecting their own barriers where they levy fees, are mostly accepted as a given by the population and peacekeepers, while within town MINUSCA stops such practices. In Paoua, MINUSCA even openly allies with one armed actor in the outer circle (the RJ) and endorses its role in creating security

---

[13] Interview with UNMISS staff member, Wau, South Sudan, November 2014.
[14] Voice of America (3 November 2014) 'South Sudanese Accuse Khartoum After Village Bombed': www.voanews.com/a/south-sudan-bombing-raid/2506137.html.
[15] Interview with a commanding officer of MINUSCA, Bangassou, CAR, 3 February 2016.
[16] Interview with a commanding officer of MINUSCA, Paoua, CAR, 27 February 2016.

outside the town.[17] The drawing of a line thus forms a very neatly delineated sphere in which MINUSCA is able and willing to tightly control security. Simultaneously, this creates a wide outer sphere in which it explicitly does not seek to take on everyday security responsibilities.

While the distinction between an inner and an outer circle is used to order the local security arena, it is also driven by actors and interests beyond the locality. UNMISS troops deploy to South Sudan on the invitation of the government. The South Sudanese government portrays its control over UNMISS's movement as a matter of sovereignty.[18] It is not just South Sudan that interprets the drawing of lines and deciding who can cross them as a prerogative of state sovereignty. Somaliland's state leaders feel similarly. All the more so if the inner circle ends at an international border, as it does on Baligubadle's southern side, which borders on Ethiopia. The local security arena for people in Baligubadle stretches across both countries because members of the Arab clan populate both sides of the border. The arena is centred in the commercial town on the Somaliland side (the Ethiopian side of town has only a few houses). The Ethiopian side is ruled by an administration that is dominated by the Somali Darood/Ogadeen clan, with whom the Somali Isaaq/Arab clan shares a history of violent confrontations in the 1970s, during the Somali conquest of West Ethiopia, and, in the 1980s, during the struggle against President Siad Barre. The Isaaq won the latter conflict and the Ogadeenis were not part of reconciliation efforts in the 1990s, meaning that enmities persist. Today, the Ethiopian police are alleged to cross the border frequently in pursuit of criminals seeking refuge in Somaliland. On numerous occasions, this has led to exchanges of gunfire between the Ethiopian and Somaliland police forces. The local dividing line is thus simultaneously a matter of national importance.

These examples share commonalities in that a dominant actor has erected a visible differentiation to prevent outer-circle insecurity from permeating the inner circle. In the CAR and South Sudan, the UN has aimed to create a small sphere in which it could adhere to its high standards of protection (rather than providing less security but for

[17] Interview with a commanding officer of MINUSCA, Paoua, CAR, 1 March 2015.
[18] Sudan Tribune (7 August 2016) 'South Sudan Denies Surrendering Sovereignty by Accepting Foreign Troops': www.sudantribune.com/spip.php?article59858.

more people in a broader area). The governments of South Sudan and Somaliland draw a line to the outer circle for sovereignty purposes and to avoid attacks from opposing actors to reach their seats of political and military power in town. Clearly marked lines divide the arena into two circles: an inner circle with a target populace, within which the checkpoint-erecting actor takes responsibility for security, and an outer circle, in which such responsibility is deliberately reduced or avoided all together. However, such visible barriers also consume resources. As a marker of a group's strength they need to be intimidating enough to discourage attacks by competitors (or be able to withstand them). And, within the delineated inner circle, a failure to live up to security expectations could lead to frustration and contestation. Therefore, some actors deliberately choose to create the division in more diffuse ways.

While road barriers are very visual demarcations between the inner and outer circles that provide particular possibilities for stably ordering the differentiation between spheres, looser forms of delineation also occur. Variable lines can be drawn without clearly visible ramifications on the ground through the narratives that actors invoke regarding how the workings of the security arena's inner circle differ from those of the outer circle.

Narratives shape the security arena beyond actual conflict events on the ground. Respondents repeatedly differentiated between the relatively safe inner town and the threatening surroundings. Obo is a case in point: an NGO suggested to its inhabitants in 2009 that to stay safe from LRA attacks they should confine their lives to a five-kilometre perimeter surrounding the town.[19] While the feasibility of this imagined safe zone is hard to judge in retrospect, for the present, all international armed forces in Obo deny the necessity of this confinement.[20] The atmosphere in Obo, however, supports the spread of rumours that something big must be going on. The calm village life of people engaging in manual trades and subsistence agriculture around straw and clay huts is pierced by dozens of heavy trucks and

---

[19] See among other mentions: Focus group discussion with Youth, Obo, CAR, 14 March 2015.

[20] Interview with UPDF commander, Obo, CAR, 18 March 2015. See also The Resolve LRA Crisis Initiative & Invisible Children 2015. Rigterink makes similar observations in south-eastern South Sudan: in a 2013 survey, 75 per cent of respondents feared an LRA attack although no attack had been reported for twelve months: Rigterink 2015: 15.

jeeps racing through town, four to five flights landing daily, and the deafening noise of helicopters taking off. Many local residents continue to voice adherence to this five-kilometre demarcation, giving up on their farms further out. However, in practice, many people regularly cross the invisible demarcation and maintain such fields further out – partly because the land near town has degraded. The narrative of the five-kilometre perimeter is more than a passive confinement. Inhabitants refer to it to voice frustration over the continuous (felt) insecurity and as criticism of the intervening parties' – the UPDF and the US army – failure to eliminate the LRA.[21] Rather than a visible differentiation, the five-kilometre mark has thus become a narrative for discussing the failures of actors in the security arena, as well as an expression of felt insecurity.

Invisible distinctions are created to formulate interests and perceptions of security in the arena and also to use as leverage. Inhabitants of Mundri go even further than using the narrative of an outer circle as criticism of dominant security actors – they use it as a threat: 'Here in town it is peaceful, but outside in the payams they are organized. Self-defence groups of Moro youth move around in the forest [to protect people]', said one of Mundri's youth leaders in late 2014. On the recent killing of a young man in the bush by cattle keepers, he added, 'you will hear the revenge of that boy, today or tomorrow'.[22] The young activists described the growing resistance in the bush through deliberately ambiguous terms that at once expressed a threat to the dominant state power and simultaneously differentiated the threat in the outer circle from the relatively non-violent interaction in the town centre. However, as state repression against Mundri town's residents mounted in the following weeks, people fled to the outskirts or even further to Uganda.

Even without visible barriers, the inner and outer circles can form distinct spheres with separate modes of ordering, making different people feel safe. In Mundri, this differentiation is brought about by extremely violent actors but, in Zeila, socioeconomic composition marks the differences. Three distinct circles can be distinguished based on the way the security arena is composed in and around Zeila:

---

[21] Cf. 'Through rumour people both concretely experience the threat of political violence and express their concerns about it.' Kirsch 2002: 57.
[22] Focus group discussion with Youths, Mundri, South Sudan, 8 December 2014.

first, Zeila town, the administrative centre, which is home to many government institutions and where the mostly ethnic Gadabuursi/ Samaron inhabitants engage in trading or government service activities; second, Tokhoshi, an artisanal salt mining area eight kilometres west of Zeila, where a mixture of clan and state institutions provide security and two large ethnic groups (Ciise and Gadabuursi/ Samaron) live alongside one another; third, the southern rural areas, which are almost universally inhabited by the Ciise clan, with its long, rigid culture of self-rule. Each part of the arena faces particular conflictual issues (political representation in Zeila, economic distribution in Tokhoshi, and inter-clan relations in the outskirts). They each have different combinations of actors that engage in resolving these issues, from state-dominated actors in Zeila to a mix of clan, state, and economic actors in Tokhoshi and clan self-rule in the desert.

While vague lines are easier to cross and erase, they can also create particular tensions as actors on both sides seek to extend their sphere. Baligubadle town is government controlled and conflicts erupt over matters such as land concessions or business permits.[23] Outside the town's borders lies the 'Banka', a community-organized grazing plain for which the government cannot distribute concessions. However, the borders between the two are far from clear, for two reasons: first, where the town ends and where the Banka starts is continuously debated, as residential land plots and development projects (such as water reservoirs) are pushing the town limits into the Banka; second, the traditional division of actors between the spheres – government ruling the town, traditional leaders ruling the Banka – is being disrupted as traditional leaders take up government posts (such as an Caqil holding the mayor's title) and government is responsible for controlling and at times installing traditional leaders. The ad hoc rather than rigid differentiation enables security actors in both circles to divide up responsibilities for conflict resolution as best fits the varying issues of the inner and outer circles but it also enables them to make their claims either inwards or outwards depending on their political agendas.

Drawing the line between an inner and an outer circle through visible barriers or through vague distinctions grants actors the opportunity to

---

[23] For example, the mayor was in the hospital during my first trip because he had been beaten by a local trader for threatening to close an 'illegally' erected shop. Interview with Arab Sultan, Baligubadle, Somaliland, 30 May 2015.

take advantage of varying possibilities in either sphere. Visible barriers delineate clear spheres of responsibility and thereby create stronger claims to authority. Vague differentiations enable actors to avoid responsibility in specific spheres and thereby reduce strains on resources. Visible lines are much harder to change than vague ones, which can lessen the probability of overlapping claims, but such competing spheres are more difficult to resolve once they have been drawn visibly. And, finally, visible barriers represent assertions of authority in the arena and thereby create points of attack for those attempting to counter these assertions. Vague distinctions are not visible on the ground but can become symbols in the debate over interests in the security arena. However, no line should be seen as impermeable. Actors frequently cross the line to utilize and engage with the opportunities and threats within different parts of the arena.

Crossing the Line

The line between an inner and an outer circle is a narrative that actors create to differentiate parts of the arena. People ascribe different characteristics to either side of the line and cross it to engage with the different opportunities on each side. Since the outer circle encompasses the inner circle, one could assume that I would have had to cross the obscure outskirts to enter my research localities in every instance. In about half of them, however, I did not: I reached Bangassou, Obo, Paoua, and Raja by aeroplane or helicopter.[24] Crossing the outer circles of these arenas by car was seen by many as too dangerous. This means that they are mostly absent from academic research and empty of international development projects. However, in those incidences that I was able to travel via road to case localities, such as Mundri, Buseri, Daami, Baligubadle, and Zeila, I traversed barriers and saw the negotiation this required as well as the hardships of travelling the roads. For example, it took seven hours to travel 180 kilometres by car from Juba to Mundri and, for the 350 kilometres from Hargeisa across the mountains and deserts to Zeila, it took thirteen hours.

---

[24] I thank the UN missions MINUSCA and UNMISS, WFP/UNHAS, and MSF for their kind support.

As a first, mundane form of crossing the line, inhabitants routinely leave the inner circle to farm, trade, and visit relatives. They enter into it to sleep, meet, or access the town's services. The ability to cross from the inner to the outer circle and back into the inner circle has vast repercussions for social and economic opportunity. Muslim traders in the CAR complain that they are particularly harassed by government security personnel at checkpoints and by Anti-Balaka groups on the roads.[25] State officials who are assigned to the peripheries often refuse to take up their positions, one of the hindrances being the costly, arduous, and dangerous journey to the peripheries – hardships that UN officials (or an international researcher like myself) can circumvent by plane. As Louisa Lombard has shown for the CAR, mobility thereby becomes an important marker of status and entitlement.[26] The mundane forms of everyday border crossings and their impact on political ordering, however, are not at the heart of this analysis and have been analysed by other authors.[27] In this chapter, I wish to complement the research on the everyday by investigating how actors (rather than individuals) strategically (rather than routinely) position themselves in the inner or outer circle, as well as why they move in and why they move out.

Actors of the outer circle might be content with the obscurity and fluidity their part of the arena provides but they might also vie for the (alleged or real) material and power resources centred in the inner circle. CAR's rebels capture towns in search of loot; Somaliland's elders meet for business and qat-chewing at the market; and South Sudan's national intelligence service monitors and at times represses urban dissent. When new actors enter the inner circle, already present actors and the populace voice demands to negotiate and possibly amend aims to enable continuous cohabitation.

It can also prove strategically beneficial for actors to move out of the core inner circle. UN peacekeepers in the CAR and South Sudan, as well as Somaliland military troops, have each detached themselves from the immediate inner circle so as to avoid the responsibilities of providing

---

[25] See Interview with Muslim trader, Bangassou, CAR, 10 March 2015; Interview with Muslim representative, Bangassou, CAR, 11 March 2015; Doui-Wawaye 2014: 31–2; Lombard 2016a: 92–3.

[26] See Lombard 2016a: chap. 3.

[27] See de Vries 2012; Lombard 2013; Schomerus & de Vries 2014; Vaughan *et al.* 2013.

daily security. Excursions all the way out of the inner circle are partly driven by actors trying to protect inner-circle stability through short-term actions, such as MINUSCA's actions around Paoua and Bangassou. On the other hand, actors might choose to move out of the inner circle indefinitely to reduce their visibility and navigate potential confrontations, like the rebels from Mundri who formed or joined the opposition in 'the bush'.

One typical moment of entering the inner circle is during military conquest or reconquest. When a Séléka group approached Bangassou in early 2013, the state army – FACA – fled (along with most state administrators and numerous quarter chiefs) rather than defending their checkpoint at a bridge north of town.[28] Local youth groups staged an uprising against the then ruling Séléka under the command of the Arab 'Colonel Abdallah'.[29] The national Séléka leadership replaced the unpopular leader with someone who at least spoke French or Sango.[30] Nevertheless, tensions persisted and international forces[31] were called into Bangassou in September 2013 to dislodge the Séléka. Large parts of the population did not welcome the peacekeeping contingent because they were Chadian Muslim troops, seen as allies of the Séléka – 'tout le monde était mécontent d'eux parce que ce sont des musulmans'.[32] The Chadian troops were withdrawn after about a week and replaced by Gabonese and Cameroonian contingents, who were later followed by Congolese peacekeepers, then under African Union tutelage (MISCA). Finally, in the aftermath of sexual abuse allegations against the Congolese soldiers, Moroccan peacekeepers under the UN flag took up this role. These events in Bangassou are indicative of the immense changes the security arena undergoes during the hot phases of civil war. What stands out is, first,

[28] See Interview with acting Prefect of Mbomou, Bangassou, CAR, 9 March 2015.
[29] No interlocutors were sure what his national origin was but they spoke of him as an 'Arab' as he only spoke Arabic. See Interview with Youth leader, Bangassou, CAR, 25 January 2016; Interview with acting Prefect of Mbomou, Bangassou, CAR, 9 March 2015.
[30] Observation of CPMM meeting, CAR, 10 March 2015; Group discussion with the Religious Platform, Bangassou, CAR, 11 March 2015.
[31] A local respondent talked of 'Chadian' foreign troops but, in late 2013, there were mostly French Sangaris forces that pushed Séléka forces out of key towns, as MISCA did not start until December 2013. Interview with Youth leader, Bangassou, CAR, 25 January 2016.
[32] English translation: 'Everybody was unhappy with them because they are Muslims.' Interview with Youth leader, Bangassou, CAR, 25 January 2016.

that one actor moving in is accompanied by another moving out and, second, that the populace plays an active role in changing the arena rather than simply being recipients of security and insecurity.

While it might seem obvious to say so, new security actors move into an arena primarily with a military aim. Thus, the international peace-keepers in the CAR initially entered Paoua and Bangassou together with a French military force (Sangaris) to evict the Séléka rebels. Additional civil and political affairs staff, military observers, and police trainers only followed more than a year later. The lack of appreciation for social and political tensions meant the UN had put no protections in place to deal with local frustration. Aggrieved inhabitants pillaged the Muslim quarters of Paoua and Bangassou, accusing the residents of having collaborated with the Séléka. They displaced thousands of people and dismantled large parts of the state administrative buildings and the markets. Despite the Séléka's and the UN peacekeepers' differ-ent intentions when entering the two towns, they both ruptured social cohesion at the local level: Muslims, especially those of Chadian origin, were perceived as benefitting to the disadvantage of 'autochthones' under Séléka rule and as collaborating with the Séléka in their reprisals against the populace. The arrival of the international interveners turned the tables to the other extreme, causing massive displacement of and violence against Muslims of allegedly Chadian origin.

When actors attempt to enter the inner circle, they bring about tensions resulting from realignments between those perceived as newly arrived and those who see themselves as the original security actors and populace – the so-called autochthones. Actors moving into South Sudan's Mundri, for example, triggered massive displacement. In late 2014, a wave of cattle keepers entered from afar into Mundri's outer circle, causing people to flee either into Mundri town or across it to the other side. Locals sporadically resisted the cattle keepers and accused the national government of sending them to steal their land. After my field research was over, I followed events on the ground through news reports and with the help of a local research assistant. Both sources reported that local resistance within the inner circle grew and culminated in the killing of the local head of the NSS by unknown gunmen during the last days of 2014.[33] Large numbers of NSS and

---

[33] Eye Radio (29 December 2014) 'National Security official shot dead': www .eyeradio.org/national-security-official-shot-dead/.

military then entered the town to seek out the perpetrators. While it did not lead to the direct, visible dislodging of a key security actor, this move probably led many individuals to leave town and join the growing rebellion in the bush.[34] This was a marked difference to just shortly before, during my stay, when most respondents said inhabitants had not joined the rebellion in significant numbers.[35] While cattle keepers entering the outer circle had first left the inner circle a relatively safe resort, the repressive response by the government after the killing of the NSS officer drastically reduced security perceptions.[36]

Individuals and groups entering are not a problem in and of themselves but the changes they provoke in the security arena can make people feel unsafe. In Raja, an alleged 10,000 Darfuri rebels had taken up camp in 2014. However, their presence was not a source of contention due to their behaviour; in fact, they frequented the market, bringing business to town, and seemed to treat the local population with respect. The problem was that they were not to be spoken of: 'Those, those we don't talk about them',[37] said one community leader. The participants of a focus group discussion interrupted a fellow participant when he raised the issue: 'Those people are guests [Arabic: duyuf], we don't need to talk about this.'[38] It wasn't the Darfuris themselves who silenced people but the government's intelligence services, which people feared had its ears everywhere. Conflict over newly arrived groups in all three South Sudanese cases became enmeshed in the larger political contestations over government repression and local resistance – a feature that strained peaceful interaction in the inner circle.

When an actor tries to establish itself in the inner circle, the initial violent steps are followed by the need for negotiation. Mediation boards formed in both Bangassou and Paoua to approach the Séléka leadership about the issues of reopening the schools or reducing arbitrary reprisals by Séléka forces. In many cases, they were successful. The Séléka, at least for the moment, accepted that, without negotiation, constant interaction in the inner circle meant continuous confrontation. While the Séléka neither wanted to take up education

---

[34] See ICG 2016: 15–16.
[35] See Focus group discussion with Youths, Mundri, South Sudan, 8 December 2014.
[36] Monthly report, and telephone call with local research assistant, January 2015.
[37] Interview with local Priest, Raja, South Sudan, 30 November 2014.
[38] Focus group discussion with Youths, Raja, South Sudan, 29 November 2014.

responsibilities themselves nor had a particular interest in stopping others from doing so, their brutal behaviour obscured the division of responsibilities. On arrival, the Séléka looted (among many other places) Catholic schools. Under these violent circumstances, educational administrators and teachers could not run the schools. Negotiating over reopening the schools returned educational responsibility back to civilian institutions, while not impinging on the Séléka's domains: looting and claiming armed authority.

The more prominence negotiations gain when security actors enter the inner circle, the more violence can be avoided during the realignment of actors and the adjustment of their forms of ordering. In Somaliland, the state forces' interventions have not had similarly negative side effects on population displacement as the interventions of MINUSCA in Bangassou and Paoua or the intervention of the SPLA in Mundri. The Somaliland national police have intervened on numerous occasions in the quarter of Daami to halt clashes among youth groups. Inhabitants complain about the heavy-handed approach and that they feel the police is biased against the Gabooye minority while being lenient with the culprits on the majority clan's Isaaq/Issa Musse side. However, the police play only a very brief role in the security process. Rather than controlling the arena, the police enter on one-off encounters to halt violence and then transfer responsibility for resolving the issue to clan elders and the courts. When the army moved into Zeila's security arena, it took similar steps. In 2012, inhabitants mounted demonstrations in town to contest the allegedly rigged municipal elections. In late 2015, teenage schoolchildren from the area's two main clans – Ciise and Gadabuursi/Samaron – started a fight.[39] In both instances, the conflict escalated among the community and the military intervened from its base outside of town. However, it did not seek to permanently enter the inner circle. Rather, after halting the clashes – in certain instances with violence, as in 2012, when two protesters were killed – the army again retreated.[40] The elders and other local dignitaries then took up negotiation to reach a compensation deal rather than dealing with the many cases through the state police and courts.

A move into the inner circle changes the balance of actors in the arena, often in violent ways. Negotiations can allow for rebalancing

[39] Interview with Imam, Zeila, Somaliland, 11 May 2016.
[40] See police and army in Figure 4.1.

Figure 4.1 Police and army parading on Independence Day, Zeila, Somaliland, 18 May 2015

after a new introduction into the arena. Somaliland's state forces in Daami and Zeila rebalanced relations between actors by retreating shortly after their entrance to leave negotiations to the already-settled actors of the inner circle. Other actors at least make smaller, often symbolic adjustments to reduce frictions. Through such adaptions, contested actors manage to negotiate their regulated access into the inner circle. Nomadic herders, present in varying forms in all three countries, provide an indicative example as they have recurrently changed the balance of the inner circle in almost all the localities studied.

The entrance of nomadic herders brings together matters of livelihoods and of ordering the security arena. In simple terms, people want to eat – many of them, meat – but due to socioeconomic competition livestock herders are seen as enemies in many of the localities under study. In Buseri, one respondent said that if you do not meet the chief 'your journey will be a failure'.[41] Positively seen, foreigners, such as Darfuri refugees, are welcomed under the condition that they submit to the authority of the chief. However, in late 2014, respondents voiced their anger over newly arrived cattle keepers who had not talked to

---

[41] Focus group discussion with Elders, Buseri, South Sudan, 22 November 2014.

their chief to decide on cattle corridors. Similarly, in Mundri, cattle keepers' elusiveness led to the spread of rumours about the underlying political agenda of their arrival: to dispossess the locals of their land in the name of the Dinka in government. While some Dinka butchers were still working in the Mundri market, the conflict placed them in danger: of the approximately 100 Dinka of pre-conflict times only two dozen remained.[42]

Whereas the Dinka cattle keepers are linked in people's minds to powerbrokers in government, nomadic herders in the CAR hold a marginal political position – so marginal that many respondents doubt their Central African nationality. Some actors are heavily identified with and populate in ordinary times the outer circle but they might occasionally enter the inner circle. The Peulh in Paoua and Bangassou are described by some as violent and accused of linkages to Chadian mercenaries or to the former Séléka. However, it seems more the case that, similarly to South Sudan, the decades-old struggle between sedentary farmers and nomadic herders has been caught up in the wider conflict issues engulfing the country. A variety of armed groups – fragments of both the former Séléka and the Anti-Balaka – are stealing or taxing cattle, as they are a lucrative commodity.[43] This persecution provides armed groups linked to the Peulh[44] with a protective narrative for their armed struggles. This in turn fuels accusations that Peulh use violence against local farmers. The Peulh are caught between violence on the part of people trying to steal their cattle on the one hand and continuously negotiating access to inner towns to sell their meat on the other. Despite negative opinions about the Peulh in all three CAR localities, locals still depend on them for their meat supply. While some access to the markets is still possible for cattle keepers in both South Sudan and the CAR, it has diminished immensely in comparison to pre-conflict times. Local livelihoods thus seem to have been trumped by the wider security issues inhabitants attribute to herders moving into their arena.

Tensions can always occur as part of the everyday movement of herders but it is through the resolution of larger security stakes that conflict over cattle keepers' entrance is reduced: before the crises in

---

[42] Interview with Chamber of Commerce member, Mundri, South Sudan, 6 December 2014.

[43] Focus group discussion with Mbororo Chiefs, Bangui, CAR, 16 August 2017.

[44] Such as Sidiki's 3R or Ali Darassa's UPC. See less recently: ICG 2014a.

both countries, cattle keepers could move without experiencing as much violence because access was negotiated (at least more than today). Somaliland's experience demonstrates the possibilities of nego-tiated access for herders. Camel herders crossing the Baligubadle Banka and town – populated by a traditionally nomadic society – have created accepted forms of passage. A camel herder is free to move as long as he does not disturb local inhabitants (just as that area's inhabitants are free to move to other areas in search of water and grazing lands). When approaching a water point, he must talk to the respective elders, who seldom refuse access. During the rainy season, when meetings at water points become common and travelling herders frequent the local mar-kets, tensions can rise, but they are recurrently resolved through dis-cussions with the respective elders and possible police intervention.[45]

Negotiation is engrained in Somaliland's political system and, in the other two countries, powerful actors who enter the inner circle also go to great lengths to allow for cohabitation and negotiation with the populace in an attempt to reduce confrontation. As the inner circle is marked by continuous interaction, security actors make changes so as to facilitate communication with already-established actors and the populace. The rebel leadership in Bangui replaced the Arab-speaking Séléka commanders in Bangassou and Paoua with French- and Sango-speaking commanders to appease the populace, which felt dominated by 'foreigners'. The UN followed step when they recalled a Chadian contingent from Bangassou that had taken over after the Séléka's departure. Locals mistrusted them, as they believed these Chadian peacekeepers to be in cahoots with the allegedly Chadian-led Séléka. In Mundri, while the short-term NSS and army intervention was harsh, the longer-term police con-tingent was put under the command of a Nuer, because his prede-cessor, a Dinka, had been mistrusted by the populace.[46] The Somaliland military and national police, after initial violent incur-sions, have granted the most room for negotiation by leaving the entire process to inner circle actors and retreating back to their bases. Based on the workings of the inner circle, it is almost impossible to abstain from negotiation and powerful actors are therefore usually willing to make some adjustments.

---

[45] Focus group discussion with Elders, Gumburaha, Somaliland, 2 May 2015.
[46] Interview with Police Officer, Mundri, South Sudan, 6 December 2014.

Without renegotiation of relative roles and responsibilities, tensions will mount and resolve themselves only through the dislocation of one of the contesting actors or large parts of the population. The South Sudanese NSS and SPLA are on the other end of the spectrum, having shown almost no willingness to negotiate in Mundri and Raja but rather using their dominant force to violently suppress local dissent – with the inverse effect of pushing people out of their originally secure inner circle and into rebellion in the bush. Aside from individuals fleeing to save their lives, moving out can also prove to be a valuable strategy to minimize risks and take advantage of the outer circle's obscurity.

Some international actors go to great lengths to stay out of the inner circle. The Congolese troops that had taken up camp at the centre of Bangassou town in late 2013 were replaced by Moroccan troops, accompanied by civilian staff, who moved to a new, air-conditioned base seven kilometres outside of town. While Congolese peacekeepers had walked through town and the market, sat idly in the old police station, and even adopted a local stray puppy to play with, the new contingent stays in the compound outside of town. Even though the new UN police and army patrol the town multiple times a day, locals are unable to interact with them (as they almost never leave the cars). They travel to and through town only in their white UN vehicles.[47] A member of the US contingent in Obo, despite having been deployed for more than seven weeks, described the height of his local interaction as waving to women from his car but only if they were not balancing a vase on their head, because he worried they might drop it.[48] The MINUSCA contingent in Obo also had strict orders not to interact with the populace. When moving between the UN base and office soldiers had to travel by car, even though the two compounds are a mere 100 metres apart.

Being physically present in the inner circle, but behaving as if one is in the outer circle – that is, refraining from interaction – is no neutral endeavour. In Obo, local inhabitants are frustrated by the lack of interaction and accountability of the US and UPDF forces. For instance, the US forces I talked to did not know about a local auto-defence group

[47] Ironically, one time a UN vehicle even passed at the exact same instant a local respondent complained about the UN's absence in Bangassou town, as if he did not see it.
[48] Interview with US soldiers, Obo, CAR, early 2015.

that was pursuing the LRA on its own terms, albeit randomly and infrequently. Without close contact, rumours about the supposed 'actual' dealings of the interveners spread. Respondents claimed the UPDF were dressing up as the LRA and attacking villages to legitimize their continued presence.[49] While international actors, such as the USA, UPDF, MINUSCA, and UNMISS, try to minimize interaction with the inner circle, they do engage with it selectively through certain actors – for instance, during weekly security meetings in Obo, through contact with state security forces, and through regular patrols. They thereby attempt to live an ambiguous half-life, limiting interaction in the inner circle but not truly moving out of it either.

Other actors have made a more definite move out of the inner circle to avoid regular interaction. Examples include the armed groups in the CAR, which have moved (or stayed) out of Paoua town, and the inhabitants of Mundri who have left town to join the rebellion in the bush. Continuous cohabitation within Paoua is implausible for the loosely organized armed group of the GP, who are described by the MINUSCA forces as 'très grands bandits'.[50] Outside of town they can engage in activities such as racketeering, including demanding fees from passing travellers, and avoid punishment by MINUSCA by fleeing from attacks on their villages. For Mundri's inhabitants, the growing and increasingly hostile presence of NSS and SPLA forces after the death of the local NSS head in late 2014 has meant that many feel too insecure to stay in Mundri town. Some people have fled to rural villages, to Uganda, or to Juba. Others pursue a political agenda of changing the security arena. They have left the inner circle because the ongoing possibility of persecution by the much stronger NSS or SPLA is considered too dangerous. The outer circle, on the other hand, already hosts numerous rebel groups which they have been able to join. Additionally, 'in the bush' their opposition is much more difficult for the NSS and SPLA to suppress.

Some actors move out to avoid the workings of the inner circle. Others do so precisely to protect the inner circle's ways of ordering. In all three countries, the main security actors feel compelled to move out when tensions mount. MINUSCA pursues Séléka groups and

---

[49] Focus group discussion with Youth, Obo, CAR, 13 February 2016.
[50] English translation: 'very big bandits', Interview with a commanding officer of MINUSCA, Paoua, CAR, 27 February 2016.

alleged bandits into distant villages, the SPLA fight various oppositional groups and their alleged supporters in the bush, the UPDF and
US forces chase the LRA across the lightly populated south-east CAR,
and the police forces in all three Somaliland localities intervene in
conflict outside of town. However, violence is spiralling in South
Sudan, security and insecurity oscillate in the CAR localities, and
security has been reinstated after outer-circle conflict in Somaliland.
The types of penetration and the perceptions of the outer circle explain
these variations.

Powerful actors in the CAR and in South Sudan penetrate the outer
circle with a precise short-term military goal. MINUSCA abstains
from establishing everyday security but confines itself to shaping the
arena by declaring where an actor can or cannot be. When actors stay
put, they are given free rein to rule or racketeer. When actors move
and forcefully install themselves in new places, MINUSCA intervenes.
Nineteen MPC fighters entered Ndim village, approximately seventy
kilometres from Paoua, in mid-February 2016. This stirred a large
controversy that former Séléka forces were again expanding in the
country, making headlines and even hitting the international news.
The MINUSCA civil affairs representative travelled to Ndim and to
MPC headquarters multiple times to request decent behaviour on the
part of the MPC. Then, however, the commander of the MINUSCA
troops in Bocaranga – without talking to his counterpart or civil
affairs in Paoua – gave the MPC an ultimatum to leave Ndim within
forty-eight hours. The MPC indeed left but they allegedly burned the
market and some houses on their way out. The MPC leaders, on the
other hand, say they were framed.[51] After leaving Ndim, the MPC
were not pursued. Similarly, in early 2016, approximately ten former
Séléka left Bema, located roughly 120 kilometres from Bangassou, to
enter a village that was around thirty-five kilometres from Bangassou
and erected a new barrier. MINUSCA troops arrived, told the handful
of fighters to get on their motorcycles, and escorted them all the way
back to Bema.[52] MINUSCA thus penetrated the outer circle with one-
off activities but did not seek to continuously control it.

---

[51] Interview with MINUSCA Civil Affairs officer, Paoua, CAR, 21 February 2016.
[52] Interview with UNPOL Officer, Bangassou, CAR, 29 January 2016; Interview
with MINUSCA Civil Affairs officer, Bangassou, CAR, 26 January 2016.

Continuously controlling the outer circle is a very different matter than controlling the inner circle. The inner circle is marked by proximity and constant interaction. Divisions of responsibility and chains of authority can and often must be resolved to allow for cohabitation. On the other hand, some actors move into the outer circle to evade stronger actors within the inner circle and to obtain profit in the less legible surroundings. Armed actors in the peripheries of Paoua and Bangassou erect barriers on the roads leading out of town. These barriers, the fees levied at them, and the possible violence a traveller might face on reaching them mark a clear difference from how security is organized in the inner circle, where the UN bars any similar attempt by armed groups. Attacks by an actor from one locality on another locality are another sign of the seemingly uncontrollable nature of security in the outer circle. During my visits to the (relatively calm) respective inner circles, cattle keepers in Mundri's outskirts attacked and burned villages, Paoua's RJ rebel group attacked the village of Pendé, the MPC attacked the small town of Ndim, and LRA attacks were reported around Obo and Bangassou. Armed actors build on the flexibilities of the outer circle, in which they can attack and then mitigate possible reprisals by stronger actors. For instance, the cattle keepers around Mundri were escorted (briefly) out of the county by government soldiers after their attacks but returned shortly thereafter. MPC forces left Ndim after the MINUSCA ultimatum but only after ransacking the town. They then moved to another village. The LRA have been constantly pursued by UPDF and US forces but, eight years into the anti-LRA mission, they still move about in small numbers. Despite their violent attacks, armed groups use the open space (in terms of both geography and authority) of the outer circle to reduce reprisals by inner-circle actors for their actions to a minimum.[53]

This evasion of sanctions for acts that in the inner circle would more likely be met with a powerful response is due to security actors' limited will to permanently move out and enforce control. As all security actors in all nine inner circles (including state and international forces) have limited means to impose their authority continuously throughout the outer circles, a more feasible alternative is to negotiate relations with outer-circle actors. The police in Baligubadle negotiate their excursions into the outer circle, where they are not in daily control, with those

---

[53] Cf. Kopytoff 1987; Mbembe 1996.

security actors that are. The police intervene only when called on by elders or when accompanied by them. While this behaviour – one-off robust intervention – is not so different from that of the other cases, the negotiated access through elders means that perceptions of such interventions can be managed. Time and again, I was struck by Somalilanders' high perception of security despite recurrent violent incidences. However, such incidences are not seen as a direct personal threat or even a plot by the government and other powerful actors in the local arenas studied – possibly more so in the eastern regions.[54] Unlike MINUSCA's one-off excursions into the outer circle for demobilization talks or attacks, Somaliland's police intervene in a clear manner, to rein in specific incidents without making any promises of larger social or political reforms. Access in Somaliland is brokered through respected local security actors, unlike the NSS's and the army's interventions in South Sudan, which circumvent or even target local stakeholders.

Negotiated access means an actor also has to convincingly portray his willingness to renege on an aim when the opposite side rejects an offer. Conflicts over land are growing in Somaliland in general and around Baligubadle in particular as inhabitants enclose parcels of public grazing land to engage in agriculture, thereby causing local herders to resist violently. The role of the state judges herein is becoming ever more important, as the public grazing area, the 'Banka', is under clan rule but rulings concerning agricultural land allocations are under the sole jurisdiction of the state.[55] In fact, government agencies often cause the problem by granting land titles bordering on or in the public grazing land. However, faced by heavy local pressure (and weak state enforcement institutions to suppress it) the court often backtracks on government land deals and the Banka thus far remains largely public.[56] State judges are therefore going against technocratic assumptions about the need for agricultural development to prevent famine and even against the assessment of the main clan's own sultan, who believes more land should be used for agriculture to grant his community greater nutritional self-sufficiency.[57] Such (violent) back and forth regarding the access to and usage of Baligubadle's outer circle feeds into

[54] See Hoehne 2015.
[55] Interview with Chief Justice, Baligubadle, Somaliland, 1 May 2016.
[56] Interview with Village Chief, Gumburaha, Somaliland, 2 May 2016.
[57] Interview with Arab Sultan, Baligubadle, Somaliland, 7 May 2016.

the perception that security (even when it deteriorates) is in people's own hands. When, how, and if inner-circle actors can move out is thus up for negotiation.

Negotiation reaches its limits when local inhabitants and actors feel they have no impact on security. In Buseri (South Sudan), the main security issue concerns the cattle keepers. This issue goes beyond the chief's means because, as he said, they have guns while he does not.[58] The chief left his inner circle to join a gathering of chiefs in Jur county. Leaders from Wau and Jur counties and from the neighbouring Warrap state (from which the cattle keepers originate), as well as the leaders of the cattle camps, came to the meeting. The chiefs from the Wau side demanded that cattle should only move in designated corridors as of January (i.e. after the harvest) and cattle keepers should arrive unarmed. According to the Bongo chief, a cattle leader replied: 'We liberated this country with the cattle so be quiet.'[59]

While the outer circle is much wider, it is not empty. Actors have to decide between trying to impose themselves on others or negotiating with those already present. Constant imposition is implausible even for the strongest actors as the outer circle is characterized by illegibility and mobility. On the other hand, even negotiated resolutions can be reneged on as soon as the inner-circle actor retreats back to town. Imposition becomes plausible only when an actor permanently installs itself outside, while negotiation can build on the strong collaboration with outer-circle actors.

How actors move in and out of the inner circle is embedded into the larger security issues people believe to be at stake. Nevertheless, even in violent contexts, everyday crossings continue, albeit to a lesser degree. A key element in understanding the impact of crossings between the inner and outer circles on security is thus whether and how everyday matters become linked to larger security issues – cattle keepers to government repression in South Sudan, community tensions to armed groups in the CAR, and agricultural development to clan rights in Somaliland. While larger tensions persist, actors can take advantage of the different characteristics of each part of the arena by moving in or moving out of the inner circle. When such crossings become more regular, disconnected

---

[58] Focus group discussion with Elders, Buseri, South Sudan, 22 November 2014.
[59] Focus group discussion with Elders, Buseri, South Sudan, 22 November 2014.

from the broader violence, and accepted, the salience of the line diminishes until it becomes irrelevant.

Erasing the Line

So far I have shown how actors order the arena both by drawing a dividing line and by crossing it. When a line can be crossed easily, the question of whether it has lost its relevance in the security arena arises. Even while talking about the difference, inhabitants very frequently cross the line for everyday activities. Part of the everyday access is accounted for by actors who straddle the inner and outer circles. In Mundri, these are, among others, the Dinka butchers. For them, the cattle camps in the outer circle are easily accessible and not a perceived zone of violence. In other words, where the obscurity of the outer circle begins is very subjective. The Peulh brokers of the CAR are the members of their community that live in town but also have cattle and relatives in the surroundings. They therefore allow nomadic herders access despite their poor reputation locally. The so-called bandits around Paoua own houses in town and I came across members of armed groups eating, drinking, or meeting friends in the immediate vicinity of the gendarmerie and the UN base. Those of the inner circle also more frequently engage with the outer circle than the narratives of its obscure violence would suggest. In Obo, many inhabitants tend their farms outside of town despite their stated fear that the LRA roams the region. In South Sudan's Buseri, inhabitants depend on nearby Wau for education, healthcare, and the market, having to cross the feared government checkpoints on their way to the city. The mundane crossings of inhabitants pursuing their livelihoods can feed into the creation of more definite bridges across the circles that could over time erase the division and have a repercussion on the make-up of the security arena.

There remains, however, a difference between crossings and the erasure of the line. For crossings, the line is an ordering narrative that actors revolve around. When the line is erased, on the other hand, it no longer plays a role in the actors' mind-sets. While the dividing line is sharp in cases such as Paoua, Bangassou, Mundri, and Raja, frequent interaction between actors and inhabitants of the inner and outer circles in Somaliland's Baligubadle and Zeila reduces the salience of such a dividing line for security. Actors can attempt to erase the line by seeking dominance in both spheres and thereby merging them into one or by creating such strong negotiated relations between inner- and outer-circle actors that the defining characteristics of each circle fade.

The logical direction of erasing the line might seem to entail inner-circle stable ordering extending into the outer spheres. However, there are also instances in which the actors from the outer circle bring obscurity into the inner circle. The Séléka entered the CAR's Paoua in 2013 and ruled with brutality. After they were chased out by French Sangaris forces, locals pillaged the Muslim quarter and displaced thousands. An ethnic divide deepened when contesting armed groups competed for stakes in the arena after the Séléka left. In Bangassou, the violence brought about by the Séléka rebellion led to such a rupture of society that even everyday interaction in town was diminished as people retracted to their ethnically divided town quarters and installed separate vigilante groups that controlled any outsider entering their quarter. In May 2017, auto-defence militias from surrounding villages entered town and attacked the Muslim quarter, killing dozens, displacing thousands, and interrupting commercial and social life. In other words, the characteristics of the inner circle gave way to those of the outer circle. Interaction was reduced as divisions spread through town and as whole parts of the population were expelled. New forms of violence emerged that made people feel they could no longer read other people's intentions and therefore needed to seek protection within a small communal group which they could still trust. The everyday came to a standstill, as markets closed (most of the traders, Muslims, had been displaced) and public services such as schools were pillaged.[60]

However, a collapse of the inner circle – that is, its assumption of the characteristics of the obscure outer circle – is uncommon and unsustainable. After the initial disruption, everyday interaction and legibility returned in each case: the Séléka began allowing for some degree of social opening (i.e. of schools); auto-defence groups have gone on the down-low in Bangassou as perpetrators are pursued by international actors; and, in Paoua, people increasingly refuted the armed groups'

---

[60] Interview with Prefect of Mbomou, Bangui, CAR, 18 August 2017; Interview with displaced Trader from Bangassou, Bangui, CAR, 20 August 2017. After finishing the first manuscript draft in late 2017, I returned to Bangassou in August 2018 and spoke to all sides to the conflict: Interview with Displaced People's Representative, Bangassou, CAR, 3 August 2018; Interview with a commanding FACA Officer, Bangassou, CAR, 4 August 2018; Focus Group Discussion with Displaced People, Bangassou, CAR, 5 August 2018; Interview with two Auto-Defence group members, Bangassou, CAR, 6 August 2018.

ethnic representation claims, making interaction in town less contentious. Erasing the line through the subsuming of the inner circle into the
outer circle thus seems to be only temporarily viable.

More lasting change is represented by the opposite direction, in
which the outer circle gradually loses its distinction from an expanding
inner circle. In Zeila, the division is fading. Through its police and the
buying-in of elders, the Somaliland state is expanding into the outer
circles, while traditional leaders try to maintain linkages to the town.
However, while police forces and elders frequently interact across
circles, social and political struggles keep the difference alive. In brief,
the state and economic institutions are situated in town, while the
traditional leaders remain mostly in the countryside. An erasure of
the line through expanding government influence into the peripheries
may be seen as a threat by those actors who risk losing their original
positions. The Ciise see themselves as the original inhabitants of the
region and thus feel they are being pushed out of power by political
change. Over the last four years, the Ciise have 'lost' a majority in the
city council, the mayorship, the leadership of Zeila's police, and the
Salaal governor's seat to members of the other large local clan, the
Gadabuursi.[61] It seems that, on the one hand, the line is being erased as
more tasks and broader responsibilities are being put into the hands of
alleged government technocrats (police, mayor, governorship), while,
on the other hand, the line is becoming more salient as actors have
fewer overlapping roles than before, when traditionally legitimized
actors from the outskirts held positions in the centre. While the line
in Zeila is much less pronounced than in the CAR and South Sudanese
cases, it is not fully erased. Indeed, the trend recently points towards
more salience over time.

In Baligubadle, on the other hand, the dividing line towards the north
of town has been largely erased. Interaction across circles is so frequent
and seldom controlled that people cannot avoid others and obscure
their actions by leaving town because elders regularly traverse the
entirety of the arena. Both the town and the countryside are inhabited
by subgroups of the Arab clan. Elders of the Banka gather nearly every
afternoon at the small market centre of Gumburaha to chew qat,
leaving the herds to their children and wives. This trading post is closely

---

[61] Focus group discussion with Ciise Elders, near Tokhoshi, Somaliland,
12 May 2016.

connected to the town of Baligubadle, through a deputy to the mayor of Baligubadle[62] and the two police officers, who often sit with the elders to chew qat. Elders from Gumburaha interact with their fellow elders from other subgroups or with higher-ranking clan members, the Cuqaal – one of whom is also the mayor of Baligubadle. When a conflict arises in the outer circle – i.e. between neighbours over their land plots or over a public construction site – the elders intervene and call in the police if necessary. The actors involved know each other from former security interventions as well as social interaction. The everyday happenings of the centre are conveyed to the periphery and vice versa. While the physical markers are thus observable both on the ground and even by satellite imagery – i.e. the wide-open plains that are sparsely populated versus the population concentration of Baligubadle town (see Chapter 1, Map 1.1) – the security-relevant distinctions are hardly felt.

Even such model cases, though, face limits on erasing the line. While towards Baligubadle's north the dividing line has nearly been erased, towards the south, where the border to Ethiopia lies, the line is all the more rigid: criminals and tax evaders cross the border to avoid the respective state forces from pursuing them and people flee across each other's territory, either to Europe through Sudan or across the Gulf of Aden to the Arabian peninsula. The poor rapport between the Ethiopian and Somaliland state agents enables culprits to seek a safe haven on the other side of the border. Thus, the erasure of the line is not driven simply by societal composition (which is similar in both the north and the south) but rather by the cooperation of actors. Towards the north, traditional elders cooperate with the state in managing the peripheries. Towards the south, the Somaliland state has an imperative to protect its sovereignty (as does the Ethiopian state) and therefore bars unhindered access towards the outer circle and into the inner circle. In sum, the distinction between the inner and outer circles continues to play a crucial role in ordering the security arena in all nine cases under scrutiny.

Actors draw a line between an inner and an outer circle to differentiate between forms and responsibilities of ordering. This line is more visible at some points, while it remains vague at others. Visible

---

[62] He is the mayor's deputy in a traditional rather than a state role – that is, a deputy Caqil.

checkpoints at town entrances are mostly on roads and are manned by the dominant security actors, such as UN peacekeepers in the CAR, the army in South Sudan, and the police in Somaliland. Relatively weak actors would not be able to maintain a permanent checkpoint as it constitutes a clear target for attacks. Therefore, many actors prefer to create more flexible forms of division through narratives of ordering. 'The bush', as a sphere of alternative ordering and a reservoir for violence and rumours, is thereby differentiated from the more regulated inner circle.

The line is drawn not only to differentiate but also to be crossed. Controlling crossings provides opportunities for making profits and claiming authority within a certain part of the arena[63] – and for avoiding permanently taking on responsibility outside the inner sphere. Actors move into the inner circle in pursuit of the alleged benefits of profit and control centred in the arena. On arrival, they choose to engage the already-present actors by imposing their will or by negotiating a reordering of the arena. Actors who wish to resist a more powerful actor's imposition can move into the outer circle to avoid a costly confrontation. Inner-circle actors then try to engage these – to them 'unruly' – outer-circle actors. However, continuous control of the outer circle is not possible without a permanent presence, while negotiated solutions can be avoided when they are no longer beneficial.

Reining in the obscure outer circle can only be fully achieved by taking its seclusion from it – in other words, by erasing the differentiation between an inner and an outer circle. When actors relate across lines strategically and for everyday activities, the line fades: actors outside the centre seem less obscure, people cannot avoid one another, and rumours about alleged threats diminish as contact increases. In some of the studied cases, the line is becoming erased. Struggles over the ordering of the security arena nevertheless continue in all nine arenas and the line allows actors to claim their authority and pursue their preferred ways of ordering. Who these actors are and how they order the arena is analysed in the following chapters.

---

[63] See also de Vries 2013: 157; Lombard 2013.

5 | Stable Ordering and Predictable Security

'Il faut être fort!' says the acting prefect of Mbomou and flexes the muscles in his arm.[1] After the Séléka rebels ransacked the entire administrative quarter, Mr Feyomona set up his office in an abandoned safari hotel in Bangassou.[2] The new prefect is a middle-aged, highly patriotic public servant who worked his way up from being a municipal administrator. He owes his promotions mostly to his cunning and resourcefulness in staying put and active even during the years of crisis the country faced from 2012 onwards. Despite his lack of administrators or a budget, or even a bicycle as a means of transport, he continually attempts to gain influence in the local security arena. After my trip in 2015, I return to the same location in 2016. The prefect had received a vehicle from the national government and a secretary, along with numerous state servants who trickle in by the day. His resolve is mounting: 'Le préfet est le premier responsable de la sécurité et de l'administration.'[3]

While the prefect might be a determined leader in the struggle to create stable state structures even in the absence of resources and respected hierarchies, he is certainly not the only patriot of this kind whom I found during my research. Many others, however, fear reprisals by the population or armed groups and thus choose to avoid asserting themselves as openly as the prefect did. Rather, they deliberately exploit the leeway granted by unassertive national governments. The central governments in all three countries vary dramatically as to how and why they penetrate the security arena on a local level: South Sudan is at the furthest end of the spectrum of attempting to violently enforce a dominant claim by state institutions in the local security

---

[1] English translation: 'We must be strong.' Interview with acting Prefect of Mbomou, Bangassou, CAR, 9 March 2015.
[2] See Figure 5.1.
[3] English translation: 'The prefect is the first person in charge of security and administration.' Interview with Prefect, Bangassou, CAR, 22 January 2016.

Figure 5.1 The acting prefect sitting at his desk on the porch of a closed-down safari hotel, Bangassou, CAR, March 2015

arena, the CAR furthest on the side of neglecting state responsibilities, and Somaliland promotes a mix of stable and fluid ordering methods.

Variations in state effectives and state security provision, as exemplified with the story of the prefect of Mbomou, are based on historical legacies of the state (see also Chapters 2 and 3). These legacies form long-term trends based on where in the security arena they become involved, ranging from CAR's confinement to the inner circle to the attempts of South Sudanese state actors to pursue armed groups in the outskirts. Legacies also establish lasting collaborations of state actors with others: whereas state actors in CAR depend on the international substitution of their security responsibilities, those in Somaliland have never witnessed intervention and would rather collaborate with traditional institutions in a marriage of necessity. These legacies shape what people believe state actors can and should do in the security arena.

A dominant expectation of the state is to provide stable ordering in the domain of security. Local inhabitants often raise this demand and non-state actors can claim their own legitimacy precisely when the state does not deliver predictable security. Internationals, on the other hand, go to great lengths to support the administrative bureaucracy and justice provision in an approach they term 'state-building'. State employees themselves, such as the prefect of Mbomou, can assert their dominant claim to the security arena based on the legal-bureaucratic expectations towards their institutions.

Nevertheless, in South Sudan, Somaliland, and the CAR, state actors find themselves face to face with other security actors of similar or even greater strength. Grabbing the monopoly of force nationally or even in a local arena is thus often a resource-draining and highly contentious endeavour. In this chapter, I investigate the fact that the vast majority of acts people take to order their security happen without the resort to physical force. I first contrast the discourses of state justice and security on a local level with the diverse empirical realities I found on the ground. These reduced practices of the state leave room for other actors to also engage in organized security provision. Second, I discuss how state actors attempt to assert their claims to authority in the security arena by resorting to the use of force. Again, the state is not the only actor trying to make a clear claim in the security arena by using physical violence. Finally, I demonstrate how stable ordering creates predictability both for security and for insecurity.

Narratives and Practices

In the CAR, the reality of the state has been marked by very limited effectives since its inception at independence. It is thus not the asserted state authority but the idea of it that saves state actors from oblivion.[4] The Bangassou prefect's strong assertions – 'il faut être fort' – have no means of materializing on the ground. State security provision is thus more aspiration than fact but remains a powerful desire shared by many in the security arena. When discussing state actors and especially their alleged deficiencies in security provision, I find it crucial to set the measures of state actors and those of the populace as a bar and take the real resources available to them into account. I thus provide a short overview of the structures and responsibilities of the state actors in the local security arena and then turn to the actual effectives I witnessed when conducting field research on-site. Afterwards, I look at the ways non-state and international actors engage the security arena to provide

---

[4] See also Lombard 2016a: 10.

predictable security. Non-state actors often officially form part of state hierarchies but engage in conflict resolution beyond their state mandate. Intervention forces tend to ignore these non-state approaches and focus on strengthening the state's predominance in security provision.

The official roles of the state concerning security provision are similar in each of the three countries: there exists a hierarchical relationship between different levels of government, from the smallest local level to the central national level. Security forces have distributed security responsibilities in the arena and officially stand under the oversight of a civilian administrator. While security forces arrest or detain violent individuals, only courts can give a ruling and pronounce a sentence. In the CAR, official relations between state actors are rather hierarchical within the local security arenas and towards the capital. In contrast, the South Sudanese security-related state actors form parallel clusters between actors perceived as local and those sent from the national government. In Somaliland, hierarchical strands resemble those in the CAR but split in a dual nature between parallel state and non-state hierarchies.

The bar that state actors set for themselves concerning security provision in the CAR's local security arenas is both very high and very much biased towards the stable ordering side of the spectrum. The CAR's state institutions are hierarchically organized on paper and in the discourses of state actors. In all three CAR security arenas, respondents describe very similar vertical chains linking state actors: the prefect stands at the top, followed by the sub-prefect, the mayor, the group chief, and finally the quarter and village chiefs.[5] Similarly, among the security forces, focus group participants put the army in first place, followed by the gendarmerie and the police. Aside from their hierarchy, state actors' respective security responsibilities are also described rather clearly: on the side of enforcement, the army is responsible for protecting the nation against foreign threats, the gendarmerie to patrol the overland routes, and the police to stop crime within the town.

In South Sudan, state actors also claim overall security responsibilities in the security arena. Officially, the country holds a more decentralized political model, in which the governors (unlike prefects in the CAR) are supposed to be popularly elected. In reality, elections were

---

[5] Quarter chiefs are in town, while village chiefs are in the countryside.

held only in 2010 and most governors have since been replaced by presidential decree.[6] State administrators below the governor are appointed at the levels of district, 'payam', and 'boma', forming a hierarchical administrative chain.[7] Respondents do not, however, situate state security forces in hierarchical chains. On the one hand, they mention state institutions they view as rather local and trustworthy, such as the police and wildlife forces. On the other hand, they speak of non-local actors they view as hostile, such as the army (SPLA) and NSS.

Security responsibilities in Somaliland are divided between state institutions enforcing an end to hostilities, while traditional institutions provide contractual resolutions to insecurity incidences. Governors are appointed by the central government (similar to the CAR), while councils and mayors are popularly elected. Unlike the other two cases, traditional chiefs are not below state actors but rather form a parallel hierarchy from oday to caqil to sultan.[8] The mid-level caqil is the most important leader for security and is officially 'employed' by the state, with a token salary by the Ministry of Interior, and is supposed to report to the governor. In cases of larger inter-clan violence, the army is responsible for intervening to prevent conflicts from escalating. In every town and village I visited, there are police forces responsible for catching criminals.

I do not want to go so far as to recount the actual written laws of the state but would rather discuss the ways state actors and inhabitants view the role of the state. These varying realities on the ground drive how the state can fill its role in the local security arena. Expectations shape the security arena by leading to aspirations when state actors move in the desired direction and to frustrations when demands are left unfulfilled.

In the CAR, state actors in the local arena struggle to make themselves heard from below by the population and above by the national government and international interveners. Claiming to assert authority

---

[6] de Vries & Schomerus 2017a: 37–8.
[7] Cf. the more flexible local justice compared to the more rigid higher level structures: Leonardi *et al.* 2010: 57.
[8] Oday is an 'elder', a man of age in the clan. Caqil is the leader of a blood-paying group, which comprises of around a hundred families. Sultan is the leader of a major clan, and the Arabic word for 'king'. The Ciise call their leader at the level of sultan 'ugas'. See Hoehne 2011: 8.

Figure 5.2 The prefectural court in session, Bangassou, CAR, January 2016

over security matters is one way they seek to stress their importance. The courts attempted to reassert themselves in each of the CAR cases after years of absence during the height of the crisis from 2013 to 2014. In January 2016, everyday security within Bangassou started moving back into former, structured channels. The police, but more so the stronger gendarmerie, arrested culprits and handed them over to the tribunal that held public trials and passed judgement.[9] After only three sessions, however, the judge interrupted his tribunal's work indefinitely: 'On sera à un moment obligé d'arrêter les procès judiciaires parce que on n'a pas une maison d'arrêt.'[10] The tribunals of Obo and Paoua fared even worse. The judge appointed to Obo only briefly held session once in February 2015, before returning to Bangui for unspecified reasons. In Paoua, experienced groups of bandits went as far as to make death threats against the prosecutor after he took up office and

[9] See Figure 5.2.
[10] English translation: 'At some moment, we will be forced to stop the judiciary process because we have no prison.' Interview with Judge, Bangassou, CAR, 4 February 2016.

started trying cases in late 2015 – the court dared not follow through on the investigations.

State officials deliberately try to keep international attention on themselves. Asserting some authority, even in the face of blatant resource limitations, is also a means to relate to other actors in the arena. The police commissioner of Paoua insisted on registering me when I returned in early 2016 – as he said, for my own security. He reassured me that, if I ever faced trouble, I should call him any time of day or night and he would then notify MINUSCA that I needed help. In other words, he wants to uphold the semblance of state sovereignty but acknowledges his institution's incapability to enact it without international substitution. In fact, the narrative of the state's primacy on stable ordering in the security arena makes state actors the primary benefactor of international assistance despite the state on the ground, in most cases, falling short of what people expect of it.

Of the three countries, the CAR has the weakest and least assertive and resourced state institutions. The police force of Paoua has only six police and thirteen gendarmerie officers, while neither police nor gendarmerie has a mode of transport and only the gendarmerie has any firearms. In Bangassou, the number of police officers stands – or rather sits idly – at three, and the gendarmerie at around fifteen. In Obo, there is one sole salaried police officer and, following the removal of the single gendarme, no gendarmerie. The army is absent in all but one case (Obo), although all three cases lie near a border.[11] Under these circumstances, the continuing adherence to the mostly imagined state force monopoly has almost absurd effects on security and justice. In none of the cases does the gendarmerie have the logistical means to patrol overland routes and thus takes on security responsibilities within town in addition to the police. Even when culprits are caught, none of the three cases has a functioning court (save Bangassou, for one month in January 2016) or a prison. Claiming the security prerogative without the means to follow through can have the inverse effect. The CAR's defunct state justice system perpetuates impunity by upholding rules of a maximum seventy-two-hour preliminary lock-up but not having judges to take over afterwards. It can happen that

---

[11] After completion of this manuscript, the army was redeployed to Bangassou and Paoua in mid-2018.

inhabitants see the rapist of one's child or the murderer of one's close relative live freely, with no state-provided justice in sight.

Compared to those in the CAR and Somaliland, security arenas in South Sudan exhibit an overabundance of state forces: Mundri and Raja each have a few dozen local police wildlife forces while also hosting hundreds of SPLA soldiers and small numbers of NSS officers. Buseri has only half a dozen police officers and a transitory army base nearby, with fluctuating, unspecified numbers of soldiers. The national forces are much more powerful than local state forces, leading to a perceived impotence of the latter towards the former. Instead of dividing responsibilities horizontally or vertically, national actors seem to trump local officials. This is not to be confused with a hierarchical relationship, where a centrally commanded common goal is pursued from top to bottom. Rather, local state actors and inhabitants feel they cannot fulfil their security aspirations against the ulterior motives of national state forces.

The Somaliland national government, while similarly impoverished as the government of CAR, spends more than half of its budget on security.[12] State security forces are thus comparatively stronger: the small town of Zeila has about twenty-five police officers, Baligubadle around thirty-five, and Daami less than a dozen (but with hundreds of backups in the nearby capital centre). Zeila additionally has a military base nearby with approximately 200 soldiers.[13] Crucially, in Somaliland state security forces in the localities under investigation here are (mostly) paid regularly on a monthly basis, unlike those in the CAR and South Sudan.[14] While in the inner circle state security forces dominate, the workings of state security provision depend on the collaboration of non-state actors. In some domains and in the outer

[12] Document 3: Somaliland federal budget 2014 in Somaliland Shillings, Source: Ministry of Finance, viewed April 2016.
[13] While these numbers seem impressive and might 'obviously' explain the better security in these cases, first, if international forces in the CAR are taken into account, then Somaliland's forces are comparatively weaker and, second, force strength has no natural, immediate impact on security improvement – as the South Sudan cases show, strength can always be abused.
[14] See confidential monthly reports from each of the nine cases, sub-question: 'Were the state forces paid this month?'; Alice Hills, to the contrary, describes police officers as being only irregularly paid (Hills 2017: 9). Her analysis is based on country-wide data from the Observatory of Conflict and Violence Prevention, while my own data stems only from the three localities mentioned, where salary arrears were at no point mentioned.

circle, non-state actors even take precedence in handling issues of security.

In summary, the adamant stable ordering narratives of state agents paired with minimal effectives in the CAR create a vast expectation gap concerning security. This is contrasted by the overabundance of state security forces in South Sudan, where the national state itself has become an insecurity bearer, creating tensions between the local and national level. In Somaliland, finally, the state does not claim a monopoly of force but public expectations of state–non-state collaboration are being met. In none of the countries is the state the sole actor engaging in stable ordering.

Traditional clan institutions play an immense role in forming people's identity and in conflict resolution in Somaliland, while other non-state actors – such as religious leaders, women and youth representatives, and entrepreneurs – play only a secondary role.[15] The clans are hierarchically structured: within sub-clans (or diyas) there are accepted wise men or elders, the odayaal (singular oday), who form the key council to resolve conflict issues, the guurti, and decide on compensation schemes, the xeer. Should the conflict go beyond them or include different sub-clans, the respective cuqaal (plural of caqil) come together.[16] If the conflict involves different clans, the sultans step in. These traditional institutions have century-old histories and it is common in new disputes to refer to past oral and written xeer; in some sense, the xeer are thus incipient legal documents.[17]

The CAR has no comparable hierarchical, traditional system that spans the country. The chief structures were, in many instances, created by French colonizers to enable managing the peripheries.[18] Even in the absence of an assertive state and with the negligent means given to them by the state, chiefs play a crucial role in resolving day-to-day conflict in their respective areas in their own right and through their charisma and standing.[19] In comparison to Somaliland, in CAR a more prominent role is played by civil society organizations, such as youth groups and

---

[15] Other important non-state institutions include a vast array of national NGOs, which usually focus on drought relief and small developmental projects, and political parties, which were not very active in any of the three local arenas. Youth and women's groups were also present in the cases but members are subsumed in clan structures when security issues are concerned.

[16] For a short pronunciation guide, see Note 118 in Chapter 2.

[17] Hoehne 2011; Lewis 1961; Renders 2007; Simojoki 2011.

[18] Woodfork 2006: 130.   [19] See Bierschenk & Olivier de Sardan 1997.

the women's organization OFCA. Churches and mosques provide for schooling and assembly. The Catholic Church is by far the most resourced and hierarchically organized religious institution in all three local arenas. In South Sudan, churches also play a role in conflict mediation and civil society organizes itself in a party organization or according to professions. Traditional leaders are of significant but varying importance.

Witnessing such non-state structures in place that deal with security in regulated manners, it is surprising that international actors rarely collaborate with them. MINUSCA in the CAR in 2015 was still operating very differently from UNMISS in South Sudan. MINUSCA took up camp in the inner circles, engaged with the local populace, and portrayed a strong physical presence to create a heightened sense of security. Since 2016, however, MINUSCA has begun to increasingly resemble UNMISS by detaching itself from everyday security. In Paoua, new police trainers spend most of their day writing reports in their base, occasionally visiting state actors and planning the construction of new gendarmeries and police stations.[20] With the UN mission becoming more established and demanding adherence to its rules, flexibility of peacekeepers on the ground is limited. Whereas Paoua's MINUSCA formerly locked up criminals, they now hand them over to defunct state justice institutions, from whose prisons culprits often escape and return to Paoua shortly after their arrest.[21] This rigidity of sticking to UN regulations fuels a key driver of the CAR conflict: rampant impunity perpetuated by the weak state.

International interveners often prefer to stabilize arenas under state leadership, despite states' often detrimental impact on security. Such support is framed as technical rather than political. Among other activities, interveners construct office buildings for state institutions and train security officers on human rights issues. In all three CAR localities, MINUSCA takes the lead in reconstructing prisons, courts, police and gendarmerie stations, and administrative offices. UN staff regularly visit the police and gendarmeries in Paoua and Bangassou to discuss training and conduct. Their aim is to rebuild the state so that it can take over security responsibilities from the interveners.

---

[20] Interview with UNPOL, Paoua, CAR, 27 February 2016.
[21] Interview with a commanding officer of MINUSCA, Paoua, CAR, 1 March 2015. Compared to: Interview with a commanding officer of MINUSCA, Paoua, CAR, 27 February 2016.

These measures deliberately reduce internationals' daily security responsibilities to encourage state ownership at the local level. State ownership, however, does not always have a positive effect on security. When the state and its populace oppose one another, peacekeepers need to interpose themselves to fulfil their mandate to protect civilians. In South Sudan's Raja, the UN peacekeeping contingent depends on the national government to grant them access to conflict sites. A complex web of actors is fuelling insecurity and mounting tensions in Raja, where the national government is hosting Darfuri rebels from Sudan, who provide support in the government's fight against rebel groups. There are no reports of the rebel troops misbehaving, which could be down to the close relations between the neighbouring Fertit groups in Darfur and Raja. Sudan, however, is angry that South Sudan has granted a safe haven to its enemies and responded by bombing the Darfuris' camp in late 2014, killing thirty-five, including an unknown number of Raja's civilians.[22] While I was researching in Raja, inhabitants feared discussing the incident due to threats from the NSS. UNMISS left Raja for a larger base in Wau, 220 kilometres further south-east. The relocation of peacekeepers from Raja to Wau took away an important mediating aspect,[23] enabling conflict to spiral, wherein an armed militia even attacked the convoy of the county commissioner.[24]

Following its stable ordering mantra with a focus on the state, UNMISS pursued support to the state. 'How can you expect to have peace, if you are not holding meetings?' said a UNDP trainer during a police–community relations committee meeting in Wau,[25] reflecting that her notion of conflict resolution is based on creating stronger links between the state security apparatus and the population, which it is supposed to serve. While in principle this sounds helpful, in the specific context of

---

[22] Voice of America (3 November 2014) 'South Sudanese Accuse Khartoum after Village Bombed': www.voanews.com/a/south-sudan-bombing-raid/2506137 .html.

[23] Focus group discussion with Women, Raja, South Sudan, 28 November 2014.

[24] I am deeply saddened by the news that one of my interviewees for this book – a bright, young radio journalist from Raja – died in the attack. My sincerest condolences go out to her family. International Press Institute (28 January 2015) 'South Sudan: Five Journalists Killed in Roadside Attack in South Sudan': http:// allafrica.com/stories/201501301195.html.

[25] Observation of Police Community Relations Committee meeting, Wau, South Sudan, 21 November 2014.

Figure 5.3 Police–community relations committee meeting, Wau, South Sudan, November 2014

South Sudan it can be counterproductive. When the state itself is perceived by the populace as a source of insecurity, forming links between state and community structures prevents the possibility to consider non-state alternatives without involving the distrusted state. During the several-hour meeting in Wau,[26] I could not lose the impression that the police chief and his colleagues saw the assembly as a way to gather intelligence rather than to be accountable – even though the chief promised to investigate any reports of corruption.[27] From a deeper perspective of the conflict dynamics, international support for state–community relations legitimized the national government's narrative that this conflict was about intercommunal tensions, which could be resolved by a neutral state. Therefore, interveners followed the credo of 'no meetings, no peace'. Many respondents in Mundri, Buseri, and Raja, on the other hand, described insecurity as being driven by the state repressing and disowning its people. A local trader said, 'You are the president of yourself, your own security, the

[26] See Figure 5.3.
[27] Observation of Police Community Relations Committee meeting, Wau, South Sudan, 21 November 2014.

government is not doing anything'[28] – thus reflecting a rather different doctrine of 'no solutions aside the state, no security'.

State actors see themselves as the natural bearers of stable ordering. Intervention forces support the state's claim to this form of ordering even when it can be counterproductive to local security provision. However, with multiple actors turning to regularized security provision, the state often has difficulties in showing its dominant claim. The prefect of Mbomou might be a very vociferous person. He tries to seek a force monopoly for the state, of which he is the highest representative: 'Je suis le président dans ma préfecture', as he says.[29] But, in reality, he has very few means to enforce control. The hierarchies among his own state institutions are contested. The populace views him as biased and authoritarian.[30] International actors hesitate to collaborate. The prefect's story thus serves not only as an example of a state actor seeking a strong role in the security arena – even the force monopoly in the distant future – but also as an example of the real deficiencies such an attempt to control faces in the security arena and for the person themselves. When its rules are not adhered to voluntarily, the state often turns to physical enforcement.

Resorting to Force

In most of the security arenas, state actors are not dominant players. In the CAR, they are outgunned by armed groups and international interveners. When state actors assert their claim to authority, they thus prefer challenging neither of the two and go after smaller targets, such as petty criminals. In South Sudan, by contrast, the state often is one of the most powerful players in the security arena. Nevertheless, asserting dominance against comparably strong oppositional forces and international interveners is a costly endeavour and often has contrary effects on security. By using excessive force, state actors risk undermining instead of asserting their claim to authority, because they reduce security in the eyes of the local population. Somaliland's balance in the security arena is simpler due to the absence of

---

[28] Interview with Chamber of Commerce member, Mundri, South Sudan, 6 December 2014.

[29] English translation: 'I am the president in my prefecture.' Interview with acting Prefect of Mbomou, Bangassou, CAR, 9 March 2015.

[30] Focus group discussion with Vigilantes, Bangassou, CAR, 1 February 2016.

international actors. Non-state and state actors continuously renegoti-ate their respective domains of authority but neither side has an interest in fully taking over from the other.

The biggest cost of enforcement is the physical danger it presents for the actors themselves. State actors deliberately confine their attempts of taking control to the inner circle, so as not to overstretch limited capacities. 'Normalement je devais organiser des services dans dix ou quinze kilomètres, mais pour l'heure il y a l'insécurité', said the gen-darmerie commander of Paoua in early 2016.[31] As in both of the other CAR cases, the gendarmerie does not even attempt to fulfil its official responsibility of controlling overland routes, but rather confines itself to town. The gendarmerie commander of Paoua is an experienced man with strong words regarding his institution's role. One could lament the paradox of a security actor abstaining from his official responsi-bility of providing security on the roads outside of town due to inse-curity. In reality, the commander's prudence is well placed and might not go far enough. While they refrain from overland excursions, the gendarmerie pursues thieves in town and jails culprits brought to them by MINUSCA. In December 2016, the gendarmerie station (which is just outside the MINUSCA military base) was attacked by armed men attempting to free their comrades in arms.[32]

The key current security concerns in the CAR are not posed by petty criminals but by armed groups. These threats go beyond what state courts are meant to handle. In Paoua, respondents ascertain that only a redeployment of the national army, the FACA, can reinstate security.[33] In contrast to the expectations respondents voice regarding a self-asserting, strong state, the events unfolding in Obo in late 2015 offer a glance at the violent reality of FACA redeployment (see Box 5.1).

---

[31] English translation: 'Normally, I would have to organize the [security] services in ten or 15 kilometres' distance, but for the moment there is insecurity.' Interview with a commanding officer of Gendarmerie, Paoua, CAR, 29 February 2016.

[32] Réseau des Journalistes pour les Droits de l'Homme (13 December 2016) 'Centrafrique : Un gendarme pris en otage entre Paoua et Bossangoa par des combattants du MPC': http://rjdh.org/centrafrique-gendarme-pris-otage-entre-paoua-bossangoa-combattants-mpc/. A local research assistant recounted an attack on the gendarmerie station in town itself that same month.

[33] See among others: Interview with Deputy of Paoua, Bangui, CAR, 17 August 2017; Focus group discussion with Tali women, Paoua, CAR, 1 March 2016.

Box 5.1 Army fuelling tensions in Obo, CAR, July 2015

A FACA contingent had been stuck in Obo during the crisis for three years with irregular salaries and no rations from the state, which were partially substituted by the Ugandan army unit that was stationed in town. Most soldiers abandoned their posts and the remaining four dozen spent their time idly in the centre of Obo town rather than pursuing the LRA with the Ugandans, as was their mission. In June 2015, the FACA contingent was finally replaced. The new captain brought along anti-Muslim sentiments from the capital, where he had fought the Séléka rebellion. In July, a smuggler was reported to the army and then caught on the road to Obo carrying weapons and ammunition to bring to nearby Mboki, allegedly for the Muslim Mororo living there. The FACA went into Obo's Arab quarter to investigate rumours concerning Muslim citizens taking up arms to attack the person who reported the smuggler to the authorities. When the captain arrived in the quarter, he allegedly aggressed the Imam, angering the inhabitants, who then chased him away. The captain mobilized his men, stationed them at key points around the Muslim quarter, and entered using force. Ugandan soldiers intervened immediately and halted the FACA. Inhabitants described the FACA as being on the verge of starting armed combat in the middle of town. The prefect held a meeting and gave a speech that was broadcast on the radio to calm things down. The FACA captain was relieved of his duties and sent back to Bangui and, by August, a new captain, who seemed to be regarded more highly by all sides of the population, took over but he still did not have his elements under full control. The FACA went back to spending most of their time idly rather than meddling in local security affairs.

The example shows the problematic role the army plays in the local arena when it asserts its authority by fuelling communal tensions rather than appeasing security concerns.

As the Obo example shows, state assertion does not always have a positive effect on security. The state can fuel tensions among communities in the local arena. Such tensions can be avoided when state actors either collaborate with locally accepted actors or take on clearly defined responsibilities. In contrast to the CAR's weak state, Somaliland's government is expanding its influence into new domains. It thereby risks losing the buy-in of traditional actors and their supporters. Daami and Zeila diverge from the official Somaliland success story. In Zeila town, criminal acts are often linked to smuggling or other illicit activities, which the state institutions take singular responsibility for pursuing. In this context, traditional conflict resolution loses importance relative to a strengthening state dealing with new forms of insecurity. The 2012 local elections decisively changed the power balance in the town's council, in which Ciise clan members had previously held a majority. Demonstrations followed and were violently suppressed. The army killed two protesters in the clashes. In late 2015, the government also replaced the governor, a Ciise, with a technocrat from another region and clan.[34] Historically, the Ciise were not supporters of Somaliland's independence and their key government positions until recently could be interpreted as their buy-in – one they are now losing.

The role of state actors in Daami's security arena is even more contested. The Gabooye minority which lives in Daami has almost no recruits in the state police and the state police has only a handful of officers in Daami quarter, despite its reputation as a haven for criminals. Events in Daami quarter show that Somaliland is not immune to tensions created by the state, similar to what happened in Obo. Cohabitation between traditional and state actors is heavily disturbed. The minority groups living in Daami see the police and state representatives (most of whom come from majority clans) as hostile to their needs, while the government believes Daami quarter to be a refuge for criminal groups. The government uses repressive means, such as security sweeps, to catch criminals, with only limited success. During the recurrent inter-clan clashes, the national police force enters the quarter and halts the fight using, at times, brutal means causing a number of injuries – Daami's inhabitants thus feel threatened by the police rather than seeing them as a possible security provider.[35]

Nevertheless, the degree of resistance to the state in Daami is much lower than in South Sudan, where stark assertion is even more detrimental to security. In South Sudan, the state security forces are large in

---

[34] The changes were probably driven by administrative and political reasons (typical rotation of commanders, the former governor was charged with corruption, and a recent reshuffle of the ruling Kulmiye party due to internal power struggles).
[35] Focus group discussion with Gabooye Youths, Daami, Somaliland, 26 April 2016.

comparison to Somaliland and massive in comparison to the CAR – at the same time, security in South Sudan is the lowest. The powerful state forces are themselves driving conflict. South Sudan's state actors originate from various militias and exhibit large continuities in membership, structures, and methods of playing out political struggles through violence.[36] On a national level, the army and government have split into different factions vying for national power.[37] Government leaders impose control of the peripheries through repression. While expectations towards the new Southern Sudanese state were high after independence, its practices seem to fall in line with those of the former rulers in Khartoum and from even earlier. Indicative of this are the garrison-style town control from which unruly surroundings are suppressed[38] and the mistrust towards local government and the frequent replacement thereof by order of the central power. This in turn furthers the impression on the local level that only violence can give one a voice.

In the local arenas under investigation, the NSS is accustomed to spying on locals (including local state actors) and installing an atmosphere of fear. In Raja, local security actors, such as religious and clan leaders or even local government, are reluctant to speak about the most pressing security issues: the Darfuri rebels in town, and the two bombing raids conducted by Sudan in late 2014. Interview partners speak in hushed voices even in their own homes, warning that NSS could be listening in. The government's attempts at forceful control led to backlashes by local actors such as when an unknown group attacked the convoy of Raja's commissioner in early 2015. Even though this local state leader had no influence on the repression by state actors, he became the target of anti-government violence. Just as in Raja, locals in Mundri would only talk to me about the government in very secure environments, where they could be absolutely certain that the NSS (or as they said, 'Dinka')[39] was not listening in. After my field research in Mundri, frustration apparently grew to such a high level that the head of its NSS bureau was killed and the local rebellion grew in strength.[40]

---

[36] Cf. Öhm 2014; Pinaud 2014.
[37] See de Waal 2014; Pinaud 2014; Rolandsen 2015a.
[38] Rolandsen & Daly 2016: 19.
[39] Focus group discussion with Youths, Mundri, South Sudan, 8 December 2014.
[40] Eye Radio (29 December 2014) 'National Security official shot dead': www .eyeradio.org/national-security-official-shot-dead/; ICG 2016: 15–16.

Actors apart from the state can also turn to violence to change the security arena in their favour. Making stable claims becomes a necessity for armed groups that wish to decisively alter the current setting rather than just to navigate a dangerous environment. Some oppositional fighters around Mundri, Raja, and Buseri joined the organized opposition, the SPLA-IO, to make their voices heard in internationally brokered agreements that were confined to the state and the main opposition groups.[41] When this pathway brought forth no progress, the opposition – and also the government – further fragmented.[42] Former Séléka groups in the CAR present themselves as stable actors for multiple purposes: as the de facto state in the north-east regions, where the central state is mostly absent;[43] as brokers with marginalized groups, particularly the Peulh; and as a means to facilitate cooperation with the UN peacekeepers.[44] Stable ordering for armed actors is a means to be heard.

For the armed group RJ in the CAR's Paoua, the aim is DDR, inclusion in the national army, and gaining state positions for their leaders. They are organized, powerful, and through stable ordering are able to make claims that fluid actors cannot: for instance, in 2014, then-leader Armel Sayo gathered his men and marched on the capital to pressure the transitional government to include him in the cabinet; he received a ministerial portfolio and the RJ returned to north of Paoua.[45] The RJ acted from a position of strength, as they were much more powerful than local state actors, on par with the UN peacekeepers, and the only structured rebel group after the Séléka left before they later returned with the successor group of the MPC. While the RJ was founded to defend against the Séléka rebels in 2013, in February 2016, the RJ made a volte-face and joined forces with the former Séléka group MPC to form the RJ/MPC.[46] The MPC and RJ alliance made the new group one of the most powerful in the country – and one of the deadliest. The MPC attempted to gain a foothold near Paoua and was thereafter seen to be the most powerful armed group,

---

[41] ICG 2016: 1.

[42] See Tchie, A. E. (1 May 2017) 'South Sudan crisis deepens as main rebel groups fragment and realign', *The Conversation*: http://theconversation.com/south-sudan-crisis-deepens-as-main-rebel-groups-fragment-and-realign-76240.

[43] Cf. Le Noan & Glawion 2018.   [44] See Lombard 2016a: 46–7.

[45] Interview with RJ president Armel Sayo, Bangui, CAR, 25 February 2015/ 5 February 2016/17 August 2017.

[46] Interview with a commanding officer of MPC, Paoua, CAR, 24 February 2016.

with the vastest territorial control, in the prefecture.[47] They were successful in becoming a signatory to the 2017 peace agreement that promised economic opportunities on disarmament.[48]

Non-state actors turn to stable ordering when they have the relative strength to press their claims against other actors in the arena. Stable ordering also signals more readable demands to which similarly ordering actors can relate. Thus MINUSCA collaborates with the RJ (but not with more loosely structured groups) and all organized rebel groups are granted a seat at the peace negotiation table, where lucrative benefits for laying down their weapons are discussed.

International actors also turn to stable ordering to express clear claims beyond their immediate mandate in the local arena. Participation in missions such as MINUSCA and UNMISS often enables sending countries to outsource financing of their militaries to the UN,[49] even if they are using the funds to repress dissent at home. The geopolitical aims of the countries contributing to Obo's LRA mission are also questionable. For Uganda, the partnership provides them with military funding from and diplomatic plus points with the USA.[50] The USA, on the other hand, has established an installation in the geographic heart of Africa, from which it can gather intelligence on other countries in the region.[51] While it is impossible to verify such activities, the mission's opaque nature fuels such concerns among local, national, and international actors alike. These concerns are not simply conspiracy theories; they are the views of inhabitants who have witnessed that the control sought through stable ordering is used not only to provide security but also to pursue ulterior motives.

Predictable Security and Insecurity

When I saw the prefect of Mbomou for the third year in a row in August 2017, we met in a restaurant in Bangui instead of his large home in Bangassou. He was as vocal as ever but his situation had

---

[47] Interview with MINUSCA Analyst, Bangui, CAR, August 2017.
[48] See Entente de Sant'Edigie (19 June 2017) 'Accord Politique pour la Paix en République Centrafricaine': www.santegidio.org/documenti/doc_1063/accor d_politique_pour_la_paix_en_republique_centrafricaine_entente_de_sant_egi dio.pdf
[49] Brosig 2017.   [50] Titeca & Costeur 2015.
[51] Interview with source from within US military base, Obo, CAR, March 2015.

deteriorated. An armed group had chased him and his family from his home even though he had warned the government and the UN peace-keepers for weeks of the imminent attack.[52] The UN only reluctantly allowed him to seek shelter on their compound the night of the attack, in which more than 100 people died.[53] In Bangui he sat idly, unable to return to his community, of which he was still the prefect, and moving about cautiously as even here he said there were people after him.[54] A few days after we met, I read in the newspapers that the president had reshuffled prefectural posts. Mr Feyomona's name was not on the list.[55]

Actors use stable ordering to make claims beyond the here and now in the security arena. State actors wish to emphasize their supreme right to control security through legal-bureaucratic means. Internationals aim to build the state's stable ordering capacities and pursue their own objectives beyond the local arena. In the CAR, claiming state authority creates aspirations even under conditions of limited effectives and triggers support by international actors. At the same time, they have to make do with very limited means on the ground, allowing for other actors to engage in stable ordering even where the state allegedly holds a prerogative. In Somaliland, pragmatic negotiations open new domains to a state with extremely few resources, by keeping costly security provision out of its sphere of responsibility. Non-state actors also use regularized practices to provide security for the populace. In South Sudan, repressive imposition is seen as a means of regime survival, while local and national state actors are suspicious of one another. Actors resort to enforcement when others do not voluntarily accept their claim to control and when simultaneously they believe to be in a relative position of strength in the local arena.

Stable ordering is characterized by clearly voiced claims, hierarchized actor relations, and structured processes of security provision. In other words, people know what they can expect. This can be a very positive aspect, as this predictability allows inhabitants to adapt their lives in a way to minimize threats and maximize security through

---

[52] Interview with Prefect of Mbomou, Bangui, CAR, 18 August 2017.
[53] BBC (29 May 2017) 'RCA : l'ONU Condamne la Résurgence des Violences': www.bbc.com/afrique/region-40082199.
[54] Interview with Prefect of Mbomou, Bangui, CAR, 18 August 2017.
[55] Interview with former Prefect of Mbomou, Bangui, 10 July 2018.

adherence to the laid-out rules. However, these rules might be untenable for some people. In a negative sense, stable ordering thus also creates very predictable forms of insecurity – for example, for those that speak out against the repressive South Sudanese regime. From an actor's perspective, seeking control is weighed against limited capabilities and even the inherent dangers of assertion against other (possibly violent) actors. Enforcing stable ordering is also weighed against the likely benefits of selective responsibilities and personal gains that more fluid ordering can provide.

6 | *Fluid Ordering and Flexible Security*

When I visited Zeila in 2015, it seemed to me ordering in the security arena provided high levels of security for all its inhabitants, until a respondent came up to me and suggested that I might want to talk to one particular elder. I searched for him over several days and finally met up with him in a tea shop in nearby Tokhoshi. He aired some of his grievances, while chewing on qat leaves, but seemed reluctant to share his opinion openly with me and in this public space. He told me that next time he would tell me more.[1] However, I could not manage to arrange another meeting with him before my departure. And thus I waited a year until I could return to Somaliland and, when I called him again, he sounded delighted. He invited me to his home, about an hour into the desert south-east of Zeila – a small, idyllic conglomeration of two clay houses painted white, a wooden shack, and a tall water tank, in the shade of which around fifty sheep were dozing. But he was not there. He had gone to meet some of his fellow elders in another village. Again we took off through the desert for more than an hour. The sand became so fine and quick that even my highly experienced driver was sweating as we nearly got stuck multiple times. Finally, thorny trees and bushes began to spot the landscape and under one of the trees sat the elder in a circle with a dozen others. I jumped out of the car and was warmly welcomed into their midst. Here, in the middle of the desert, in the shade of a thorny tree, next to a small village, they felt very free to talk about their grievances towards the government and seemed happy to see that I was listening.[2] They talked about the historical tensions with the now ruling Isaaq during the 1980s, their perceived political marginalization in the new state, being pushed out of town into the outskirts, and the lack of development in their home areas.[3]

[1] Interview with Ciise Caqil, Tokhoshi, Somaliland, 17 May 2015.
[2] See Figure 6.1.
[3] Focus group discussion with Ciise Elders, near Tokhoshi, Somaliland, 12 May 2016.

Figure 6.1 Meeting with Ciise elders, near Zeila, Somaliland, May 2016

More than just an anecdote about my exciting travels through Somaliland, there are multiple aspects to this story that resemble what I also saw in other security arenas. First, the aspect of the alternative story: during my research, I was expected to grant state actors courtesy visits first and only then talk to other actors, granting the views of the state the benefit of a first impression and non-state actors an alternative to these views. Second, non-state actors seek safe spheres, often in outer circles, in which they feel freer to discuss sensitive issues with me. Third, the differentiation of an outer circle becomes clear through the arduous travel and the primacy the non-state actor holds in navigating it – e.g. sending me first to the house, then to a village, all of which we had great difficulties to find without marked roads or even visible tyre tracks.

Non-state actors do not act in a vacuum, an 'ungoverned space',[4] but rather relate to other actors with other ordering ideas in the arena, most notably the state and international interveners. Non-state actors thus force all others in the arena to think about

---

[4] As suggested by Clunan & Trinkunas 2010.

possibilities of cohabitation of different ordering forms. While in Chapter 5, I decipher a certain tendency of state actors towards stable ordering narratives, in practice they do not naturally form accepted hierarchical chains of command with clear distributions of responsibilities in the security arena. In some instances, state actors deliberately try to widen the space in which they can compete over stakes in the arena. Advancing fluid ordering is often needed for self-preservation of all types of actors and offers agents particular benefits for personal gain. At times fluidity can also enable dynamic solutions to complex problems that are appropriate to meagre resources. Through fluid ordering, actors can flexibly collaborate with others as well as adapt to movements and new issues in the security arena. At the same time, the lack of clear regulations and enforced controls creates spaces for self-enrichment and violence against the populace. I thus analyse how actors deliberately use more fluid forms of ordering for its particular benefits but also to compensate for the minimal resources available for stable ordering.

In the CAR, state actors are endowed with the fewest resources from the central government. They are nonetheless highly reluctant to provide flexible solutions to security concerns. The deliberate absence of state actors in many areas and domains grants space to both civil and violent non-state actors to take up matters of security. In Somaliland, as a contrast, fluidity is made official policy and underlines the country's relative success story. For many in the countryside, the state is of secondary importance to the role of traditional elders for security. In towns, however, the balance has turned, although all interlocutors still ascribe non-state actors with at least complementary roles in security provision. South Sudan's national government tries to impose its authority using violence, while giving leeway to forces for unaccounted violence on the local level, which further fuels local resistance. The repression exerted by national state actors in South Sudan leads people to form alternative security actors in opposition to the government. Within this violent context, non-violent approaches to security in South Sudan lose influence.

Mediated security provision is presented as an alternative to stable ordering that avoids imposition on other, often stronger actors. Peaceful actors that do not or cannot resort to violence play absolutely crucial, and under-researched, roles in providing security to inhabitants,[5] and I thus wish to emphasize their impact on security by focussing on their ordering of the security arena in the first half of this chapter. Only thereafter do I turn to those that take up arms and are more commonly studied in conflict contexts.[6]

Mediated Security Provision

Mediation is more commonly studied in international diplomacy.[7] However, its principles also hold on the local level, that is, the discussion of a resolution between two belligerent parties with the aid of a third. While it can be beneficial for the third party to be neutral, this is not a definitional characteristic and, in the local context, is often impossible. Local relations and historical appreciation of the mediating actor can even be advantageous in resolving deeply rooted conflicts.[8] Mediation is a process in which the parties search for a compromise that both sides can accept. In some instances, they might agree on forms of enforcing the mutual decision after it is taken but the process itself needs to be without force. Actors aiming at providing security to the populace without taking up arms must tread carefully. Their lack of armament makes them directly vulnerable to attacks but simultaneously less likely to be attacked in the first place because they are not threatening. They can thus engage the arena by navigating the spaces that are open solely to them – e.g. speaking to armed actors of varying types – while staying aware of their constant exposure.

Non-state actors in the CAR formed mediation committees during the Séléka rebellion (2012–13) to negotiate resolutions for public grievances with the respective local rebel leaders and to reduce intercommunal tensions. Bangassou's Comité de Paix et Médiation de Mbomou (CPMM) formed in April 2013[9] and members describe it as the model that other towns then replicated.[10] A Catholic abbot leads the mediation board and joins forces with representatives from protestant churches, local mosques, and civil society. Paoua's Comité d'Appui Spirituel aux Autorités Locales (CASAL) is less extensive, including half a dozen key religious leaders, but is informally headed by a former rebel leader. Finally, in Obo, the Catholic abbot joined with his

[5] See Clunan & Trinkunas 2010; Logan 2013; Mac Ginty 2010a; Molomo 2009.
[6] See Arjona *et al.* 2015; Cederman *et al.* 2010; Gurr 1970.   [7] Böhmelt 2011.
[8] Lederach 1997.   [9] See Figure 6.2.
[10] Observation of CPMM meeting, CAR, 10 March 2015.

Figure 6.2 The CPMM holding a meeting, Bangassou, CAR, January 2016

protestant and Muslim counterparts and half a dozen civilian representatives to adapt the model from other towns.

The CAR boards hold no significant traditional authority and are new short-term marriages of convenience – unlike, for example, in Somaliland, where mediation is led by traditional authorities with long historical continuity. CAR's mediation boards are new creations with no force that can be mobilized. They thus continuously renegotiate their position in the security arena without the ability to enforce changes in their favour. The boards are internally weak as membership fluctuates and their representativeness of society is not clearly delineated – e.g. alleged representatives of 'the youth' or 'the Muslims' are at times unknown or contested in the respective part of the community. With such a weak standing in the arena, the Obo board was never established as an important player,[11] while the Bangassou and Paoua boards became mired in controversies.

---

[11] As the Séléka could never take control of the town (due to a US and Ugandan presence) and intercommunal tensions were rarely expressed in open violence, the board stopped its work after a few sessions.

During the Séléka rule in Paoua (March–October 2013) two peace committees competed as vehicles of negotiation between local inhabitants and the rebel leadership. The first, CMPP, included several civilian leaders and was headed by a representative of a well-established political party.[12] However, after the departure of the Séléka, the committee was soon brandished as an election vehicle for its leader.[13] Many members switched to the second mediation board, CASAL, while the other one dissolved. CASAL seeks out contact to armed groups to try to appease tensions by building on their respect as men of god and because CASAL's leader is himself a former commander of a regional rebel group.[14] Currently, they play a key role as brokers in the demobilization negotiations between international actors and the armed groups. However, members of CASAL complain that their role in these negotiations is reduced to that of mere interpreters.[15] Bangassou's mediation board, CPMM, similarly suffers from a lack of enforcement capabilities. While there are numerous accounts of their mediators intervening to prevent revenge attacks between Muslim and non-Muslim groups, the committee can only ask for forgiveness and offer advice, not provide justice. In March 2015, the Muslim members of the CPMM resigned, reasoning that the committee was covering up crimes against their community's traders.[16] With the return of the state justice apparatus by early 2016, a former member questioned why the committee was still in place.[17] The committee is flexibly repositioning itself in search for new duties aside from intercommunal interventions, such as assisting electoral preparations.

In contrast to the CAR's three mediation boards that have either no measurable security impact (Obo – also because the Séléka did not reach there), are contested in the arena (Bangassou), or can only

---

[12] The Mouvement pour la Libération de Peuple Centrafricain (MLPC) was founded in 1982, has its base in the north-west of the country, and ruled CAR from 1993 to 2003. See Mehler 2011: 119–20.

[13] See Interview with Sub-Prefect, Paoua, CAR, 27 February 2015.

[14] Many of the fighters in the RJ were remobilized men from the former APRD, which was led by Abdelnour Wafio until 2012. Interview with former APRD-leader, Paoua, CAR, 27 February 2015.

[15] Interview with former leader of APRD, Paoua, CAR, 18 February 2016.

[16] In 2015, criminals targeted Muslim traders as their goods were one of the few forms of wealth remaining in town, which meant violence took on an intercommunal connotation.

[17] Interview with Muslim Youth representative, Bangassou, CAR, 24 January 2016.

facilitate negotiation (Paoua), elder meetings in Somaliland play a key role in the security arena. This stems both from the strong internal structure of traditional institutions and from their accepted standing in the security arena by state actors and the populace. Baligubadle is a case in point of the Somaliland system: strong clan-based compensation mechanisms and a police force that intervenes only when and as long as necessary to restart the clan compensation process. Baligubadle is predominantly inhabited by only one clan, the Isaaq/Arab. Elders permeate all strata of administration, including traditional councils and governmental offices. The importance of clan elders in Baligubadle is so ingrained that, in a discussion with herders in the Banka, a young man just simply refused to believe that I had no affiliation to any clan.[18] For him, his clan signified the defining marker of his place and his rights in the security arena. However, the Baligubadle model is the exception rather than the rule in modern Somaliland.

The importance of traditional institutions varies from one security arena to another in Somaliland. In downtown Zeila, many people cannot even name their respective elders or caqil and state councils are filled mostly by economic and social representatives. Ciise clan members have felt disempowered by the state and the clan of the Gadabuursi/Samaroon since they lost their hold on the mayor's office and city council following the 2012 municipal elections, which were riddled with significant irregularities.[19] The Ciise and the state interact mostly according to a live-and-let-live attitude, whereas clan leaders deal with their conflicts in the countryside, the state controls the town, and the meeting points in rural villages are mixed. Traditional institutions in Zeila thus function in parallel, rather than complementarily, to the state.

Cohabitation in Daami is even more tenuous. Inter-clan compensation is imbalanced and the harmony between state and customary institutions struck by discord. Daami is a very particular case, as it is mostly inhabited by the diverse minority group of the Gabooye, who historically have no clan system of their own. To be able to engage with other clans in times of conflict, they imitated the Somali clan system by selecting leaders on all three levels in the early twentieth century.[20] On

---

[18] Focus group discussion with Youths, Gumburaha, Somaliland, 3 May 2015.
[19] See Kibble & Walls 2013.
[20] Historically, the 'customary' roots of the Gabooye are rather shallow: Gabooye is a blanket term used for those Somalis who previously were clan-less servants,

the traditional side, the Gabooye's attempt to adopt the clan system results in only a feeble copy of the workings of other clan families: they have much less livestock and funds to pay for compensation deals, they are organized by vocational casts, which undermines cohesion based on lineage, and they are stigmatized by other clans that refrain from building social links with them, such as through inter-clan marriages.[21] The local opinion of the state is marked by suspicion, as the Gabooye feel largely underrepresented politically and live in economically destitute situations.[22] Thus, while elders are expected to have a hand in the Somaliland model, in reality, the Gabooye feel marginalized from participating equally. In general traditional authority in Somaliland has the strongest standing of the three countries but significant in-country variations remain.

Similar to the CAR, South Sudan's churches play a key role in mediated conflict resolution.[23] In all three arenas, churches contribute to society through education, interfaith dialogue, and, in Buseri, even by training locals to peacefully approach cattle keepers. Chiefs play a similarly ambiguous role in South Sudan as they do in the CAR: they are heavily bound to the state and, while some groups hold long histories of traditional authority, such as the Zande that inhabit both South Sudan and the CAR, the hierarchies of other groups formed due to pressure from British colonizers.[24] Even more, during the long years of civil war, chiefs were torn between having loyalty to the government or to the rebels and were frequently replaced. They thus cannot build on a generational standing comparable to clan leaders in Somaliland.[25] The civil wing of the SPLA, the SPLM party, also plays a role that spans the country, at times upholding loyalty to the national leadership, as in

---

travelling with the recognized clans to conduct those services considered undignified for Somali nomads – such as shoemaking, barbering, and so forth. In the early to mid-twentieth century, colonial authorities granted the Gabooye permanent settlements. One of these confined areas, Daami, was then near Hargeisa but, due to population growth, is now part of the city. The inhabitants decided to create their own clan structures to be able to claim their rights in the Somali system. With Somaliland basing its political system on these customary institutions during the struggles of the 1990s, Gabooye's recognition as a clan remains a pressing issue. See Vitturini 2017.

[21] Focus group discussion with Gabooye Youths, Daami, Somaliland, 26 April 2016.

[22] Interview with Village Chairperson, Daami, Somaliland, 23 April 2016.

[23] See Öhm 2014: 145, 174–7.   [24] See Leonardi 2013: 41ff.

[25] See Lewis 1961.

Raja, but in others also ready to voice criticism, as in Mundri. Intended to be a unifying institution in the lead-up to independence, the SPLM is thus divided similarly to its military counterpart in the ongoing civil war.

Aspiring mediators in South Sudan act in an extremely dangerous environment. Rather than their accustomed neighbourly quarrels, the populace expects chiefs, party members, youth leaders, and priests to deal with the big security issues of the day, such as the movement of cattle keepers and the war between government and opposition. The government, on the other hand, expects chiefs to act as their interlocutors by transmitting messages from the governor to the people. The key government messages in November 2014 were to not join the rebellion and instead to send recruits to the national army.[26] In the context of state repression and the use of chiefs as government messengers, South Sudan's non-state actors are hard struck: whereas CAR's mediation boards use the leeway of an absent state, South Sudan's face a repressive one.

Non-state stakeholders nevertheless try to provide independent security. The chief of Buseri met with his counterparts from both the agricultural community and the side of the cattle keepers to discuss ways in which there can be movement of cattle without the destruction of crops. Buseri's chief described how, during a meeting with cattle keeper leaders and other chiefs, he was simply told off, whereas, before that, when cattle keepers arrived unarmed, he could talk to them.[27] An initiative of the local church in Buseri to train people to peacefully engage the cattle keepers is equally unable to halt the threat emanating from them. In Raja, elders form a kind of advisory board to the Executive Director – a local state administrator – but mention their inability to confront government repression in the area.[28] A sheikh, in principle an influential leader, described how his daughter was taken from him by a soldier but he could not pursue the culprit because 'somebody with the gun has a lot of power'.[29] Raja's non-state actors cannot address the presence of Darfuri rebels, which is used as a pretext for Sudan to bomb the town, or get the government to reduce their imposition of an atmosphere of fear. Mundri's civil leaders, on the

---

[26] See Interview with Sultan, Raja, South Sudan, 28 November 2014.
[27] Focus group discussion with Elders, Buseri, South Sudan, 22 November 2014.
[28] Focus group discussion with Sultans, Raja, South Sudan, 27 November 2014.
[29] Ibid.

other hand, speak up and seem to form a web with local state actors to resist the national government's repression. They try in vain to provide solutions to the arrival of cattle keepers and to government repression. The national government leaves no space for mediated security aside the state in any of the three local arenas, as they interpret public statements on security as a threat to their rule.

Based on these varying structures, conglomerations of non-state actors, and their role in the security arena, actors face different challenges and opportunities to make their mark on ordering the local security arena and, in some instances, provide security through mediation. When state actors take the prerogative based on legal-bureaucratic authority, non-state actors take recourse using other sources, such as religious and traditional authority or economic influence. In Somaliland, traditional elders, state forces, and religious leaders fluidly relate to one another to deal varyingly with both low levels of conflict daily and the occasional large threat. The state encourages elders to handle most issues through long-held traditional structures of conflict mediation. In the CAR, mediation boards sprang up in all three arenas during the recent crisis. At first glance, these boards share similarities: they include religious, social, and political leaders and mostly deal with intercommunal tensions. However, their different positions in the respective security arenas have granted them varying levels of influence on security. The window of opportunity for non-state mediation in South Sudan closed during the civil war that started in 2013. Traditional leaders try to address cattle movement and government-oppositional fighting but their endeavours seldom come to fruition. In sum, space for mediated security in South Sudan is minimal, in Somaliland elders have great means to negotiate security resolutions, and in the CAR civil society actors attempt to take on a similar role to that in Somaliland through the formation of mediation boards.

Towards state actors, unarmed non-state actors often seem to hold only a secondary role. Chiefs were appointed by colonial authorities in the CAR and South Sudan. They hold minimal authority beyond their small quarters or villages in most of today's CAR. During South Sudan's previous and current civil wars, chiefs became caught up between violent demands for loyalty from state actors and from those who oppose this.[30] In all three countries, so-called traditional

---

[30] See Leonardi 2013: 167ff.

authorities are on the payroll of the state. The state, not in the Weberian sense, but as an institution that comes from the capital and flexibly adapts to the local arena, is a focal point in all cases studied.

It should not be understated how recurrent it is also for state and international actors to turn to fluid ordering despite both actor types' claimed emphasis on stable ordering. State forces are granted opportunities for fluid ordering when expecting accountability neither from above nor below. Such fluid ordering opportunities are quickly criticized by external observers who worry armed forces will eschew costly public security responsibilities to seek a personal profit. Indeed, such can become the case, as an example from the CAR's Obo shows, where the town's gendarmerie brigade commander[31] became engulfed in a scandal that would cost him his job: A Ugandan soldier driving a US army vehicle ran over a local girl. The Ugandan army allegedly offered CFA 4 million (around EUR 6,100) in compensation to the deceased's family. They made this unofficial deal outside the courts, with the facilitation of the local gendarme. Only CFA 1 million reached the family and the gendarme was alleged to have kept the rest. The lack of stable channels of accountability in extreme events can lead people to seek more ad hoc responses to make state actors account for their abuses. Large public protest followed and Obo's gendarme was reassigned to Bria where he was said to face trial.[32] In an earlier incident in the same town, the prefect stood accused of having taken a government vehicle destined for the municipality for his personal use. Again people took to the streets, during which demonstrators stole and dismantled the vehicle.[33] The prefect became so frightened that he rarely left his home. On the one hand, these protests can be seen as improving security in the arena as state actors are held accountable for abuses of office. On the other hand, the fluid nature of these heated, spontaneous protests without due process might have allowed room for false accusations and undermined the state's role in security provision. Because of the intense public reaction, some state actors became inoperable: the recalling of the only gendarme in Obo meant the bureau was closed and the prefect, rather than steering his community, began hiding from it. Similar accusations of malpractice against state security forces are

---

[31] A euphemism, as he was the only member in his 'brigade'.
[32] The gendarme in question refused to comment on the affair.
[33] Interview with Gendarmerie, Obo, CAR, 17 March 2015.

voiced in Bangassou and Paoua,[34] making Obo far from an isolated case.

On the other hand, flexible processes have a positive impact on security when actors use them to substitute for stable ordering processes that are lacking resources on the ground. State actors in the CAR at times try to bend rigid state justice regulations to halt the rampant feeling of impunity. In Bangassou, the gendarmerie detains around fifty accused or sentenced criminals in makeshift rooms at the station indefinitely rather than releasing them back into the public as they are legally obliged to do in the absence of functioning prisons or tribunals. Obo's police commander acts similarly: in 2015, he jailed an accused murderer in a makeshift hut behind his office for around three months. However, he had difficulties finding the means to feed him, the iron-sheet hut became very hot, and he feared he could not protect the culprit from angry neighbours seeking revenge. He thus brought the culprit and the family together and – with no court justice in sight – they agreed on a compensation scheme in which the culprit would pay CFA 300,000 (EUR 460) to the deceased's family and CFA 50,000 (EUR 75) to the state. Afterwards, the perpetrator was released and the police commissioner said the situation calmed down. Nevertheless, in three other cases of murder, the culprits were granted preliminary release, only having to regularly present themselves at the police station. This, however, the commissioner could not enforce due to the limited means available to him.[35]

One way actors flexibly contend with limited official means is by strengthening their position through unofficial recruits. CAR's state security services increase their minimal effectives – think one salaried police officer for the prefectural capital Obo with around 8,000 inhabitants – by recruiting voluntary auxiliary forces. This is the case for the police in Obo and Paoua and the gendarmerie in Paoua and Bangassou.[36] The gendarmerie in Bangassou also collaborates with local vigilantes as well as hiring auxiliaries.[37] These auxiliary recruits, while

---

[34] One gendarmerie commander in Bangassou was said to be particularly corrupt, as he extorted fees from alleged and real criminals for their release, without granting a trial.

[35] Interview with Police Officer, Obo, CAR, 10 February 2016.

[36] See Figure 6.3.

[37] The gendarmerie denied both in an interview but I met an auxiliary officer at the station and talked to vigilantes who alleged collaboration with the gendarmerie. Interview with Gendarme, Bangassou, CAR, 28 January 2016; Interview with Youth leader, Bangassou, CAR, 25 January 2016.

Figure 6.3 Police forces in front of their police station, Paoua, CAR, March 2015

unarmed, are drawn from the local arena and thus bring local biases with them into decentralized state structures that are supposed to stay independent of personal and communal struggles. As the auxiliaries receive no official pay and even the state employees face recurrent salary arrears, CAR's state security forces try to make ends meet by leveraging fees for the pursuit of criminal cases.

Although not legally grounded, practices of recruiting auxiliary forces and leveraging fees are not a key security concern for respondents in the CAR or in South Sudan, while respondents nevertheless dismiss the excessive fees as bad behaviour. Respondents in South Sudan's Mundri and Buseri have similar complaints about unofficial police fees to those of people in the CAR. 'For your statement to be written [at the local police] you need to pay twenty-five pounds', a Buseri woman who had been the victim of theft complained.[38] This creates unequal access to justice based on wealth. However, people also realize that, similar to the CAR, the salaries of police officers in South Sudan are often late and sometimes not paid for months.[39] People in all three local South Sudanese arenas are thus relatively understanding of the fees levied by local police officers.

More important to inhabitants than paying small fees is whether state actors offer flexible solutions within the limited means available to them. Local state actors in Mundri are seeking to create such fluid spaces to deal with pressing security concerns. In late 2014, the acting commissioner, police forces, and wildlife forces acted in concert with party leaders and youth and women representatives to follow up on rumours of a training camp for rebels allegedly being founded nearby. They posted notices on the market asking for the support from local traders in the way of fuel and mobile phone credit to send a delegation to a nearby town where tensions were rising after locals had killed a military intelligence officer who had been conducting secret investigations. Local state actors therefore take on responsibilities not officially part of their role and, rather than imposing themselves through arrests, they seek dialogue with inhabitants.

Even when the local state is comparatively better resourced, fluid ordering can reduce tensions that more rigid stable ordering could create. State forces in the arenas I visited in Somaliland at least are paid regularly (albeit this does not always seem to be the case).[40] They are, however, no less in danger of facing violent resistance to their imposition. Police officers repeatedly explained to me that clans remain armed and they therefore cannot simply enforce their decisions on them.[41] The police of Baligubadle, for example, have one or two functioning cars, around

---

[38] At that time around USD 5. Focus group discussion with Women, Buseri, South Sudan, 25 November 2014.

[39] Focus group discussion with Women, Buseri, South Sudan, 25 November 2014; in addition, Cherry Leonardi *et al.* find the police to be staffed mostly by 'undertrained former SPLA soldiers' with high illiteracy rates. Leonardi *et al.* 2010: 47.

[40] Cf. Chapter 5, Note 14.

[41] Interview with commanding officers at National Police Headquarters, Hargeisa, Somaliland, 24 May 2016; Interview with Police Officer, Baligubadle, Somaliland, 1 May 2016.

thirty-five officers in town, and only two personnel in the centre of the nomadic Gumburaha Banka. In any single given incident, they can use force to arrest people who are fighting. However, they are unable to project their power everywhere at all times, especially throughout the vast, open plains of the Gumburaha Banka. Collaborating with clan elders thus becomes a measure of extending security provision and reducing dangerous side effects.[42] On numerous occasions, respondents described incidences in which the police intervened without the accompaniment of the respective elder of the accused – often they were shot at and had to retreat to find the elder to de-escalate the situation.[43] The police arrest the culprit and often even the victim or their respective families to put pressure on the elders to strike a compromise. If the elders cannot come to an agreement, the police transfer the case to the state court. The judge can then sentence the culprits and have them incarcerated. Imprisonment is, however, rarely the end of the story.

Justice in Somaliland certainly does not follow principles of due process and equitable sentences by Western standards. Rather than seeking punishment and an abstract form of justice, state channels aim at establishing security. State institutions therefore allow for almost limitless flexibility in their decisions. In Baligubadle, the state judge only steps in when the traditional process stalls. He then first tries to pressure the elders to find a solution and, if they do not, he sentences the culprits after a rather minimal 'due' process: 'Two witnesses is enough for me to make my decision', as he explained his court proceedings.[44] However, even after the ruling and sentencing, the respective elders of the victim and the accused can still strike a compensation agreement and present it to the court, after which the culprit will be released no matter his crime. At this late stage, however, both sides have to pay a high fee for the annulment of the court ruling.[45] The state institutions, it seems, deliberately try to keep people from using the limited state resources. And state actors are ready to fluidly share security responsibilities with non-state actors rather than enforcing a rigid state monopoly on the use of force.

Some international actors at times follow a similar approach of sharing security responsibilities and negotiating flexible solutions. Despite the UN being a bureaucratic behemoth, UN officials on the ground have

---

[42] Interview with Deputy Mayor, Baligubadle, Somaliland, 3 May 2015.
[43] Focus group discussion with Youths, Baligubadle, Somaliland, 3 May 2016.
[44] Interview with Chief Justice, Baligubadle, Somaliland, 1 May 2016.   [45] Ibid.

a surprising degree of flexibility. In Raja, civil society representatives were dreading the departure of UNMISS's local civil affairs officer, who was leaving because Raja's UN base was closing. This officer had engaged not only with state actors but also with civil society actors, joining them frequently for meetings outside the office, thus taking on the position not only of intervener but also of friend.[46] When talking to him, it became obvious that this extra effort to enter society granted him access to local knowledge on the conflict that none of his colleagues had, who stuck to the rule book and stayed within the compound. A civil affairs officer in Paoua adopted a similar approach by engaging armed groups. He visited them frequently, talked to all sides, and noted each group's demands. He facilitated this access by collaborating with members of the local mediation committee, who acted as translators and helped him to establish a rapport with the local groups. This flexible, unarmed approach to armed groups allowed international actors to discuss and resolve matters – such as preparing eventual disarmament measures – without resorting to violence to uphold an imagined state monopoly on the use of force.

The question thus arises as to what are the underlying processes of ordering that enable mediated security in some arenas but undermine them in others. One necessity for mediated security is sufficient leeway for flexible outcomes. When seeking flexible outcomes, actors negotiate numerous pathways to resolve security concerns, without either participating actor seeing violence as the sole method to achieve its aims. In South Sudan, actors that propose alternative, fluid approaches find themselves face to face with the highly militarized national government. Under such conditions, peaceful mediation does not have sufficient space to even attempt to appease tensions, as voicing an opinion is potentially interpreted as opposition to the government. Somaliland's elder boards build on a generational standing, broad public support, and a large degree of leeway granted by the state to take up security matters. Finally, in the CAR, the unassertive state leaves an opening for other actors to take on security duties. However, because CAR society is characterized by more fluid ethnic and group affiliations than society in Somaliland,[47] meditation board members lack the ability to build on social cohesion. The Catholic abbot can by no means rein in all 'the Catholics' and nor can other leaders such as

---

[46] Interview with UN Civil Affairs officer, Wau, South Sudan, 19 November 2014. The spontaneous, amicable exclamations by a number of people on the ground, when mentioning the UN CA officer's name, support this viewpoint.
[47] Cf. Woodfork 2006: 9.

'the youth' representative. While they meet regularly and debate a range of issues, the boards have no enforcement capacities or partners. The credibility of enforcing eventual mediation outcomes is thus a second key condition for mediation success. Actors that feel their peaceful means of ordering bear no fruition can turn to fluid violence.

Fluid Violence

Fluid violence stands out because it is so hard to pin down. Who is participating in violent acts, who is leading them, and what the members want are not clearly shown. Actors on the ground choose deliberately to engage in fluid violence for the benefits it might accrue. It is a way to stay relatively safe from counterattacks by more powerful actors: it is hard to arrest a leader or attack members when neither are clearly specified. Fluid ordering is used particularly often in security arenas in which the stable ordering actors of the state are not providing the desired security and the risk of confronting another powerful actor is high. In other words, fluid violence allows actors to navigate a potentially dangerous arena even without access to significant resources.

When powerful stakeholders cause widespread insecurity, inhabitants are faced with the dilemma of wanting to resist but also wanting to survive. People in Raja, South Sudan, are particularly aggrieved with their national government. They cannot openly voice their dissent as the arena is filled with powerful actors: large SPLA contingents are stationed in town and at multiple points north of it (towards the contested border to Sudan) and the town hosts government-allied Darfuri rebels. Directly attacking either of these actors would amount to suicide. Raja does not experience the schism along the lines of ethnicity and loyalty to ambitious political leaders that drives conflict in the rest of the country. The inhabitants of Raja face Sudanese bombings and government repression in a civil war that has little to do with them. Choosing fluid resistance, rather than forming a stable rebellion, leaves future pathways open to multiple opportunities as an alternative to an all-or-nothing confrontation with the government. Where fluid violence meets a stably ordered state or international response, the two eschew one another, with neither side able to defeat the other. South Sudan's conflict remains so violent in Mundri and Raja because neither side is able to rein in the other. Locals who sympathize with armed oppositional groups seek a response to their security concerns but the rebels cannot deliver these as they are forced into hiding by the stronger government. The government wants to control the local arena and therefore does not allow non-state actors to deal even with local issues, as the government feels this would allow rebellion to grow. It is unable to fully rein in opposition, however, so long as rebels fluidly eschew government control. This results in a mutually hurting stalemate that continuously reinforces itself.[48]

Non-state armed actors proliferate also outside the South Sudanese context where inhabitants wish to defy a dominating order that they feel is undermining their security. Because the Somaliland policing system is disrupted by mistrust in Daami, the quarter is considered the most dangerous of the Somaliland capital and a safe haven for its worst criminals. Daami quarter lies just outside downtown Hargeisa and is inhabited by a population comprised mostly of the Gabooye minority. Youth groups claim to defend their community against aggression and marginalization from the dominant clans, especially the Isaaq/Issa-Musse clan that lives in the neighbouring quarter.[49] These youth groups can be only loosely differentiated from football clubs, gangs, and the general population.[50] As these youths do not voice clear demands or have an outlook on integration into the state, the route of fluid ordering provides opportunities: in this way, they can make their political and social claims without taking on the heavy task of providing security or risking a full-scale confrontation with the much larger group of Issa-Musse or even the state (see Box 6.1).

The gains groups can achieve through fluid ordering are comparatively moderate but so are the risks. Auto-defence groups formed in Obo and claim to create security against LRA attacks and for inhabitants at night. However, their activities are confined to the occasional search party after an alleged LRA attack and bringing information on culprits or the criminals to the police.[51] More influential are the 'Comités des Vigilantes' of Bangassou that youth groups formed in each of the town's three districts to resist the Séléka rulers in late 2013.[52] They armed themselves with the

---

[48] Contrast this with Zartman's concept of a mutually hurting stalemate opening opportunities for negotiated solutions: Zartman 2000; Zartman 2001.
[49] Focus group discussion with Gabooye Youths, Daami, Somaliland, 26 April 2016.
[50] Focus group discussion with Women, Daami, Somaliland, 25 April 2016.
[51] Interview with Auto-Defence leader, Obo, CAR, 9 February 2016.
[52] Interview with Youth leader, Bangassou, CAR, 25 January 2016; Focus group discussion with Vigilantes, Bangassou, CAR, 1 February 2016.

Box 6.1 Clashes in Daami quarter, Somaliland, March 2016

In late March 2016, Isaaq/Isse Musse youth called a passing Gabooye girl 'Midhgan' – a term considered a slur for Somali minority groups. As other Gabooye youths confronted the slanderers, more and more youths gathered around, and soon young people from both sides were throwing stones at each other as well as at bystanders and their property. The clashes continued for two days and two nights. Three people were badly injured, two cars destroyed, and multiple houses damaged. The police intervened from its nearby district headquarters. Gabooye citizens felt the police were targeting them specifically rather than keeping people apart. The police arrested forty allegedly implicated youths on the spot as well as both the Gabooye/Musse Dheriya Caqil and the Isaaq/Isse Musse Caqil to force them to call their sons to the police station (since they believed their sons to be the leaders of the trouble on both sides). The sultans – the highest clan rank – of each side then came to the police station and struck a compensation payment deal between the two clans to pay for the physical and property damages committed by both sides. After three days in jail, everyone was released but, as one Gabooye youth leader put it: 'The clash can come back any moment, they don't even greet another although they live among each other.'

---

limited weapons at their disposal, including machetes and simple hunting rifles. They erected roadblocks and staged a popular resistance against the Séléka, who ultimately left by late 2013. After the departure of the Séléka, they took matters of justice into their own hands to stop the rampant criminality that filled the power void as inhabitants looted houses and shops. The vigilantes of Bangassou shift security in the arena by creating more felt security for their small target populace while fuelling larger tensions in the arena. Vigilantes regroup around youth leaders of the ethnically homogeneous quarters[53] rather than spanning across quarters. One vigilante went as far as stating: 'Thieves need to be killed instantly.'[54] No evidence shows that they actually follow through on such threats. However, the unclear rules, regulations, and even membership dissipate any real responsibility for security and allow leeway

---

[53] Interview with Youth leader, Bangassou, CAR, 25 January 2016; Interview with Muslim Youth representative, Bangassou, CAR, 24 January 2016; Interview with Police Officer, Bangassou, CAR, 28 January 2016.
[54] Focus group discussion with Vigilantes, Bangassou, CAR, 1 February 2016.

for criminal activity.[55] The creation of auto-defence groups is thus linked to the unravelling of intercommunal communication channels (both between ethnicities and religions). These vigilantes pursue short-term protective narratives that are best furthered through fluid ordering and do not aim to gain larger political stakes through stable control.

Fluid protection is not only against the visible. Local security issues that people of the CAR want resolved include obscure forms of retribution, including witchcraft and popular justice.[56] However, from my own research, I judge this trend to be overstated. In fact, people mentioned only one popular justice event in all my discussions, in which, years ago, one person was buried alive by a mob around 100 kilometres from Obo; people spoke with shock and horror of the event. For this matter, my research might be biased, however: Peter Geschiere links witchcraft to the notion of intimacy.[57] As my research approach searches for broad comparative insights rather than deep individual narratives, respondents might simply not have felt that our relationship was intimate enough to discuss witchcraft. If mentioned at all, it was discussed matter-of-factly – a reference to a person in jail for witchcraft in Paoua[58] – rather than as a specific form of interaction in the arena. Another factor might be that witchcraft creates a shadow world behind the everyday[59] but has not (yet) been linked to the new ongoing conflict.

In a more mundane sense, local defence groups with fluid membership and elusive claims create a felt alternative to the state for their supporters without, at least initially, directly confronting more powerful actors in the arenas. The benefits of fluid ordering are, however, not confined to some relatively weak non-state actors. Even more powerful players of the state and international forces can use it to their strategic or personal advantage. Spaces open for state actors when hierarchies are not enforced, attributions of responsibilities are unregulated, and activities can be varied according to individual officers' whims. While

---

[55] Respondents at times spoke of vigilantes and at others of bandits and many could not clearly differentiate the two. In one interview, a man explained to me that vigilantes recruited from bandits as a sort of communal reintegration idea – a trend that also existed in Somaliland's community police.
[56] See Lombard & Batianga-Kinzi 2015.   [57] Geschiere 2013.
[58] Interview with Police Officer, Paoua, CAR, 2 March 2015.
[59] Geschiere 2013: 4.

these characteristics offer state actors possibilities to provide flexible solutions and to collaborate with non-state actors, state actors can interpret security responsibilities in such ways to racketeer the population and they can engage in practices of abuse of civilians. While other actors will find ways to oppose the state, fluid ordering cannot provide regulated mechanisms to account for abuses and thus often violence can spiral.

The spiral of violence in South Sudan's Mundri was the most detrimental example of the dangers of fluid ordering. With the civil war raging with particular intensity in the regions east of Mundri, such as Jonglei, cattle keepers arrived in 2014 with their livestock and their arms. They engaged in multiple skirmishes with local communities that defended their farming land against the cattle keepers' arrival. Mundri's commissioner met with the encroaching cattle keepers without informing other local stakeholders, such as the youth representative or the city council chair. Respondents accused him of taking bribes during this meeting in exchange for allowing the cattle keepers to stay and avoid state justice for the crimes they had committed.[60] Local resentment of the commissioner grew so strong that he decided to take an indefinite 'sick leave' away from Mundri and pass authority on to his modest executive director as acting commissioner.

In Buseri, similarly, inhabitants complained about the abuses committed by strong state actors outside the village: 'There is another area behind there, unclear whether they are retired [soldiers] or something, but they are the ones that cause these troubles.'[61] The description bears characteristics of the outer circle, as the respondent speaks of an 'other' area that is unclear and emanates trouble. Locals accuse these soldiers of coming to Buseri to aggress people at the market and abuse or even rape women.[62] Aside from their unaccountable abuses, state forces flexibly interpret what is their responsibility in the security arena and what is not: despite the multitude of state security actors in the arena – the army, local police, a large police force in nearby Wau town – none provide a solution to Buseri's most pressing security concern: the arrival of armed cattle keepers. Local leaders explain this with the

---

[60] Focus group discussion with Youths, Mundri, South Sudan, 8 December 2014.
[61] Focus group discussion with Women, Buseri, South Sudan, 25 November 2014.
[62] Focus group discussion with Youths, Buseri, South Sudan, 24 November 2014.

fact that the cattle keepers and the state forces in Wau 'are the same people'.[63]

National state forces are not the only ones that deliberately refrain from their official tasks and use open spaces for fluid violence. The more internationals engage in daily interaction, the more openly friction can arise between them and the local population as well. When foreign soldiers patrol the roads by foot, buy their food at the market, and interact personally with the local populace this can create uncontrolled instances that individuals can misuse. Between my first and second visits, there were numerous allegations of sexual abuse voiced against UN peacekeepers – mostly Congolese – and French Operation Sangaris troops. In Obo, rumours of UPDF soldiers gruesomely raping local women have fuelled resentment towards the mission.[64] In Bangassou, Congolese soldiers were said to have sexually abused minors and, in Paoua, Cameroonian forces were alleged to have used a peacekeeper-run bar for promiscuous activities. These allegations have been a key factor behind MINUSCA's increasing detachment.[65] MINUSCA officials in Obo cite the avoidance of sexual scandals as a main reason for forbidding their soldiers to interact with locals. A high-ranking MINUSCA commander proudly claimed that he ordered his soldiers never to step out of a car or to talk to local inhabitants.[66]

Despite these stories of sexual misconduct by UN peacekeepers making international headlines, the issue was not of key concern in Bangassou. A women's representative explained to me why: 'Quand les femmes se présentent [dans leur bases] comme ça, ils [les soldats congolais] sont dans le besoin.'[67] It is not that sexual abuse is accepted in

[63] Focus group discussion with Elders, Buseri, South Sudan, 22 November 2014. Similarly also during Focus group discussion with Youths, Buseri, South Sudan, 24 November 2014.
[64] Focus group discussion with chiefs, Obo, CAR, 15 March 2015; Focus group discussion with Youth, Obo, CAR, 14 March 2015.
[65] Cf. UN General Assembly (23 June 2016), 'Report of an independent review on sexual exploitation and abuse by international peacekeeping forces in the Central African Republic', A/71/99: www.un.org/News/dh/infocus/centafricre pub/Independent-Review-Report.pdf.
[66] Interview with a commanding officer MINUSCA, Obo, CAR, 12 February 2016.
[67] English translation: 'When women present themselves like that [in their military base], they [the Congolese soldiers] have needs', Interview with Vice-President of OFCA, Bangassou, CAR, 2 February 2016.

society but rather that the Congolese soldiers' acts were situated among other equally real threats of sexual abuse by various local individuals in the arena. She added that women went to the Congolese because sexual relations could earn them food or money and that the Congolese did not explicitly seek them out. UN headquarters decided to remove the Congolese from the mission and replace them with a more detached contingent from Morocco; however, this decreased the sense of security in the arena: 'Les Congolais, ils étaient venus pour faire la sécurité, ils ont fait leur travail, avec eux les Séléka avaient peur, après leur départ les Séléka ont décidé de revenir.'[68]

This detachment not only worsens security perceptions; it also fuels local suspicions that internationals pursue ulterior motives to their peacekeeping mandate. International actors can pursue self-interests that negatively impact local livelihoods and security. In Paoua, the Cameroonian contingent is in control of the remaining open trading route between the CAR's Paoua and towns in Cameroon. Traveling in a military armed convoy is the only way to bring goods across. Local respondents accuse peacekeepers and their Cameroonian trading partners of unfairly gaining from this trade monopoly.[69] Similarly, in Bangassou, after the DRC contingents' arrival, trade started flowing into the CAR from the DRC rather than from Chad to the DRC via the CAR.[70] Ugandan military drivers in Obo exploit their monopoly on the South Sudan–Uganda trade route (through which only heavy military trucks can pass due to road degradation caused by these same trucks) to extract heavy fees from merchants trying to restock.[71] In none of these instances has a concerted effort to engage in clandestine trade been proven. However, many international interveners are not in the CAR to purely provide security. Neighbouring interveners (which formed the brunt of the initial AU and UN mission) positioned themselves near to their own borders. This provided them with advantages in terms of enhancing military operational capability, securing political control

---

[68] English translation: 'The Congolese, they had come to create security. They did their job; with them the Séléka were frightened. After their departure the Séléka decided to return', Interview with Vice-President of OFCA, Bangassou, CAR, 2 February 2016.

[69] Interview with Kaba chief, Paoua, CAR, 29 February 2016.

[70] Interview with Muslim trader, Bangassou, CAR, 10 March 2015.

[71] Interview with Trader, Obo, CAR, 12 February 2016. Other stories were told about Ugandan soldiers selling their fuel, ammunition, and even weapons to the populace, as well as trafficking timber with military planes and trucks.

beyond their borders (often to protect their borders), and extending their economic spheres.

Modifiable Security

Non-state alternatives are at times romanticized through labels of local ownership, grassroots movements, and bottom-up peace-building.[72] How non-state actors impact security in the arena, however, is rather ambivalent, depending on the opportunities they view in their arena. When state or international actors are dominant, non-state actors providing stable ordering would make overlapping claims to authority; they can avoid overlaps by providing fluid ordering as an alternative to the stable ordering state actors. Turning to fluid ordering can also function as a survival strategy when dominant actors try to repress opponents: South Sudan's army and intelligence cannot halt the incipient rebellions in Raja and Mundri because the latter grant them no clear lines of attack. Nor can MINUSCA in Paoua defeat the 'bandits', as these become indistinguishable from the villagers among whom they live.

State actors can also find benefits in turning towards fluid ordering in the arena. Foremost it can help them stay safe by avoiding more powerful actors. They can seek to provide flexible solutions to security problems even when they are fitted with minimal resources and face a dangerous environment. They can collaborate with non-state actors by being open to negotiating respective domains of responsibility. Fluid ordering also enables state actors to make a personal profit and even to commit abuses against the populace without being held accountable in official hierarchies. Foreign soldiers can use uncontrolled spaces for sexual abuse, while their hierarchies might use the intervention beyond its mandate for political and economic advances.

In South Sudan, the space for mediated security is the narrowest of all three countries. Varying actors try their best to provide room for discussion and finding peaceful resolutions but feel rebuked by armed actors and the national government. On a local level, non-state actors often find a sympathetic ear for their grievances but also witness the powerlessness of local state actors when faced with the national political dynamics of intra-state civil war or war with Sudan. As a last resort, some people thus turn to resistance against

---

[72] See Richmond 2011.

the national government. In their rebellion, they follow character-istics of fluid ordering, such as moving into the outer circle 'bush' and talking in whispers and of rumours. This move protects them from a direct confrontation with the more powerful national state and its allies while reducing their ability to reorder security nation-ally or even in their nearest inner circle.

State actors in the CAR simply do not have the means to repress alternatives or opponents to the state with the kind of force the army and intelligence in South Sudan can assert. Peaceful mediation boards fill the vacuum left by a mostly absent state justice and security appa-ratus. While mediators achieve some notable successes through dialo-gue, their lack of any enforcement capabilities has disenchanted some of their members and followers, who then left the boards or withdrew their support. All three arenas are marked by armed actors that are seen as protectors to some and threatening to most others. In Bangassou and Obo, state security actors at times collaborate with auto-defence groups to pursue criminals. However, in Paoua, armed groups far outpower the state and no avenues of state co-optation are feasible. Rather, armed actors can threaten the state and effectively confine it to the inner circle.

In Somaliland, traditional institutions and state institutions often cohabitate in complementary ways. While the state officially puts forth a stable ordering structure and narrative, in reality, they allow for a vast amount of fluidity when traditional institutions wish to take over security duties. While both the state and the traditional institu-tions within themselves divide responsibilities clearly and establish relatively stable structures, it is the sphere between them that remains fluid: they renegotiate their respective responsibilities on a case-by-case basis, clan elders hold state positions, and the state leaders can fill clan positions. This cohabitation functions precisely in Baligubadle. However, it is struck by discord in Daami, due to the weak standing of traditional institutions among the Gabooye and of the Gabooye among other clans, as well as in Zeila, where traditional actors are pushed into the outer circle and interrelations to inner-circle state actors are weakening. Somaliland's comparative security is thus based neither on stable nor fluid ordering but on the complementary mix of the two.

7 | *Mixing Ordering Forms*

The CAR's Mbomou prefecture with its capital Bangassou has been the most recent region to be drawn back into conflict. After being chased out of Bambari by MINUSCA, the Unité pour la paix en Centrafrique (UPC) of Ali Darassa moved south, causing numerous deaths among the local population of Mbomou, which resulted in increased local demands for protection or even reprisals. MINUSCA did not forcefully intervene to halt the UPC from expanding into numerous towns. Auto-defence groups claimed they thus needed to take security into their own hands but were then confronted by MINUSCA, which killed one of their leaders in Nzacko. Auto-defence groups accused MINUSCA of supporting the 'Muslim' UPC (the Moroccan contingent is also seen as 'Muslim')[1] and therefore attacked peacekeepers both on the road at Yongofongo and at their base in Bangassou. When the auto-defence groups attacked the town's Muslim quarter in May 2017, the peace-keepers failed to protect the Muslim population, despite the presence of a large contingent near Bangassou. More than 100 people are estimated to have died in the attack.

Mansur Olsen's much-cited analysis of roving bandits describes how armed groups seek the benefits of violent expropriation while eschewing the costs of authority or counterattacks by moving about. Olsen also speaks of stationary bandits who must take on some governing responsibilities in the area in which they are active in order to continue their extractive practices.[2] I broaden these differences by speaking of the forms of ordering the arena as more fluid, encompassing roving banditry, and more stable, encompassing stationary ruling. As shown with the example of the attack on Bangassou, armed actors at least partly use fluid forms of ordering or moving about to eschew direct combat to stay safe against relatively strong actors. Indeed, I find no

---

[1] See Interview with Sultan Bangassou, Bangui, CAR, 22 August 2017.
[2] Olson 1993.

clear distinction between groups that only use fluid and those that only use stable ordering – armed groups can thus be roving some areas while trying to become stationary in another point of the arena.

Many studies suggest that stationary rebel groups tend to create stability and provide public goods as a by-product of their self-interests – basically making them incipient state-builders.[3] Some non-state armed groups might indeed seek to create a space where the actor, its members, and supporters feel permanently secure, even when hostile security actors remain in the wider arena. However, this is not always the case. On the other end of the spectrum, actors can deliberately avoid seeking control to eschew taking on costly responsibilities for citizens and goods and to make themselves less traceable to other hostile actors. State actors also don't naturally tend to only one end of the ordering spectrum. They react to incentives or disincentives to engage in either fluid or stable ordering in a given arena to ascertain whether enforcing a monopoly on the use of force is feasible and strategic. In choosing their forms of ordering they must navigate the different parts of the arena and interact with other types of actors. As state actors tend more towards centres and inner circles, non-state actors position themselves rather towards the peripheries and outer circles and thereby complement the picture of how security is ordered in the local arena. International actors more readily support stable ordering of the state and mostly ignore fluid approaches to security provision. Actors mix forms of ordering or join with other actors to complement what one form of ordering alone cannot achieve. In this chapter, I seek out first how actors use the varying opportunities for ordering from centre to periphery and inner to outer circle. Afterwards, I investigate how actors of different types compete and complement one another by using different ordering forms.

Ordering Different Parts of the Arena

Mixing forms of ordering on a national scale can increase the centre's power over its peripheries. This approach is most clearly encouraged in the Somaliland cases. This does not mean that the state is not trying to assert itself. In fact, since the mid-1990s, the gradual trend is of the state expanding its relative influence. In the three localities visited, the

---

[3] E.g. Branović & Chojnacki 2011; Cheng 2018; Tilly 1990.

state is attempting to gain control over economic activities (smuggling in Zeila), political sovereignty (defending the border to Ethiopia in Baligubadle), and as the guarantor of security (ending gang violence in Daami). The state legacy of devolved colonial government and the clan-based rebellion in the late 1980s, however, have brought forth very influential clan institutions and non-negligible religious actors. Some non-state actors mistrust the ever-strengthening state and resist the expansion, if necessary, with violence. Even in the mind-set of the individuals filling state offices, the clan plays a key, beneficial role that they personally adhere to and therefore cannot simply abolish.

The violent imposition of the dominant role of (mostly national) state actors over all others in South Sudan is driven by the government's fear of growing opposition in the country and the risk of losing power. However, compared to the CAR and Somaliland they have eliminated space for fluid ordering in the peripheries, such as in Mundri and Raja, which led to the opposite of what the government sought: it pushed people into open rebellion. South Sudanese militia leaders have used the threat of violence, or actually taking up arms, to gain a better position in government, after which they rein in their forces– although keeping the possibility of remobilization on the table.[4] In Mundri, youth leaders seek regulated access to local state actors to obtain responses to security issues but nevertheless invoke the threat of armed groups roaming in the countryside in a sort of dual-ordering strategy.

In the CAR, MPs spoke of the forces they could raise, if necessary, or lamented that other MPs have contacts to ill-defined armed groups to use as threats.[5] One MP told me that he could put 4,000 armed men on the street to topple the president if he wanted to but he preferred not to, yet.[6] The sultan of Bangassou claimed he had nothing to do with the attack on Bangassou in May 2017 and instead that he had tried to calm the situation down in collaboration with the state and international actors. At the same time, he claimed that his communications secretary was in daily contact with the commanders of the auto-defence groups that had mounted the attacks.[7] He also showed me a document on

---

[4] See HSBA 2013; de Waal 2014: 361.
[5] Interview with CAR Member of Parliament of Bambari, Bangui, CAR, 23 August 2017.
[6] Interview with CAR Member of Parliament, Paris, France, August 2017.
[7] Interview with Sultan Bangassou, Bangui, CAR, 22 August 2017.

a proposed change of law he allegedly drafted, which proposed to reinstate traditional authorities in a prominent position in the CAR's political system.[8] This is an illustrative mix of his attempt at institutionalized stable ordering, along with the backbone of a threat of fluid violence.

So far, international actors have yet to buy into the questionable story of the Bangassou Sultan and favour leading local improvements of security provision themselves. And MINSUCA's preferred tool remains state-building. Besides the larger theoretical questions concerning the feasibility of external state-building,[9] trainers in Paoua and Bangassou openly speak about two key obstacles in their daily work. First, they cannot access rural offices because there are no stations or police officers outside of main towns, thus effectively restricting the state to the inner circle. Second, state forces only behave well while being accompanied, returning to corrupt dealings thereafter.[10] From a theoretical point of view, both dilemmas could at least be tackled (if not necessarily resolved) by combining stable state-building with fluid intervention. For instance, police trainers could travel to the peripheries and engage with non-state alternative security providers, who are more commonly present outside town centres while the UN emphasize reducing corrupt practices within town.

However, interventions confine themselves to working with state actors and these state actors are mostly centred in the inner circles of the nine arenas. This is particularly the case in the CAR, where no state actor takes on responsibilities outside towns. Local state leaders of the CAR experience next to no interference from national state actors. When state actors are truly willing to compromise on official rules in the pursuit of pragmatic justice – as in the case of Obo's police commissioner – flexible solutions can lead to a felt increase in security. Most often, however, the state actor's real fluidity is contrasted with an adamant stable ordering narrative. State actors abuse their office flexibly for (often modest) self-enrichment but remain unmovable on matters that could call into question their broader state claim to authority. Eschewing fluidity entirely, however, would endanger state actors that

---

[8] Document 4: Projet de loi portant statut de la chefferie traditionnelle en République Centrafricaine, Bangui, CAR, dated 22 January 2017, received August 2017.

[9] See Call & Wyeth 2008; Chandler 2005; Menkhaus 2006; Schneckener 2010.

[10] Interview with UNPOL Officer, Bangassou, CAR, 29 January 2016.

face far stronger and better-resourced security actors in the arena.
Fluidity is thus used for self-preservation, neither creating lasting solutions to security nor producing larger incidences of insecurity itself but
fuelling a lasting driver of insecurity in the CAR: rampant impunity for
perpetrators of violence.

Why using fluidity in addition to stable ordering works in some cases
and further deteriorates security in others again comes down to what
actors make of the legacy of the state on the local level. In South Sudan,
the state is internally divided. Some local state actors, such as the police
and acting commissioner in Mundri, provide opportunities for negotiation to address complex security matters on top off their official
administrative roles. However, they are confronted by close surveil-
lance of national intelligence services and the violent behaviour of the
SPLA. Mundri's security forces also conduct ad hoc excursions into the
outer circle but largely because they see it as an unruly sphere of
potential rebellion. In Raja, monitoring is even tighter. Some state
actors use fluidity for abuses against the local populace. Such fluid
interpretations of state office that seem to undermine national interests
are repressed, while abuses against the local population are often left
unaccounted for as long as they do not threaten regime survival. Local
state actors try to provide security through continuous administration
and dealing with smaller offences. However, they have minimal impact
on the key security threats: the movement of armed cattle keepers and
the spiral of repression and rebellion. Local expectations of what the
state should do – be open to dialogue – and expectations on a national
level – enforce control – are increasingly at odds with one another:
national state actors interpret locals voicing their grievances as resistance, while locals ascribe hidden motives to national state actors'
refusal to engage in mutual dialogue. In such a context, stable and
fluid ordering are seen as opposing forms of ordering for national,
inner-circle, and local, outer-circle actors that neither side wants to
use in complementarity.

In Somaliland, state actors maintain a small presence even in remote
villages but mostly negotiate excursions into the outer circles with
elders who are permanently present and respected in the zone of intervention. In Baligubadle and Zeila, both in Somaliland, the leeway given
to traditional and religious actors and their conflict resolution institutions might hold the key to the arenas' relative stability despite limited
state resources and strength. Fluid cooperation goes so far as to leave

the last words on security and justice to elders rather than judges. This is a pragmatic move in two senses: it increases security even with limited state resources and, second, means eschewing responsibilities left to traditional structures to save capacities for domains seen as more important to the state or the individual official involved. These solutions, while filled flexibly with varying content on a case-by-case basis, are not local inventions but are promoted within the Somaliland political system on all levels of the state and supported by large parts of the population.

While Somali traditional authorities prefer and often even pride themselves on peaceful means of conflict resolution, respondents do at times voice the need to be able to contest an expanding state.[11] In Zeila, security is also quite high but the breaking points are much more prominent than in Baligubadle and triggered more frequently. The demonstrations by (mostly Ciise) inhabitants in response to the 2012 elections were a fluid attempt to voice a grievance without positioning oneself too definitely. If, instead of loosely organized demonstrations, clan leaders had mobilized their kin for a concerted effort against the state, conflict would have been much higher and the possible losses of life, possession, and position would have become a real threat (mostly to the weaker side of the Ciise clan). Despite their continuing ad hoc criticism of the government, clan leaders thus prefer to confine their realm of influence to rural areas, where they continue to hold definite control.[12] Security in Zeila and its surroundings remains high because increasing government stakes are either uncontested or only contested in fluid manners that eschew open confrontation.

The role of fluid violence in Somaliland is intricate: on the one hand, I have shown that mediation by elder boards is key to providing security; on the other hand, the story is incomplete without recognizing the potentials for violence that traditional authorities can exert to protect their domains from the influence of the state. Clans in Somaliland do not openly mobilize militias because only the state officially has a standing army. It is, however, an open secret that clan

---

[11] Interview with Deputy Mayor, Baligubadle, Somaliland, 3 May 2015.
[12] Focus group discussion with Ciise Elders, near Tokhoshi, Somaliland, 12 May 2016.

members remain armed and that clan structures are fit to wage conflict if necessary.[13] Markus Hoehne argues that Somaliland's traditional actors are switching from a network to a state logic of stabilization through territorialization.[14] My own findings support this argument: with the state of Somaliland becoming ever stronger, clans strengthen their hold on territories by providing security to defend their position in the political arena. In Baligubadle, clan control is clearly felt in the surrounding Banka (public grazing land), which is mostly void of government security agents but marked by high levels of security provided by clan leaders. However, government officials and farmers have attempted numerous times to expand private land grants for farmers and livestock entrepreneurs into the Banka, arguing that land is the government's jurisdiction.[15] In numerous such incidences, those leasing the land and government forces securing it were attacked by locals, causing the government to revoke the titles.[16]

Across the nine arenas, local state actors embed themselves in larger centre–peripheral relations and the demarcations of an inner and outer circle. Part of the answer on how actors mix ordering forms is based on historical legacies, which produce actors with different ideas regarding the type of ordering. The CAR state institutions are heavily influenced by the French model and the French-style national administrative training of its civil servants. CAR's state actors are officially under central rule but they are disconnected from the capital's resources and orders. Somaliland was ruled with a light administrative footprint during colonial times. Today, Somaliland's state actors are more clearly under central control but are given leeway for negotiations of their relative roles in the local arena. The state in South Sudan has its origins in a militia movement and is staffed in many key positions by military personnel.[17] Its state actors struggle between violent national imposition in the war between government and opposition forces and the limited use of local leeway for alternative solutions.

---

[13] Interview with commanding officers at National Police Headquarters, Hargeisa, Somaliland, 24 May 2016.

[14] Hoehne 2016.

[15] Interview with Chief Justice, Baligubadle, Somaliland, 1 May 2016.

[16] Interview with Arab Sultan, Baligubadle, Somaliland, 7 May 2016; Focus group discussion with Youths, Baligubadle, Somaliland, 3 May 2016.

[17] See Öhm 2014; Pinaud 2014; Rolandsen 2015a.

Finally, enforcing control is a highly risky business that actors only engage in when they feel they are in a relatively strong position. Actors tend to focalize their forces where they can have most of an impact. For state and international actors, this means deploying effectives first to centres and inner circles from which peripheries and outer circles are engaged as a lesser priority. Through comparatively higher capacities in inner circles they can control towns through stable ordering, while in the outskirts they also engage in more fluid ordering. Non-state actors are present in all parts of the arena – using their established traditions of stable ordering for daily influence but also the opportunities of fluid violence from the outer circles to challenge state and international actors. While some narratives in the arenas express state actors' intent to assert their prerogatives, practices on the ground in all three countries show fluid ordering forms and collaboration with non-state actors. For state actors, combining ordering forms often seems more strategic than choosing one side only. Mixed ordering is a pragmatic choice of actors in the arena. Allowing fluidity where key interests are not at stake frees up limited resources for primary domains. Somaliland's state has taken this strategy the furthest and CAR officials as a matter of necessity, while South Sudan's national security actors strain their resources by seeing a vast array of actors and their activities as a threat to the regime.

Collaboration and Competition Between Actors

While fluid violence eschews the risks of presenting a clear target, only through more stable forms of violence can actors make rigid claims in the security arena. The competition between different types of armed non-state actors as well as with state and international actors continuously changes which opportunities and costs each side of the ordering spectrum provides. In the Bangassou arena, inhabitants (particularly those of the surrounding villages) feared the arrival of the more stably organized UPC of Ali Darassa, a Séléka successor group. Loose auto-defence groups used fluid violence not as a defensive strategy but as a deadly offensive one as seen in the introduction to this chapter. This example shows the dilemmas posed by the multitude of armed groups: the UN directly combatted and simultaneously spoke to the UPC and embedded them in structured processes such as the demobilization programme and peace negotiations. More fluid groups were not part of such direct communication channels. Local inhabitants saw this imbalanced collaboration as the UN taking sides. The auto-defence forces exacted their violence fluidly in many ways: their weapons were makeshift, their strategies improvised and at times near insane – think attacking a fortified UN camp with propane cooking cans, self-fabricated rifles, and machetes – and their targets broadly defined. This, however, also made preventing the attack or apprehending the culprits and supporters immensely difficult. The line between attackers, supporters, and bystanders is blurred and the civilian population acts as a shield against reprisal attacks. Supporters are rumoured to be manifold, ranging from MPs in the capital and the sultan's associates to the former president Bozizé – none of which, however, could be proven.

I focus on the competition between more fluid and more stable armed actors and their relationships to other actors in this section, as to which Paoua offers up another intricate example. Over multiple years, the arena hosted rebel groups that acted more towards the stable ordering and far on the fluid ordering end of the spectrum. During my second research trip in early 2016, the RJ still solidly controlled north of town and the Groupe des Patriots (GP) were embedded fluidly in their home villages west and south of town, while the MPC had no original stronghold in the arena but nevertheless entered the arena violently by attacking distant villages. I present this case in more detail to analyse the dynamics between competing types of armed groups.

The RJ present a protection narrative to residents north of Paoua: they defend them against attacks by so-called Chadians – armed cattle keepers most likely with links to the military in N'Djamena – and against Séléka rebels.[18] They are also seen as an ethnic defence force for the Kaba. While they extort the population, they do so in a structured fashion, demanding regular 'formalités' of 1,000 or 2,000 FCFA (2–3 EUR) from traders.[19] The GP diverge strongly in narrative, structure, and behaviour. In 2014, numerous ethnic Tali split from the RJ, citing discrimination by the ethnic Kaba leadership and their frustration at not rising in

---

[18] Focus group discussion with Group Chiefs, Paoua, CAR, 2 March 2015; Interview with RJ president Armel Sayo, Bangui, CAR, 25 February 2015.

[19] Interview with representative of RJ political party, Paoua, CAR, 21 February 2016; Interview with Trader, Paoua, CAR, 29 February 2016.

the ranks.[20] They positioned themselves in their home villages west and south of Paoua and now claim to defend its mostly Tali inhabitants against RJ attacks. They are structured loosely into three to four subgroups with unclear chains of command and membership.[21] Other inhabitants and actors of Paoua would refer to the GP also as Anti-Balaka groups or bandits because the GP extorted travellers in a highly arbitrary manner: at times, they would take 500 FCFA per passing motorbike and, at other times, they stole the motorbike and killed the driver.[22]

Commanders of MINUSCA seem biased against fluid ordering, loose auto-defence groups. The town's peacekeeping military commander deemed a robust intervention strategy the best way to create security

Figure 7.1 Auto-Defence members and villagers gather for a meeting with the IOM and CASAL, Pendé, CAR, March 2016

[20] Focus group discussion with Tali Chiefs, Paoua, CAR, 20 February 2016; Interview with former leader of APRD, Paoua, CAR, 18 February 2016.
[21] In meeting with three of these groups I was unable to differentiate GP members from locals (excepting the three to four leaders) as they did not wear different clothing, seated themselves within the population, and spoke of similar grievances as other locals. See Figure 7.1.
[22] Interview with MINUSCA Civil Affairs officer, Paoua, CAR, 21 February 2016.

against what he perceived to be the biggest threat in the arena: banditry.
He thereby acted in contrast to his own Civil Affairs officers, who were
discussing disarmament with the alleged 'bandits'. Mandjou (see Box 7.1)
and his section of the GP surely engaged in what the MINUSCA commander called 'banditism' but some significant parts of the population
also saw them as protectors against the RJ, whom they considered
a menacing force of Kaba dominance.[23] Their view of the RJ was not
entirely false, as the RJ had gained stakes in national government through
a ministerial post for its leader during the transitional government and
had collaborated with the UN mission. With UN capacities focussed on
fighting bandits, other changes were allowed to happen in the security
arena, such as the establishment of the RJ to the north of town and the
arrival of the MPC, which would soon become the dominant non-state
force and the main local security concern.

Box 7.1 Killing Mandjou, Paoua, CAR, January 2016

The events that surround the killing of the Paoua GP leader Mandjou
reflect the fluid and stable mix of international enforcement. In
January 2016, MINUSCA Civil Affairs and local CASAL mediators
entered negotiations with Mandjou about his inclusion in a communal
disarmament process – as a fluid actor with unclear stakes in the arena,
the GP was not eligible for the 'real' DDR packet reserved for stable
groups such as the RJ. Mandjou was hesitant but agreed to further
meetings. A day later, a ministerial delegation came to Paoua, including
the minister of defence, who gave a speech in front of 400 people. The
minister asked all Anti-Balaka (meaning the GP) to come forth, scolded
them, and then offered to pardon them should they disarm. Mandjou
took up the microphone and rebuked the delegation and Armel Sayo in
particular, the residential minister, who was also the president of the rival
RJ. The next day, Mandjou was seen armed and acting aggressively in
Paoua market. Someone informed MINUSCA, who came in force and,
allegedly in self-defence, killed Mandjou. The Paoua site commander
described this event as a success in the 'lutte contre le banditisme', while
Civil Affairs saw its reputation among other GP groups tarnished.
Although bandit activity briefly dropped after this event, by late
February, armed banditry was again on the rise around Paoua.

---

23 Observation of IOM and CASAL meeting with Anti-Balaka, Pendé, CAR,
     2 March 2016.

The GP never became a signatory to any peace agreement because they are loosely organized and act too fluidly. They pursue more diffuse economic and political agendas: Tali inhabitants feel that Kaba dominate political and administrative positions and the recent crisis brought by the Séléka resulted in the closure of the cotton mill of Pendé town, which employed hundreds of Talis.[24] With their limited organizational means they pursue their objectives fluidly: the GP has created a felt popular resistance (rather than an army) against 'the Kaba' without risking a large-scale confrontation and extract material goods on the road that they cannot gain otherwise. Thus, despite repeated attacks by the much stronger RJ and the MINUSCA on their home villages in early 2016, the GP survived simply by fleeing into the bush and returning when the attack was over.[25] But they also failed to gain a seat at the DDR and SSR negotiation tables that only stable ordering actors can attain. By 2017, all GP groups had either fled attacks by the MPC or pre-empted their defeat by accepting lesser communal violence reduction programs from the UN.[26] Their grievances and those of the populace were not addressed in any larger political setting.

Violence in Paoua spiralled due to competition rather than collaboration between actors with different ordering ideas. Some actors have difficulties accepting that turning to loose auto-defence groups is one way for inhabitants to seek alternative ways of security provision. International actors seldom seem open-minded towards collaborations with those actors that deviate from stable ordering norms, even when it is state actors themselves that decide to find solutions aside their written mandate. When I presented the example of a police commissioner in Obo offering a proven murderer to pay compensation to the family rather than to incarcerate him as an alternative form of justice provision at a summit of international humanitarians in the CAR's capital, numerous participants were appalled.[27] The police commissioner of Obo, however, claimed that compensation increased the perception of security: the deceased's family at least had something,

---

[24] Ibid.
[25] Interview with MINUSCA Civil Affairs officer, Paoua, CAR, 21 February 2016.
[26] Interview with MINUSCA Analyst, Bangui, CAR, August 2017.
[27] 'Dilemmas of Protection and Policing in the Central African Republic', presentation held at the Humanitarian Forum, Bangui, CAR, 7 March 2016.

which was better than the usual impunity, and the threatened revenge attacks did not materialize.[28]

In Somaliland, on the other hand, compensation is key. Actors in the Somaliland security arena are guided by principles originating from their national or even local context. Judging the Somaliland security resolutions in light of their promotion of human rights or gender equality, they are far from perfect. For instance, deaths in one group are weighed up through deaths in another group[29] and crimes against women are compensated with half the amount of those committed against men. In each of the Somaliland cases, inhabitants feel safe not necessarily because there were no security incidents but rather because such events are pragmatically dealt with through the limited means available. As one respondent put it: 'The problems can be happening . . . every time it is out of our hands. The solutions depend on the problem that is happening.'[30] Somalilanders do not witness significant foreign military interveners in their arena and therefore cannot assign responsibility to real or alleged international actions. Threats are described as mundane processes that necessitate a resolution by the actors in the arena through combining their forms and opportunities of ordering.

Any security arena at any time witnesses multiple forms of ordering. Actors can view another actor as a competitor based on its way of ordering, such as when stably ordering interveners feel threatened by fluidly ordering 'bandits'. Actors can, however, also precisely build on these differences to complement one another. This coexistence is often based on different types of actors, such as police and traditional leaders, coming together. Non-state actors in the CAR that act without arms cannot pair up with the state to enforce decisions – because the state is itself too weak – and have not been able to establish an eye-level or even less of a decider–enforcer relationship with international actors. When compared to the tensions between actor types in the CAR and in South Sudan, in Somaliland this collaboration works relatively well. On top of the leeway non-state actors find here for

---

[28] Interview with Police Officer, Obo, CAR, 10 February 2016.

[29] In other words, if clan A kills ten members of clan B and clan B kills eight members of clan A, then compensation only has to be paid by clan A to clan B for the remaining two deaths. Such a weighing of deaths happened after conflict between the clans of the Arab and Ogadeeni in the Baligubade border area, where the Arab only had to pay for the extra deaths they caused to the Ogadeeni. Interview with Arab Sultan, Baligubadle, Somaliland, 30 May 2015.

[30] Interview with Arab Sultan, Baligubadle, Somaliland, 30 May 2015.

open negotiations, they can also rely on the more powerful state to enforce their mediated decisions. A key to the strong mediating capability in Somaliland's Baligubadle (and a reason for the weaker ability in Daami and Zeila) is the reinforcement between flexible outcomes and the ability to enforce decisions. Decisions are enforced through the clan leaders' strong standing in society and the police using its limited means to punctually but decisively force deviators to adhere to the decisions of the traditional elders.

In Baligubadle and Zeila, clashes can happen but people do not fear violence getting out of hand. State and clan actors frequently compete over the distribution of responsibilities. Conflict – at times heavy conflict – is the outcome of overlapping claims that only a return to a fluid division of responsibilities can appease. In principle, the state and clans always have overlapping claims regarding security and, most currently, land. However, when relations are negotiated fluidly these overlaps need not cause insecurity as responsibilities can flexibly be reallocated, often in complementary ways. Dialogue between actors with different ordering ideas might be the key to security in Somaliland. While state enforcement in the CAR is often marked by a strong dichotomy in letter and action, and in South Sudan central state and local state actors violently compete, in Somaliland the functioning of the state and its imposition is pragmatically negotiated.

Mixing Ordering and Providing Security

Stable ordering can raise explicit claims to restructure authority in the security arena, while actors engaging in fluid ordering can pursue their interests in varying open spaces without challenging dominant actors and their ordering directly. Actors also choose one or the other with respect to their own safety: stable ordering claims are readable and its actors thus vulnerable to open contestation, while fluid ordering enables them to avoid the grasp of other, more powerful actors. Some actors mix fluid and stable ordering to combine risk avoidance and making clear claims.

The authority a state prerogative can instil in people's minds – especially for international actors – is faced with resource constraints that demand flexibility on the ground. The CAR is the perfect example of this duality. In the CAR, state actors adamantly portray regularized security and justice but, due to the limited means available to them, officials must flexibly navigate the security arena. Confronting armed actors stronger than the occasional petty thief is simply beyond their means and thus an overly risky endeavour. Simultaneously, their assumed authority to levy fees for the pursuit of criminal cases, at road blocks, or during payment of fines gives them a means to profit from their state role by flexibly bending official state rules. The cohabitation within state actors of stable narratives but flexible enforcement allows them to survive and gain a (often modest) profit, as long as they eschew public protest and accept their rather minimal influence in the security arena, compared to armed rebel groups and international interveners.

While actors in the CAR mix ordering forms as a matter of survival, in South Sudan state actors mix ordering with more specific goals in mind. The national state tries to control the domain of regime security by repressing any voice they see as dissenting. On the other hand, they are very lax on how their soldiers behave in the local arena, granting a large leeway for violence – which might even be encouraged when it is aimed at alleged opposition forces or supporters. State actors are so powerful and violent that even the UN mission dares not directly confront them and rather focusses on detached forms of intervention and on flexibly interpreting its mandate to eschew dangerous responsibilities. Non-state actors resort to fluid ordering to avoid control by and violence from a paranoid national state.

In Somaliland, the state attempts to enforce its control where and on whom it believes its key political and economic interests are at play. In all other domains, including most aspects of daily life and most events in peripheral and outer zones, the state flexibly collaborates with non-state actors. Elders provide traditional mediation, while relying on the state to enforce their decisions on deviators. International actors train and equip state security forces but are not present in any of the arenas physically. Rather than a three-way relationship between internationals and state and non-state actors, competition or collaboration in Somaliland forms a more manageable dyad between the state and traditional institutions.

In sum, Somaliland's non-state actors play complementary roles welcomed by the state, while, in the CAR, civilian leaders try to fill the void left by an absent state. In South Sudan, with no room to talk, many people turn to armed resistance against the repressive state. After delving into the historical to present relations between centre and periphery, inner and outer circle as well as stable and fluid ordering and the mix thereof, one question remains: why should actors engage themselves in the security arena in the first place?

8 | *Embedding into and Detaching from the Arena*

I arrived in Bangassou for the first time in March 2015. I followed my usual routine of talking to people about relevant security actors and then seeking them out one by one. Fortunately, I did not have to walk very far to get from the acting prefect to the gendarmerie, from the chiefs in the quarters to the market traders, or from the market traders to the Congolese peacekeepers based at the old police station. Two Congolese sat idly next to the iron barrier at the entrance of their unimpressive base, which had low walls that could be breached at multiple points. One of the soldiers was playing with a stray puppy to pass the time. The guards greeted me politely and quickly woke one of the deputy commanders (his superior was on patrol), who spent close to an hour discussing the security situation with me – albeit with a degree of suspicion and in a reserved manner. He described how his soldiers were embedded in the local community: they patrolled the streets, bought food on the market, and generally were in close contact with the local population.[1] They were so deeply entrenched that it was difficult to view them solely as an external force independent of local dynamics.

When I returned a year later, a lot had changed. The acting prefect was now the prefect. The gendarmerie had new staff and was hosting the court judge. Most crucially, the old police station stood empty, as the Congolese had been removed from the mission after accusations of sexual abuse.[2] The replacement peacekeepers were stationed at a new compound seven kilometres out of town. Surrounded by high mounds of earth and barbed wire, it was much more imposing and secure.[3]

---

[1] Interview with a commanding officer of MINUSCA, Bangassou, CAR, 9 March 2015.

[2] La Croix (5 February 2016) 'Abus sexuels en Centrafrique, vive réaction de l'ONU': www.la-croix.com/Monde/Afrique/Abus-sexuels-Centrafrique-vive-reaction-ONU-2016–02-05–1200737898.

[3] See more generally: Duffield 2010.

International civilian UN staff received me in their air-conditioned tents and only later could I speak to members of the Moroccan military contingent. On paper, the UN peacekeeping mission was operating under the same robust mandate; on the ground, however, things had transformed drastically in Bangassou's security arena. Now the peacekeeping contingent was confined to military operations, leaving the talking to civilian officers. The latter preferred interacting through meetings and training sessions, while eschewing everyday security matters.

Placing this example in the wider picture of ordering the security arena shows how security actors struggle between asserting their role as a key player in the arena in order to create security and avoiding day-to-day responsibilities by leaving most matters to other actors. Robust daily interventions like those used by the Congolese in 2015 can more immediately increase the feeling of security in an arena. They also necessitate a great deal of fluidity because encounters become much less controllable when interveners patrol the streets, work with other actors, and gain information through widespread local contact. When violence occurs, embedded interveners must react due to their immediate presence, even if the specific incident does not concern them or falls under their mandate. Staying behind compound walls, on the other hand, allows peacekeeping contingents to engage in stable, controlled forms of ordering and to avoid being compelled to act in extremely chaotic events. Similar benefits and dangers occur for state and non-state actors but the question of embedding poses itself most acutely to international actors that newly arrive in the arena.

South Sudan and the CAR are often described as suffering from too much rather than too little foreign interference.[4] Interestingly, the two countries are at different stages in their experiences of interventionism: South Sudan has seen large-scale missions since at least 2005 and therefore has highly institutionalized, detached, and stable structures, whereas the CAR experienced the deployment of a comprehensive intervention more recently, in late 2013, meaning peacekeepers were still negotiating their positions rather fluidly in 2015. By 2016, the UN was increasingly detaching the CAR mission, similar to how it had done in South Sudan. With the negative repercussions of ill-adapted

---

[4] See Baxter 2011; Lombard 2016a: 61–72; Marchal 2015b; Rolandsen 2015b; Schomerus 2012.

interventions in mind, some authors argue that Somaliland's success is precisely due to the lack of international intervention and the subsequent prominent role of local leadership.[5]

My comparison provides a rich diversity of contexts under which to investigate the impact of embedding or detaching by international peacekeepers and other external forces, such as national militaries. I first look at robust embedding and how this engulfs actors in fluid ordering. I then investigate how and why actors choose to detach themselves for stable ordering purposes. I conclude by determining how embedding or detaching impact people's security.

Everyday Security Matters

The more robustly interveners engage in the security arena through day-to-day security provision, the more deeply they must meddle in local affairs through fluid ordering. On the one hand, close contact through deep embeddedness generates knowledge and the ability to quickly respond to threats. On the other hand, embedded interveners have to deal with unpredictable security events, such as demonstrations and community disputes. Although locals perceive robust interventions to have a more immediate effect on increasing security, such approaches can create insecurity by facilitating their troops to commit fluid violence in a similar fashion to uncontrolled state and non-state actors.

Individual staff can make contact with a wide array of non-state actors and it is also partly engrained in the notion of intervention to collaborate with local actors – though this typically relates to state actors. Peacekeepers can also bend the rules of their mandates to offer flexible solutions. In the CAR, respondents regularly position the MINUSCA – for the Obo, it is the Ugandan army (UPDF) – at the top of the official security forces hierarchy, as if they were just another state force, albeit more powerful than even the army. State security forces themselves frequently mention the need to call on MINUSCA forces to deal with cases that are brought to them.[6] During my visit to Bangassou

---

[5] See Ahmed & Green 1999; Ali *et al.* 2008: 56; Phillips 2016.
[6] Interview with a commanding officer of Gendarmerie, Paoua, CAR, 29 February 2016; Interview with Police Officer, Paoua, CAR, 29 February 2016; Interview with Gendarme, Bangassou, CAR, 28 January 2016.

in early 2015, the Congolese troops – by then part of MINUSCA – reluctantly filled the void left by the state justice institutions' absence. They patrolled daily and prosecuted criminal offences. However, the contingent was neither able nor willing to emulate the complex judicial process officially found in the CAR – that is, investigations, public trials, and long-term imprisonment. Their interventions were more short-term in nature, designed to stop criminals from pillaging Muslim shops or to forcefully end intercommunal violence.

When interveners fluidly stretch their official mandate's boundaries, they can end up taking sides in local disputes rather than arbitrating them. International interveners in the CAR thus find themselves in a dilemma. On the one hand, the state is so weak that MINUSCA and other international actors (i.e. until these missions closed, Sangaris, EUFOR, and UPDF) seek to take on security provision under their own reign. On the other hand, their deep involvement in local politics engulfs them in local tensions and in security responsibilities they are unable or unwilling to handle. The UPDF commander in Obo, for instance, candidly stated that 'unfortunately, I am the prefect' even though 'we don't belong here'.[7] The UPDF is co-opting state forces alongside their officially mandated activity, which is to pursue the LRA. In return, they demand that these forces do not engage in predatory behaviour against the local population. Far from their official mandate, they are flexibly engaging in the arena to reduce tensions that could have negative repercussions for the mission's success and its members' safety. The UPDF has forcefully meddled in local affairs to halt the FACA from razing the Muslim quarter (see Chapter 5, Box 5.1). In another incident, the Ugandan commander sent soldiers to the town centre to halt a public protest against the Obo prefect, who had been accused of taking a vehicle from the municipality for personal use. However, the protests did not subside and, in the heat of the confrontation, the UPDF killed two (most likely unarmed) protesters. Being deeply embedded in the local arena (stationed in town and propping up the prefect) led the UPDF to intervene in this local protest despite it not being covered by their mandate and their own safety not being under threat.

Peacekeepers substitute the state in everyday security matters seemingly due to a sense of responsibility for the arena. However, the will

---

[7] Interview with UPDF commander, Obo, CAR, 18 March 2015.

to provide security does not mean peacekeepers are able to navigate the fluid realities of local ordering. MINUSCA's Cameroonian peacekeepers in Paoua delve deeply and violently into local affairs but interpret this as part of their mandate.[8] Such robust intervention does not provide for clear channels of security or a hierarchical setting in an arena. Rather, such interventions remain fluid, often seemingly arbitrary. MINUSCA cooperates with the RJ armed group and often acts on information provided by the RJ. However, this alliance has seen MINUSCA become entangled in a complex web of local conflict. For instance, during an internal leadership dispute, one RJ sub-commander attacked MINUSCA in August 2014 and died in the resulting battle.[9] The remaining RJ leaders distanced themselves from the culprit and affirmed their alliance with MINUSCA. Then, in early 2016, the RJ allied with the former Séléka group of the MPC at the same time that the MPC was fighting another Cameroonian MINUSCA battalion not far from Paoua. By picking sides, MINUSCA had got pulled into a struggle whose changing dynamics they could not follow.

Deep meddling necessitates gaining strong knowledge of local dynamics or collaboration with those actors that have it. The Somaliland model is a case in point. The army's positioning in Zeila's security arena resembles that of the peacekeepers in the CAR and South Sudan: they sit relatively near in the outer circle, refrain from everyday affairs, and communicate only with state actors. The army intervenes harshly but matters of security are immediately channelled back to the relevant inner-circle structures, which are heavily embedded on the ground. While concerned Zeila elders complain about rigged elections, political misappropriation, and inter-clan tensions, they do not attribute an independent role to the army in the security arena (despite its relative power dominance).[10] The army cannot be seen independently from other state actors in the inner circle, such as the police or administrators, because they form part of the same hierarchies in national government. Thus, despite grievances, traditional elders feel they are still somewhat able to influence change in the security arena.

---

[8] Interview with a commanding officer of MINUSCA, Paoua, CAR, 27 February 2016.

[9] Interview with a commanding officer of MINUSCA, Paoua, CAR, 1 March 2015; Interview with UN security expert, Bangui, CAR, 25 February 2015.

[10] See Focus group discussion with Ciise Elders, near Tokhoshi, Somaliland, 12 May 2016.

Intriguingly, local respondents in the CAR similarly try to integrate interveners in security channels at the top of a hierarchic relationship containing police and gendarmerie. At the same time, respondents are frustrated when a detached intervention force does not fulfil its expected security role in the arena. Thus, unlike the police and peace-keepers in the CAR, the police and army in Somaliland answer to the same (relatively unified) government in Hargeisa. The police live among the population and people can report misbehaviour to an array of state actors or, if one does not trust them, traditional elders. Despite mutual distrust, collaboration between state and local actors is slowly picking up pace even in Daami because both sides are dependent on each other for security. Daami is a very unsafe quarter and the state is needed to create more security there. However, the state cannot tackle the issue of criminal activity in Daami without gaining locals' trust and receiving their information.[11]

The deeper interveners embed themselves, the more openly friction can arise. Interveners will be able to impact security dynamics, such as combat between different armed groups, more immediately to restore a sense of security. At the same time, external forces can misinterpret dynamics in the security arena, pick sides, and thereby unbalance relations between different groups. This in turn can heighten conflict and position the interveners as a party to rather than an arbiter of the fighting. Everyday contact – foot patrols, buying food at the market, personal interactions – can also lead to uncontrolled instances that individuals can use for abuses against the population. A solution to the dangers of fluid embedding can be found when the external forces gain deep knowledge of dynamics in the security arena and can be held accountable locally for abuses. Intervention forces, however, prefer to avoid the problems brought forth by deep embeddedness by detaching their forces from the arena. This, however, has its own negative side effects on local perceptions of security.

Detaching from the Security Arena

When actors detach themselves from everyday activities in the arena, they can engage with other types of actors and conduct operations in a more orderly fashion. They reduce the unpredictability of daily

---

[11] Interview with Police Trainer, Hargeisa, Somaliland, 25 April 2016.

contact and its potential dangers. However, by retracting from constant interactions in the inner circle, they cease to comprehend the erratic workings of everyday security and engage only with those actors and stable ordering forms they wish to promote while neglecting or curbing more fluid alternatives. Overall, detachment reduces inhabitants' sense of security, because locals can no longer influence key actors and their ordering in the security arena. In other words, external actors may increase predictability for themselves by stabilizing arenas through clear channels of communication and hierarchies but they may also reduce predictability for those outside the opaque sphere detached actors create (particularly peacekeepers and armies).

Externals' non-intervention in local affairs can fuel perceptions of insecurity. In 2016, I observed the new police trainers in Bangassou buying cigarettes on the market – euphemistically described to me as an intelligence-gathering and contact-making strategy[12] – while ten metres away from them a fist fight broke out among a large group. The peacekeepers did not intervene, instead driving off once they had finished their shopping. A young Muslim citizen described his view on the mission as follows: 'Nous sommes inquiets de leur stratégie de sécurisation. Eux, ils ont une base là-bas, ... on les appelle, mais ils viennent tard.'[13] His impression would turn out to be very true during a security incident that targeted his community a year later. In May 2017, an armed group attacked Bangassou, targeting both the MINUSCA compound outside of town and the Muslim quarter at its centre, killing at least seventy and displacing several thousand.[14] It is difficult to imagine that such an attack would not have been anticipated in 2015 when the Congolese peacekeepers were present in the town centre and constantly interacting with locals. It is also fully implausible that it would have occurred without immediate intervention, because an attack on the town would have been an attack on MINUSCA.

---

[12] Interview with UNPOL Officer, Bangassou, CAR, 29 January 2016.

[13] English translation: 'We are worried about their securitization strategy. They have their base over there ... we call on them, but they arrive late.' Interview with Muslim Youth representative, Bangassou, CAR, 24 January 2016.

[14] Interview with Prefect of Mbomou, Bangui, CAR, 18 August 2017; Interview with displaced Trader from Bangassou, Bangui, CAR, 20 August 2017; Interview with Sultan Bangassou, Bangui, CAR, 22 August 2017; UNSC (26.7.2017), 'Letter dated 26 July 2017 from the Panel of Experts on the Central African Republic extended pursuant to Security Council resolution 2339 (2017) addressed to the President of the Security Council', S/2017/639, p. 19.

People from the Muslim quarter sought refuge in the Catholic cathedral rather than at the UN base. The cathedral was attacked by armed people and looted over the following two months. The Catholic bishop complained, 'How should we understand what happened right in front of them [MINUSCA]?', suggesting that a mere ten to fifteen people were able to attack the church compound.[15] With MINUSCA stationed outside of town and slow response protocols in place, they had lost control over local security – something which could not be said about their Congolese predecessors. By avoiding interactions with locals, they lacked the knowledge to anticipate such an attack and even became targets themselves.

By detaching themselves from the local arena, the peacekeepers create a parallel sphere of discussion for themselves and solely engage in the arena they are supposed to secure through biased channels (mostly through state actors). In Obo, three international actors coexist: the UPDF, the US army (both hunting the LRA), and MINUSCA (which is organizing elections and rebuilding the state). Local and international security actors meet at weekly security meetings. However, internationals complain that locals are rarely on time or do not show up at all. As an observer at two such meetings, I witnessed internationals heavily driving the agenda and paying little attention to local suggestions or grievances; internationals simply talked and argued among each other. In one such tactless debate, a MINUSCA member was arguing with a Ugandan soldier over the cost of a helicopter transporting election material. The amount mentioned was USD 8,000 per hour of flight time,[16] which equals almost exactly the amount of Obo municipality's public budget for one entire year.[17] Detachment, both physically (absence from the inner circle) and mentally (lack of face-to-face interaction with locals), creates parallel spheres in an arena.[18] Actors on each side find it difficult to engage one another to complementarily provide security.

---

[15] Crispin Dembassa-Kette (28 July 2017) 'Bishop in C. African Republic wants more effective UN peacekeepers after "failure to protect"': www .worldwatchmonitor.org/2017/07/bishop-in-c-african-republic-wants-more-effective-un-peacekeepers-after-failure-to-protect/.

[16] Observation of Weekly Security Meeting, Obo, CAR, 10 February 2016.

[17] The realized budget of 2014 was around EUR 4,000, and the expected 2015 budget was EUR 8,800. Document 1: Budget of Obo municipality 2014 and 2015, Obo, CAR, received February 2016.

[18] Cf. Veit 2010: 192–8.

Leaving everyday matters to local institutions is also described to promote their autonomy. However, detached intervention can risk undermining local drive. For example, in Bangassou, where the mediation board wanted to start an election information campaign in early 2016, they requested a small amount of UN funding for motorbike fuel and travel expenses.[19] The UN mission could not think in such minimal budgetary terms and requested to expand the campaign with large vehicles and public parades.[20] It thereby introduced a clear economic dimension and alienated many of the more idealistic proponents.[21] Similarly, during my visit to Paoua in 2016, members of its mediation board, CASAL, were frustrated that MINUSCA and the International Organization for Migration (IOM) had been increasingly treating them as translators (for both language and cultural aspects) for disarmament-related programmes rather than as equal partners in the negotiation of social cohesion. And the arbitrary behaviour of the UN against armed actors (see Chapter 7, Box 7.1) severely threatened CASAL's trustworthiness in the local population's eyes.

The irony of detached intervention is that, despite aiming to encourage local ownership, it reinforces international actors' biases towards stability by focussing on state actors and thereby undermining fluid local alternatives. Owing to having increasingly limited contact with locals, interveners become dependent on their state partners for information – the same state agents that often drive conflict through repression (South Sudan) or are often negligent, thus giving rise to impunity (CAR). The points I raise are not unheard of; indeed, I met plenty of attentive individuals in UN missions that came to similar conclusions. Unfortunately, large parts of the explanation for why international actors detach themselves from the security arena have little to do with the expected effect on local security provision and a lot to do with UN missions avoiding responsibility. In other words, the dynamics within investigated peripheral security arenas are secondary to decisions taken centrally, where matters of mission protocol, avoiding international scandals, and troops' security take precedence over adaptation to the local context.

It is no simple request to demand that peacekeepers provide security by fluidly engaging in daily activities and with the myriad of actors in

---

[19] Interview with Catholic Abbot, Bangassou, CAR, 4 February 2016.   [20] Ibid.
[21] Ibid.

the arena. South Sudan and the CAR are at war. Interventions come at a cost, often of many lives. The UN mission in South Sudan has lost sixty-six peacekeepers since 2011, while MINUSCA in the CAR has lost eighty-one since only 2014.[22] De Waal estimates that South Sudan had more than 300,000 uniformed security actors at the onset of civil war in late 2013.[23] With only 13,500 peacekeepers, UNMISS cannot confront all or even a decisive part of these armed forces. My analysis of the negative security ramifications of detached interventions should not be misread as criticism of individual peacekeepers, who indeed often risk their lives in these missions. Nevertheless, the negative effects of detachment remain and need to be analysed in order to improve interventions' impacts on security – especially when detachment is driven by reasons other than the safety of peacekeepers.

A key reason for why missions employ detachment strategies is that they feel accountable to the contributors and donors of intervention and not to the locals they are supposed to protect.[24] Avoiding an unfavourable international reputation thus takes precedence over avoiding a negative local one. UNMISS receives bad press from national and international journalists. Therefore, they hermetically seal off their mission to outsiders. A colleague and I tried for weeks to get authorization to talk to local police trainers in Wau about their daily work. Even though individual police trainers would have been happy to talk to us, UN administration first ignored and finally denied our request, saying we should talk to the UNMISS spokesperson at headquarters instead. If we as 'Western-looking' researchers who have contacts inside the mission and who can enter secure UN bases without much questioning face such difficulties, it is infinitely more challenging for locals to understand the intentions of interveners.

Not knowing what the intervention forces are doing can fuel the spread of rumours and misunderstandings. Detached stable ordering by MINUSCA frustrates the populace's security expectations and does little to dissipate rumours about the interveners' hidden aims.[25] Numerous inhabitants, including influential leaders in Bangassou and

[22] United Nations Peacekeeping Operations (28 February 2019) 'Fatalities by Mission and Appointment Type': https://peacekeeping.un.org/sites/default/files/statsbymissionappointmenttype_3_20.pdf.
[23] de Waal 2014.
[24] Cf. Chandler 2005: 3–4; Whalan 2017: 314; Weinstein 2005.
[25] See also Veit 2010: 194.

Obo, go as far as to call the LRA a US and Ugandan creation in order to widen their influence in Central Africa; some even say that UPDF soldiers dress up as LRA fighters and attack communities[26] – though I found no evidence to support this theory. In my opinion, the interveners' limited success in tracking down the LRA stems from a cautious tactic,[27] on the one hand, and the opportunities the ongoing LRA mission creates,[28] on the other. Following problematic and even deadly interventions by the UPDF in the local arena, the mission tried detaching itself to focus on their anti-LRA operation. However, the extensive military presence of both the UPDF and the USA (i.e. two big bases and continuous aeroplane and helicopter take-offs) create the feeling of life on the front line. Although not directed against the population, this threatening scenery drastically decreases the sense of security, even though interveners themselves describe the likelihood of an actual LRA attack around Obo as negligible.[29] However, they have failed to effectively communicate their strategy to the local communities.

Demonstrations against peacekeeping missions in the CAR and South Sudan are growing, with some even calling for their withdrawal.[30] Given that frustration often arises from insufficient

---

[26] Focus group discussion with Youth, Obo, CAR, 13 February 2016.

[27] American forces do not directly engage in combat against LRA fighters; they leave the final steps to their comparatively untrained and under-resourced Ugandan partners. Their strategy is one not of heavy fire but rather of seeking the voluntary defection of fighters. One reason for this is that LRA combatants travel with civilian hostages who could be caught in the crossfire. Diplomatic entanglements further problematize the search, as, for most of the year, the LRA is not in CAR territory but in the contested Kafia Kingi region (currently under Sudanese control) or the DRC. Both countries can no longer be accessed by Ugandan or significant US troops, because relations between the USA and Sudan are strained and because the DRC government has banned the Ugandans from their territory due to their illicit economic activities carried out under the guise of their anti-LRA mission. Neither the USA nor Uganda seem to be ready to affront these two countries in order to track down the LRA. At the time of writing, the LRA mission was surprisingly closed down as the LRA was allegedly no longer operational. See Interview with source from within US military base, Obo, CAR, March 2015; Interview with UPDF commander, Obo, CAR, 11 February 2016; Titeca & Costeur 2015.

[28] Titeca & Costeur 2015.

[29] Interview with UPDF commander, Obo, CAR, 11 February 2016.

[30] Deutsche Welle (24 October 2016) 'Une Journée "Ville Morte" Meurtrière à Bangui': http://dw.com/p/2Refk; UNMISS (20 July 2016) 'South Sudan: Demonstrators Protest Outside UN Compound Without Incidents': www.un.org/apps/news/story.asp?NewsID=54515; Glawion 2018.

peacekeeper presence, demanding a withdrawal seems to be paradoxical. However, I reason that it is the creation of parallel spheres of ordering that creates the feeling of insecurity. On the one hand, the presence of at least a detached intervention may lead to fewer security breaches than no intervention at all. On the other hand, security handled by secluded interveners also seems to move the issue beyond what locals can influence. The feeling of powerlessness creates insecurity. Speaking out against detached interveners becomes a way of taking security back into one's own hands.

Always Impacting Security

International actors have greater possibilities to detach themselves from local and even national debates because they are backed by resources (training, salaries, arms, vehicles) that come from abroad. They are primarily accountable to their home governments and UN headquarters. In controversial instances (e.g. sex abuse scandals in the CAR), national and local considerations play a secondary role compared to international reputations. Detachment signifies less of an impact on processes in the security arena not, however, less of an impact on perceptions of security. Actors always impact whether people feel secure or insecure in any case. It is hard to judge whether or not international interventions' propensity to detach themselves undermines security in a local arena since we cannot assess how the CAR or South Sudan would have fared in the absence of intervention. However, by using the three cases of Somaliland as counterfactuals, I am able to identify two differences produced in ordering the security arena that are most likely due to the absence of intervention: embeddedness of strong actors and pragmatic responses. Unlike the intervention-shaped societies in South Sudan and the CAR, Somaliland – despite still experiencing some degree of conflict – has been a relative success story, which might in part stem from the local sense of ownership of security.

Locals and some international advocates demand robust interventions, which require dealing with everyday challenges and force peacekeepers to intervene in unruly outer circles and engage with actors who oppose the state. Such an approach has the benefit of enabling missions to clarify and negotiate the terms of involvement and to have an immediate, and often positive, impact on local security.[31] The hazard is that interveners can become enmeshed in local struggles and politics and thus create a sense of insecurity. And members of the intervention force have more opportunities to misbehave and delegitimize the entire mission, particularly in the eyes of foreign audiences. Therefore, many international actors have been increasingly choosing to detach themselves from the everyday matters of local security and to interact with other stakeholders in the arena according to strict protocols only. This approach has allowed them to build more stable structures and hierarchies, which are usually biased in favour of the state, and to situate themselves between the inner and outer circles without fully engaging in either. Although this well-intentioned strategy can protect peacekeepers from being harmed or causing harm, it often causes perceptions of security to deteriorate. Detached interveners create a parallel sphere to which local actors do not have access and which prevents internationals gathering local knowledge. In sum, interventions face the dilemma of being robustly embedded to protect civilians versus detaching to engage in state-building. The former requires fluid ordering, while the latter is best achieved through stable ordering.

---

[31] Jeni Whaler claims peacekeepers need considerable autonomy in the interpretation of the mandate to gain local legitimacy: Whalan 2017: 314–15.

Conclusion

Observations from the CAR, Somaliland, and South Sudan form the basis of this analysis of local security. I chose these countries as they combine low degrees of state monopolization of authority and violence and a multitude of actors involved in security. They thus offer particular opportunities to view security from the bottom up – that is, how actors order issues of security locally and what these varying processes of ordering mean for inhabitants' perceptions of security.[1] Over the last four years, I travelled multiple times to investigate three local arenas in each of the three countries (though only once to South Sudan due to ongoing conflict). The arenas differed in terms of sociospatial distance to the capital, population size, and the presence of various security actor types. In each of the nine security arenas, I gathered data through an explorative mix of qualitative methods. With the help of the CAS approach,[2] I then compared the cases to find generalizable patterns of how different ways of ordering impact security.

The security arena concept supplies a framework that facilitates mid-N comparisons. In this study it helped me to develop useful tools and comparable dimensions across cases. For instance, I was able to conduct similar group discussions in all localities to let respondents map their arenas according to the dimensions of their actors and their interactions. Interviews with as many security actors as possible were the main way to gain an understanding of the arena. Based on this empirical data, descriptive parts became comparable, such as which type of actors are present and what their relative influence is. More importantly, the security arena concept enabled me to compare ordering processes. This includes analyses on how actors enter the arena, what their specific ordering opportunities in different parts of the arena are, and towards which ordering forms different types of actors tend.

---

[1] Lind & Luckham 2017.   [2] Ahram *et al.* 2018.

What puzzled me was that I observed strong variance where the labels 'fragility' and 'conflict' would suggest similarity. The CAR, Somaliland, and South Sudan have very different historical backgrounds, which has led them to develop highly diverging national political and security arenas.[3] And despite being part of these conflict-affected countries, their local security arenas varied widely in terms of their levels of security and insecurity. Nevertheless, I also deciphered a surprising amount of similarity in the ways different actors ordered security when relating to different parts of and actors in the arena.

I thus asked the following question: *what are the effects of varying forms of ordering on perceptions of security in the local arena?* The answer lies in observing how actors try to order their security arena and why. Towards the stable end of the ordering spectrum, I found that actors established institutions, channels, and hierarchies; towards the fluid end, they negotiated procedures and relations, and preferred to keep multiple options open. Stable ordering lends more predictability in an arena, while fluid ordering creates more modifiability.

The security arena concept served as the basis on which to compare the nine cases, whereas struggles over how to order the arena ranging from fluid to stable are the triggers of change. I identified how certain parts of and actors in security arenas leaned towards one or the other end of the ordering spectrum. These results strongly call into question the viability of linear fragility indexes because different forms of ordering always coexist, including in consolidated European nations. Although I did find some of the characteristics described in fragility studies on the ground – notably the minimal presence of state actors in the CAR's peripheries – I found 'fluidity' to be a better alternative to 'fragility' and a better opposite to 'stability'. In the fragility/stability dichotomy, the latter has a positive, active connotation regarding security and the former a negative, passive one. On the fluidity–stability ordering spectrum, both sides are active and neither is negative or positive per se. Rather, the spectrum only describes how ordering processes take place and leaves open to analysis the outcome for security.

The fluidity–stability ordering spectrum is not meant to describe an exclusive approach – that is, there is no 'stable arena' or 'fluid arena'. Based on their angles, the actors in this analysis chose different ways to

---

[3] See Glawion *et al.* 2019.

order their arenas, creating a mix of forms. This coexistence is not a problem in itself, as the case of Somaliland shows. Trouble arises when actors violently clash over the 'right' forms of ordering, which then creates insecurity. This insight could contribute to the hybrid orders debate, which assesses the cohabitation of different types of actors and ordering but could benefit from a clearer theorization of why hybrid systems at times increase and at others reduce security.[4] By researching the fluidity–stability ordering spectrum, I attempted to provide some answers to open questions in the hybridity debate – namely, those raised by Luckham and Kirk about how people navigate hybrid orders and perceive security, how links between state and non-state actors form empirically, and what impact international actors have on the ordering mix.[5] All the while, I sought to follow Kate Meagher and colleagues' call to problematize hybrid orders and clearly depict the 'dark side' of any part to the hybrid story.[6] Indeed, I found no circle of the arena, none of the actor types, and neither side of the ordering spectrum to be in itself more beneficial to security; rather, security depended on actors creating mutually beneficial combinations among all aspects.

The ordering spectrum also relates to the oligopolies of violence debate, as they both propose a multipolar security arena.[7] However, in lieu of an economic model, the ordering lens could remove some of the market aspects that do not hold up empirically in social relations. Empirically, the oligopolies' singularity of one pole[8] is called into question by findings showing that one actor is able to act both fluidly and stably, depending on the context. Rational, profit-maximizing actions explain part of the story but cannot account for decisions that are often based on changing (even factually unfounded) perceptions of potential benefits. The oligopolies of violence theory's key finding that more competition leads to less security[9] is partly supported by my findings, as competition does increase the chances of tense overlaps between parts and responsibilities in the security arena. However, even though more actors tend to make mutually beneficial cohabitation difficult, the key to security still lies in how actors align their ordering

---

[4] See the research gaps suggested in Albrecht & Moe 2015: 2; Bagayoko *et al.* 2016: 20.
[5] See Luckham & Kirk 2013: 17–19.   [6] Meagher *et al.* 2014: 5,12.
[7] Mehler 2004; Mehler *et al.* 2010.   [8] See Lambach 2007: 7–8.
[9] Mehler *et al.* 2010: 10–11.

in the arena; only thereafter does the question of how many become relevant.

Local knowledge on ordering can be expediently gained through analyses of public authority,[10] which are complemented by security arenas. Both concepts encourage scholars to view security as essentially being the outcome of local ordering struggles,[11] though the security arena specifies characteristics within public authority struggles to make them comparable across cases. In addition to the locally rooted findings of public authority analyses, the security arena concept puts strong emphasis on embedding the local into the national and international arenas.[12] While public authority analyses set ambitious goals for single-case insights, I suggest feeding comparative insights back into some of these in-depth studies in order to further develop our findings.

This is not a criticism of the other approaches mentioned, because they did not set out to investigate what I pursued in this analysis. However, while I respect the merits of those approaches for their respective research domains, I do suggest that the security arena concept holds additional value to those scholars who wish to comparatively study the links between ordering in non-monopolized settings and individuals' perceptions of security. With some adaptation to each research endeavour, the security arena concept could provide the tool to fill the gap between single case studies and quantitative comparisons of security.

When my respondents described their security arenas in their own words, they distinguished between different parts and actor types. Many respondents differentiated between an 'in here' and an 'out there' – a distinction I conceptualized as the inner and outer circle of the security arena at the local level. I also find that this distinction reverberates between the centre and its peripheries on a national level. Respondents also described different types of actors, which I have broadly categorized as 'state', 'non-state', and 'international'. In analysing the varying parts of and actors in the security arenas, I was able to detect common tendencies, which call for deeper analysis pertaining to centre–periphery relations, the distinction between inner and outer circles, competition or complementation between stable and fluid ordering forms, and embedding or detaching interventions. In the

---

[10] Hoffmann & Kirk 2013.   [11] Cf. Vandekerckhove 2011.
[12] Cf. Baker & Scheye 2007; Schlichte & Veit 2007.

sections that follow, I retrace my four key findings on ordering security and further underline them with brief empirical illustrations.

First: Centre–Periphery Relations

The historical development of how centres and peripheries relate to one another sets the context in which actors in local security arenas can act. The three countries I looked at provided two problematic and one relatively successful model of extending the centre into the peripheries. In South Sudan, the centre tries to impose itself on peripheral actors; however, these actors have a long history of fighting for their self-governance and thus turn to resistance. In the CAR, the state claims primal authority throughout the territory on paper but, in contrast to South Sudan, does not attempt to enforce its claim and has no means to do so. This dichotomy between a narrative of a state monopoly and its real absence, however, leaves little room to engage non-state actors in the peripheries in a mutually beneficial mix of ordering. Somaliland shows characteristics found in the two other case-study countries: it has militarized peripheries that historically fought against today's rulers in the capital (similar to South Sudan) and extremely limited means to enforce its control (similar to the CAR). Somaliland's government is pursuing a third path between violent imposition and utter neglect of its peripheries. It has been slowly expanding its stable state ordering across the country while allowing an array of self-rule by non-state actors and continuously renegotiating the relations between fluid and stable spheres. In short, negotiations between actors in the centre and the periphery create higher levels of security for both sides than do central actors neglecting the periphery or seeking its submission. My findings confirm a strong path dependency, which should also inform the literature on state-building and state decay and can indeed explain some of the observations that are not explicable through a local snap-shot alone.

Some of the security dynamics observed in the local security arenas are best explained within the wider frame of national centre–periphery relations. While two of Somaliland's cases, Baligubadle and Zeila, have the highest levels of security among the nine security arenas under investigation, the other – Daami quarter in the capital – is seen as being rather insecure. At first sight, it might seem paradoxical that the case closest to the centre is the least secure. However,

Somaliland's secret to success is its fluidly ordered mutual cohabitation between different actors. Daami's closeness to central power leaves the quarter with little leeway to fluidly order its own relations and to build mutual trust between the state and non-state actors. The people of Baligubadle, on the other hand, are historically and ethnically very close to the regime in the capital Hargeisa. The vast open lands and the sufficient distance to the capital also offer traditional institutions with plenty of room to self-govern. In South Sudan, armed cattle herders entered the outer circles of Mundri's and Buseri's arenas, causing local actors to feel as if they had no way to negotiate their peaceful passage. Tensions have mounted because national actors have interpreted local resistance to cattle herders as part of an anti-government rebellion, whereas locals have interpreted the cattle herders' presence as a central government strategy to expropriate them. In Raja, the central government is creating an atmosphere of fear among local actors, resulting in a marked rupture between locally rooted and centrally controlled actors, even within state hierarchies. In the CAR, the centre and periphery are so strikingly disconnected from one another that state actors play an almost negligible security role in all three of the local security arenas I visited. There, it is the UN peace-keeping mission – rather than the state – that tries to keep the centre and periphery together by organizing national elections, aiding in the deployment of state officials, and taking up camp in all sixteen prefectures.

In sum, local state actors in the CAR have to make do with few resources, while international actors predominate. In South Sudan, security actors face divisions and suspicions even within state institutions. In Somaliland, state actors do not claim a monopoly of force; rather, central actors promote cohabitation of state actors and non-state actors in the peripheries. Nevertheless, how actors act at the local level within this frame set by historical legacies and central governments can vary.

Second: Inner/Outer Circle Distinctions

In local security arenas people distinguish an inner circle of constant, more regulated interaction among security actors from an outer circle that often serves as an open space, where the absence of solid information facilitates the spread of security-related rumours and the use of violence. The line nevertheless can be and is crossed frequently. Actors move into the inner circle in pursuit of the perceived benefits of profit and control centred in the arena, while others move out of the inner circle to engage with unruly actors on the outskirts. When actors from across the divide begin to interact meaningfully, the divide starts to fade: actors outside the core of the arena seem less obscure, security actors in the outer circle can still move about, but they cannot avoid one another, and rumours about alleged threats diminish as contact increases.

In the Somaliland success stories of Zeila and Baligubadle, state actors order the inner circle through relatively stable institutions while leaving most issues in the outer circle to non-state actors. Interrelations are strong as the state depends on traditional actors to oversee outer circles and traditional actors rely on the state for enforcement. Many inhabitants in Zeila and Daami, however, have questioned this mutually beneficial cohabitation. Ciise clan members in Zeila feel marginalized by the state and have withdrawn to the outer circle, rarely contacting the state in the inner circle. Daami's Gabooye inhabitants are surrounded by the capital and its powerful institutions and thus cannot retract from them. Frictions have erupted into clashes between youth groups and the police. While the lines between inner and outer circles are blurred in local arenas in Somaliland, in the CAR those circles are heavily demarcated. In towns, the CAR state attempts to uphold a semblance of control in the three local arenas examined here but it is completely absent outside of them, where a vast number of armed groups control territory and extort local communities. Some armed groups have even attempted to move into the inner circle to attack those who they believe oppose them. In South Sudan, the state and its alleged proxies violently moved into the peripheral arenas allegedly in pursuit of rebel groups. Their repressive means saw people displaced from the inner circles to the arenas' outer circles, where some join or form rebel movements. Inhabitants interpret the outer circle both as a dangerous sphere containing armed non-state proxy groups and as an open space where people can join non-state armed groups in resistance to the repressive state. This, in turn, fuels the vicious cycle between state imposition in the inner circles and local resistance from the outer circles.

In brief, actors in Somaliland's security arenas take advantage of the different natures of the two circles, bridging the divide through constant interaction and sharing responsibility for public security. The division between the two circles is most visible in the CAR, where the comparatively secure inner circles are patrolled by international and state actors and the outer circles are seen as being highly dangerous and containing groups that do indeed sometimes attack the locality. In South Sudan, the state controls the inner circle in a garrison fashion, while facing threats from the outer circle. The inhabitants of the arenas are caught up in this binary narrative and feel forced to pick sides to survive.

Third: Stable to Fluid Ordering Spectrum

With regard to positioning across the inner and outer circles, actors more commonly use stable ordering for inner circles and often turn to fluid ordering for outer circles. State actors portray their ordering of security as stable – that is, hierarchic and regularized. On the ground, however, the state engages with alternative security actors and in more fluid ordering forms. Individual members of intervention forces can fluidly engage the populace but the mission hierarchy is biased towards stable ordering and collaboration with state actors. Non-state actors often employ fluid ordering in security arenas and thereby force all others in the arena to consider the cohabitation of different ordering forms. They can also adopt more stable forms of ordering so as to present themselves as suitable state substitutes and partners in the eyes of the populace and international actors, respectively.

In Somaliland, state and traditional non-state actors mix stable and fluid ordering complementarily across the inner and outer circle to achieve their shared goal of providing security. In Daami, however, the minority Gabooye are underrepresented in state institutions and their invented 'traditional' structures are not fully accepted by other clans. In the CAR, the coexistence of international, state, and non-state actors is undermined by the reluctance of either type of actor to open avenues for the peaceful concomitance of stable and fluid ordering. The state's approach to this cohabitation is somewhat schizophrenic in that state actors are adamant on appearing to stick to official laws, while the national government refuses to provide the necessary resources to enforce these laws. Unarmed non-state actors thus work in parallel to state actors rather than closely with them, whereas armed groups challenge the state directly and often come out of such altercations as the victor. Conflict between state and non-state actors is also a key security concern in South Sudan. In Raja, the government is hosting Darfuri rebels in the town's outskirts, who serve as allies against the opposition. At the same time, the government has threatened its own population to stay silent about the presence of the rebels. Central state actors interpret non-state actors' discourses within the framework of rebellion instead of listening to their local security concerns. Therefore, when armed cattle herders entered the outer circles of Mundri and Buseri, local inhabitants in those security arenas did not feel able to request protection from the national government and instead turned to fluid ordering by non-state and local state actors.

Actors mix ordering forms to deal with many security issues in Somaliland. However, actors also separately dominate distinct parts of security arenas, with state actors stably ordering inner circles and the capital and non-state actors and traditional institutions providing fluid ordering in the peripheries and outer circles. In the arenas studied in South Sudan, the spheres experience similar differences in ordering forms. However, the state is so repressive in the centre and inner circles that it pushes people towards the outer circles, where they join or form resistance groups. In the CAR's local arenas, actors use different ordering forms in all parts of the arena, whereas the state cannot even stably control inner circles or the capital. State and international actors are reluctant to provide flexible solutions, while non-state actors find no means to enforce their mediated decisions. In sum, actors using different ordering forms complement each other in Somaliland, compete in South Sudan, and eschew one another in the CAR.

Fourth: Embedding or Detaching Intervention

To protect civilians, international and national interveners would have to engage the full spectrum of the local security arena: from centre to periphery, from the inner circle to the outer circle, and all actors be they ordering more fluidly or more stably. However, peacekeepers are sent by a decades-old international bureaucracy, the UN, and by relatively structured militaries in their home countries. They therefore have an inherent bias towards stable ordering as well as the inner circle, capitals, and state actors. International interveners face a dilemma. On the one hand, regulations and international pressure call for peacekeepers to intervene in an orderly manner to avoid scandals (e.g. unaccountable violence and sexual abuse). On the other hand, local inhabitants demand robust intervention, where internationals take care of everyday security matters in an embedded and, if necessary, messy fashion. In other words, and this might go against the expectations of those who send and mandate peacekeeping forces, robust interventions necessitate the acceptance of fluid ordering, while stable ordering is more easily achieved through detachment.

Interveners' reluctance to adopt fluid ordering leads to paradoxical engagements like those in the CAR, where a large proportion of peacekeepers are stationed in the capital despite the vast majority of fighting occurring in peripheral localities and their outer circles. In the local security arenas, MINUSCA prefers to engage with those actors that resemble their own organization form: first, the state and, second, rather structured armed groups. In South Sudan, UNMISS dares not confront the national government. It also refrains from investigating rumours about cattle herders and rebels in the outer circles. Instead, it remains on its bases, from where it can engage in the security arena according to its stable ordering ideas. Both missions thereby avoid actors on the fluid ordering side of the spectrum and in the open spaces that are hard to control. International actors that focus on stable state actors and retract from the fluid side of ordering can become a real threat to peace. Deceived by the failed promise of protection, people turn to self-justice and in some cases may spread rumours about peacekeepers' involvement in conflict. Many local respondents voiced their frustration over UNMISS's inaction to protect them against government abuses, while the government is itself using UNMISS as a scapegoat for the ongoing conflict. In the CAR, MINUSCA's lack of clear communication and its one-sided engagement with structured armed groups has caused rumours to proliferate that the peacekeepers are taking sides. Since mid-2017, MINUSCA has itself become the direct target of attacks. Peacekeepers have thus become a party to the fighting and are no longer mere arbiters. The army in Somaliland at first sight acts in a similarly detached way in local arenas. However, they are bound to the same government in Hargeisa as other local state actors and strongly cooperate with elders and officials when insecurity arises. While they remain detached from daily life, their way of dealing with security issues is thus strongly embedded in the local security arena.

Although international actors can choose to relate only to the state and the seemingly stable inner circle of the arena, experiences on the ground show that fluid ordering actors will not let themselves be ignored. The one clear recommendation that springs from this analysis is that interveners should engage both sides of the coin (the periphery and the centre, the outer and the inner circle, as well as non-state and state actors), as avoiding one side of the coin could disrupt the functioning of existing local security practices.

Research Outlook

This analysis produced several key findings, which should be subject to further study and, if needed, improved. First, the historical development of international and national centres and peripheries explains a significant part of where and why certain actors choose to engage in more fluid or more stable forms of ordering. Insecurity arises when peripheries are neglected or subdued to amass resources in the centre only. Second, the central and inner circles are rather stable, while outer parts of arenas lend themselves to fluid ordering. Cutting the two circles off from one another risks encouraging violent crossings of the dividing line to gain control of the inner circle or to subdue 'unruly' outer circles. The two circles need to be bridged through collaboration of actors with different ordering ideas to promote security. Third, state actors and internationals portray a narrative of stable ordering, while non-state actors allegedly favour fluid ordering to pursue security provision. My observations show, however, that all types of actors vary their ordering along the full spectrum of the arena. Stable ordering practices can be used by all actors to provide more predictability for security, while fluid ordering opens avenues for constant modifications. Fourth, when national armies or international peacekeepers enter a local arena, they must position themselves between and towards both poles of the ordering spectrum in order to serve all sides. The new intervention paradigm of 'stabilization' biases missions towards only one side of the ordering spectrum and risks harming those fluid ordering practices that play crucial roles in providing local security.[13]

Although this study dealt with the limitations of this research endeavour (explorative research, unbalanced data, limitations of the actor lens, and restricted generalizations) in a way that allowed me to produce meaningful results, further studies should look to tackle these

---

[13] See also Karlsrud 2019.

issues head-on. The explorative nature of this research could be further overcome by building on the data gathered here and using it for future comparisons of the same local arenas in a more structured manner. Hopefully, the data can be rebalanced as soon as a positive change in South Sudan's political context makes sensitive research access to the country once again possible. The actor lens can be complemented by explicitly researching less categorizable instances of security and insecurity, such as perceptions of domestic violence and safety. Finally, to test the generalizability of the findings beyond the context of sub-Saharan Africa, further research should be conducted in comparable countries in other regions, such as, among others, Lebanon, Libya, Haiti, or Timor-Leste. This book should thus be viewed as an additional piece of the puzzle rather than as a comprehensive answer to the question of security patterns in non-monopolized local security arenas.

Finally, I wish to bring this analysis back to Obo and apply these arguments to the realities on the ground, which have evolved significantly in the meantime. The Ugandan troops, whose commander had jokingly called himself the prefect of the region, withdrew in mid-2017. Despite having had their own scandals, the Ugandans were also known for their tough stance against armed groups trying to create trouble in their region of intervention, the Haut-Mbomou prefecture and its capital Obo. During the crisis in 2013, Ugandan forces drew a red line at the Chinko River that no armed group was allowed to cross – and indeed no armed group did cross it. But now that the Ugandan troops have left, security has deteriorated. The Abbé of Zémio – a town in the same prefecture but 200 kilometres from Obo – expressed his despair as an armed group ransacked the town in August 2017 and displaced thousands, who then sought refuge in his church compound:

Vous avez été prévenus et vous avez décidé délibérément d'abandonner cette ville. Cette ville est sacrifiée et je vous tiens pour responsables de tous ceux qui sont morts et de ceux qui se préparent à mourir. Merci d'avoir oublié ces femmes et enfants innocents.[14]

---

[14] English translation: 'You were warned, and you have deliberately decided to abandon this town. This town was sacrificed, and I hold you responsible for all who died and those who prepare themselves to die. Thank you for forgetting these innocent women and children', quoted in: RJDH (18 August 2017) 'Centrafrique: Les deux prêtres témoins des atrocités de Zémio à l'Est, lancent des cris de désespoir': http://rjdh.org/centrafrique-deux-pretres-temoins-atrocites-de-zemio-a-lest-lancent-cris-de-desespoir/.

I greatly enjoyed playing football, sharing a laugh, and discussing life with Abbé Jean-Alain during my visits in 2015 and 2016, when he was still in Obo. I tried calling him after I read his name in the news but my efforts were in vain as the phone lines were down in Zémio during my latest visits. It is stories like these that undeniably touch researchers, even though our duty is to remain objective. In analysing processes of ordering security from the bottom up by putting the perceptions of people on the ground centre stage, this research heeds Abbé Jean-Alain's call and carries it forth into the academic community. In that sense, Abbé Jean-Alain, the readers of this book will surely remember you, the innocent women and children you so bravely sheltered, and what such actions mean for ordering local security arenas.

References

Primary Sources

Document 1: Budget of Obo municipality 2014 and 2015, Obo, CAR, received February 2016.

Document 2: Paragraph on employment in Somaliland, written by expert group on Security Sector Assessment, dated 31 October 2012, received May 2015.

Document 3: Somaliland federal budget 2014 in Somaliland Shillings, Source: Ministry of Finance, viewed April 2016.

Document 4: Projet de loi portant statut de la chefferie traditionnelle en République Centrafricaine, Bangui, CAR, dated 22 January 2017, received August 2017.

Interview with UN Civil Affairs officer, Wau, South Sudan, 19 November 2014.

Observation of Police Community Relations Committee meeting, Wau, South Sudan, 21 November 2014.

Focus group discussion with Elders, Buseri, South Sudan, 22 November 2014.

Interview with Balanda Elder, Wau, South Sudan, 22 November 2014.

Focus group discussion with Youths, Buseri, South Sudan, 24 November 2014.

Focus group discussion with Women, Buseri, South Sudan, 25 November 2014.

Focus group discussion with Sultans, Raja, South Sudan, 27 November 2014.

Focus group discussion with Women, Raja, South Sudan, 28 November 2014.

Interview with Sultan, Raja, South Sudan, 28 November 2014.

Focus group discussion with Youths, Raja, South Sudan, 29 November 2014.

Interview with local Priest, Raja, South Sudan, 30 November 2014.

Interview with Chamber of Commerce member, Mundri, South Sudan, 6 December 2014.

Interview with Acting Commissioner, Mundri, South Sudan, 8 December 2014.

Focus group discussion with Youths, Mundri, South Sudan, 8 December 2014.
Interview with Police Officer, Mundri, South Sudan, 6 December 2014.
Interview with RJ president Armel Sayo, Bangui, CAR, 25 February 2015.
Interview with UN security expert, Bangui, CAR, 25 February 2015.
Interview with Sub-Prefect, Paoua, CAR, 27 February 2015.
Interview with former APRD-leader, Paoua, CAR, 27 February 2015.
Focus group discussion with Youth, Paoua, CAR, 28 February 2015.
Interview with a commanding officer of MINUSCA, Paoua, CAR, 1 March 2015.
Focus group discussion with Group Chiefs, Paoua, CAR, 2 March 2015.
Interview with Police Officer, Paoua, CAR, 2 March 2015.
Interview with acting Prefect of Mbomou, Bangassou, CAR, 9 March 2015.
Interview with a commanding officer of MINUSCA, Bangassou, CAR, 9 March 2015.
Interview with Muslim trader, Bangassou, CAR, 10 March 2015.
Observation of CPMM meeting, CAR, 10 March 2015.
Group discussion with the Religious Platform, Bangassou, CAR, 11 March 2015.
Interview with Muslim representative, Bangassou, CAR, 11 March 2015.
Focus group discussion with Youth, Obo, CAR, 14 March 2015.
Focus group discussion with chiefs, Obo, CAR, 15 March 2015.
Interview with Gendarmerie, Obo, CAR, 17 March 2015.
Interview with UPDF commander, Obo, CAR, 18 March 2015.
Interview with source from within US military base, Obo, CAR, March 2015.
Interview with US soldiers, Obo, CAR, 18 March 2015.
Interview with Prefect, Bangassou, CAR, 22 January 2016.
Interview with Muslim Youth representative, Bangassou, CAR, 24 January 2016.
Interview with Youth leader, Bangassou, CAR, 25 January 2016.
Interview with MINUSCA Civil Affairs officer, Bangassou, CAR, 26 January 2016.
Interview with Gendarme, Bangassou, CAR, 28 January 2016.
Interview with Police Officer, Bangassou, CAR, 28 January 2016.
Interview with UNPOL Officer, Bangassou, CAR, 29 January 2016.
Focus group discussion with Vigilantes, Bangassou, CAR, 1 February 2016.
Interview with Vice-President of OFCA, Bangassou, CAR, 2 February 2016.
Interview with a commanding officer of MINUSCA 2, Bangassou, CAR, 3 February 2016.
Interview with Catholic Abbot, Bangassou, CAR, 4 February 2016.
Interview with Judge, Bangassou, CAR, 4 February 2016.
Interview with Armel Sayo, President of RJ, Bangui, CAR, 5 February 2016.
Interview with Sub-Prefect, Obo, CAR, 8 February 2016.

Interview with Auto-Defence leader, Obo, CAR, 9 February 2016.

Interview with Police Officer, Obo, CAR, 10 February 2016.

Observation of Weekly Security Meeting, Obo, CAR, 10 February 2016.

Interview with UPDF commander, Obo, CAR, 11 February 2016.

Interview with a commanding officer MINUSCA, Obo, CAR, 12 February 2016.

Focus group discussion with Youth, Obo, CAR, 13 February 2016.

Interview with former leader of APRD, Paoua, CAR, 18 February 2016.

Focus group discussion with Tali Chiefs, Paoua, CAR, 20 February 2016.

Interview with MINUSCA Civil Affairs officer, Paoua, CAR, 21 February 2016.

Interview with representative of RJ political party, Paoua, CAR, 21 February 2016.

Interview with Catholic Abbot, Paoua, CAR, 24 February 2016.

Interview with a commanding officer of MPC, Paoua, CAR, 24 February 2016.

Interview with a commanding officer of MINUSCA, Paoua, CAR, 27 February 2016.

Interview with UNPOL, Paoua, CAR, 27 February 2016.

Interview with Kaba chief, Paoua, CAR, 29 February 2016.

Interview with Trader, Paoua, CAR, 29 February 2016.

Interview with a commanding officer of Gendarmerie, Paoua, CAR, 29 February 2016.

Interview with Police Officer, Paoua, CAR, 29 February 2016.

Focus group discussion with Tali women, Paoua, CAR, 1 March 2016.

Observation of IOM and CASAL meeting with Anti-Balaka, Pendé, CAR, 2 March 2016.

Focus group discussion with Mbororo Chiefs, Bangui, CAR, 16 August 2017.

Interview with Deputy of Paoua, Bangui, CAR, 17 August 2017.

Interview with RJ president Armel Sayo, President of RJ, Bangui, CAR, 17 August 2017.

Interview with Prefect of Mbomou, Bangui, CAR, 18 August 2017.

Interview with displaced Trader from Bangassou, Bangui, CAR, 20 August 2017.

Interview with Sultan Bangassou, Bangui, CAR, 22 August 2017.

Interview with CAR Member of Parliament of Bambari, Bangui, CAR, 23 August 2017.

Interview with MINUSCA Analyst, Bangui, CAR, August 2017.

Interview with Inspector General of the Armed Forces, Bangui, 20 August 2017.

Interview with CAR Member of Parliament, Paris, France, August 2017.

Interview with former Prefect of Mbomou, Bangui, 10 July 2018.

Interview with Displaced People's Representative, Bangassou, CAR, 3 August 2018.

Interview with a commanding FACA Officer, Bangassou, CAR, 4 August 2018.

Focus Group Discussion with Displaced People, Bangassou, CAR, 5 August 2018.

Interview with two Auto-Defence group members, Bangassou, CAR, 6 August 2018.

Focus group discussion with Elders, Gumburaha, Somaliland, 2 May 2015.

Interview with Deputy Mayor, Baligubadle, Somaliland, 3 May 2015.

Focus group discussion with Youths, Gumburaha, Somaliland, 3 May 2015.

Interview with Arab Sultan, Baligubadle, Somaliland, 7 May 2016.

Interview with Ciise Caqil, Tokhoshi, Somaliland, 17 May 2015.

Focus group discussion with Youths, Zeila, Somaliland, 18 May 2015.

Interview with Arab Sultan, Baligubadle, Somaliland, 30 May 2015.

Interview with Village Chairperson, Daami, Somaliland, 23 April 2016.

Focus group discussion with Women, Daami, Somaliland, 25 April 2016.

Interview with Police Trainer, Hargeisa, Somaliland, 25 April 2016.

Focus group discussion with Gabooye Youths, Daami, Somaliland, 26 April 2016.

Focus group discussion with Arab Elders, Baligubadle, Somaliland, 30 April 2016.

Interview with Chief Justice, Baligubadle, Somaliland, 1 May 2016.

Interview with Mayor, Baligubadle, Somaliland, 1 May 2016.

Interview with Police Officer, Baligubadle, Somaliland, 1 May 2016.

Interview with Village Chief, Gumburaha, Somaliland, 2 May 2016.

Interview with Imam, Zeila, Somaliland, 11 May 2016.

Focus group discussion with Ciise Elders, near Tokhoshi, Somaliland, 12 May 2016.

Focus group discussion with Women of Ilays women's group, Zeila, Somaliland, 16 May 2016.

Interview with commanding officers at National Police Headquarters, Hargeisa, Somaliland, 24 May 2016.

Secondary Sources

Abrahamsen, R. & M. C. Williams 2008. 'Public/Private, Global/Local: The Changing Contours of Africa's Security Governance', *Review of African Political Economy* 35, 118: 539–53.

Abrahamsen, R. & M. C. Williams 2009. 'Security Beyond the State: Global Security Assemblages in International Politics', *International Political Sociology* 3, 1: 1–17.

Acemoglu, D. & J. A. Robinson 2012. *Why Nations Fail: The Origins of Power, Prosperity, and Poverty*, New York: Crown.

Adam, H. M. 1995. 'Somalia: A Terrible Beauty Being Born?', in Zartman, I. W. (ed.), *Collapsed States: The Disintegration and Restoration of Legitimate Authority*. Boulder, CO: Lynne Rienner, 69–89.

Adler, E. & P. Greve 2009. 'When Security Community Meets Balance of Power: Overlapping Regional Mechanisms of Security Governance', *Review of International Studies* 35, S1: 59–84.

Ahmed, I. I. & R. H. Green 1999. 'The Heritage of War and State Collapse in Somalia and Somaliland: Local-Level Effects, External Interventions and Reconstruction', *Third World Quarterly* 20, 1: 113–27.

Ahram, A. I. 2011. 'The Theory and Method of Comparative Area Studies', *Qualitative Research* 11, 1: 69–90.

Ahram, A. I., P. Köllner, & R. Sil 2018. *Comparative Area Studies: Methodological Rationales and Cross-Regional Applications*, Oxford: Oxford University Press.

Albrecht, P. & L. W. Moe 2015. 'The Simultaneity of Authority in Hybrid Orders', *Peacebuilding* 3, 1: 1–16.

Ali, M. O., K. Mohammed, & M. Walls 2008. *Peace in Somaliland: An Indigenous Approach to State-Building*, Hargeisa: Academy for Peace and Development.

Aliyev, H. 2017. 'Precipitating State Failure: Do Civil Wars and Violent Non-State Actors Create Failed States?', *Third World Quarterly* 38, 9: 1973–89.

Ansorg, N. 2017. 'Security Sector Reform in Africa: Donor Approaches Versus Local Needs', *Contemporary Security Policy* 38, 1: 129–44.

Arjona, A. 2017. 'Civilian Cooperation and Non-Cooperation with Non-State Armed Groups: The Centrality of Obedience and Resistance', *Small Wars and Insurgencies* 28, 4–5: 755–78.

Arjona, A., N. Kasfir, & Z. Mampilly (eds.) 2015. *Rebel Governance in Civil War*, New York: Cambridge University Press.

Autesserre, S. 2009. 'Hobbes and the Congo: Frames, Local Violence, and International Intervention', *International Organization* 63, 2: 249–80.

Autesserre, S. 2010. *The Trouble with the Congo: Local Violence and the Failure of International Peacebuilding*, Cambridge: Cambridge University Press.

Baberowski, J. 2015. *Räume der Gewalt*, Frankfurt: S. Fischer.

Bagayoko, N., E. Hutchful, & R. Luckham 2016. 'Hybrid Security Governance in Africa: Rethinking the Foundations of Security, Justice and Legitimate Public Authority', *Conflict, Security and Development* 16, 1: 1–32.

Bajpai, K. 2003. 'The Idea of Human Security', *International Studies* 40, 3: 195–228.

Baker, B. 2010. 'Linking State and Non-State Security and Justice', *Development Policy Review* 28, 5: 597–616.

Baker, B. & E. Scheye 2007. 'Multi-Layered Justice and Security Delivery in Post-Conflict and Fragile States', *Conflict, Security and Development* 7, 4: 503–28.

Baldwin, D. A. 1997. 'The Concept of Security', *Review of International Studies* 23, 1: 5–26.

Balthasar, D. 2013. 'Somaliland's Best Kept Secret: Shrewd Politics and War Projects as Means of State-Making', *Journal of Eastern African Studies* 7, 2: 218–38.

Basedau, M. & P. Köllner 2007. 'Area Studies, Comparative Area Studies, and the Study of Politics: Context, Substance, and Methodological Challenges', *Zeitschrift für Vergleichende Politikwissenschaft* 1, 1: 105–24.

Baxter, P. 2011. *France in Centrafrique: From Bokassa and Operation Barracuda to the Days of EUFOR*, West Midlands and Pinetown: Helion Co. and 30° South Publishers.

Bayart, J.-F., S. Ellis, & B. Hibou 1999. *The Criminalization of the State in Africa. La Criminalisation de l'état en Afrique*, Oxford: James Currey.

Bellin, E. 2004. 'The Robustness of Authoritarianism in the Middle East: Exceptionalism in Comparative Perspective', *Comparative Politics* 36, 2: 139–57.

Bennett, A. 2008. 'Process Tracing: A Bayesian Perspective', in Box-Steffensmeier, J. M., H. E. Brady, & D. Collier (eds.), *The Oxford Handbook of Political Methodology*. Oxford: Oxford University Press, 702–21.

Bennett, A. & J. T. Checkel (eds.) 2015. *Process Tracing: From Metaphor to Analytic Tool*. Cambridge: Cambridge University Press.

Berdal, M. R., D. Malone, & International Peace Academy. 2000. *Greed and Grievance: Economic Agendas in Civil Wars*, Boulder, CO: Lynne Rienner Publishers.

Berman, E. G. & L. Lombard 2008. *The Central African Republic and Small Arms: A Regional Tinderbox*, Geneva: Small Arms Survey.

Bhavnani, R., M. G. Findley, & J. H. Kuklinski 2009. 'Rumor Dynamics in Ethnic Violence', *The Journal of Politics* 71, 3: 876–92.

Bierschenk, T. & J.-P. Olivier de Sardan 1997. 'Local Powers and a Distant State in Rural Central African Republic', *The Journal of Modern African Studies* 35, 3: 441–68.

Bigo, D. 1988. *Pouvoir et Obéissance en Centrafrique*, Paris: Karthala.

Birnbaum, M. 2002. *Krisenherd Somalia: Das Land des Terrors und der Anarchie*, Munich: Wilhelm Heyne Verlag.

Blocq, D. S. 2014. 'The Grassroots Nature of Counterinsurgent Tribal Militia Formation: The Case of the Fertit in Southern Sudan, 1985–1989', *Journal of Eastern African Studies* 8, 4: 710–24.

Boege, V., M. A. Brown, & K. P. Clements 2009. 'Hybrid Political Orders, Not Fragile States', *Peace Review* 21, 1: 13–21.

Böhmelt, T. 2011. *International Mediation Interaction: Synergy, Conflict, Effectiveness*, Wiesbaden: Springer.

Bourdieu, P. 1985a. 'The Social Space and the Genesis of Groups', *Theory and Society* 14, 6: 723–44.

Bourdieu, P. 1985b. *Sozialer Raum und 'Klassen'*, Frankfurt: Suhrkamp.

Bradbury, M. 2008. *Becoming Somaliland*, Bloomington, IN: African Issues.

Brady, H. E. 2008. 'Causation and Explanation in Political Science', in Box-Steffensmeier, J. M., H. E. Brady, & D. Collier (eds.), *The Oxford Handbook of Political Methodology*. Oxford: Oxford University Press, 217–70.

Branović, Ž. & S. Chojnacki 2011. 'The Logic of Security Markets: Security Governance in Failed States', *Security Dialogue* 42, 6: 553–69.

Braudel, F. 1980. *On History*, Chicago: University of Chicago Press.

Brosig, M. 2017. 'Rentier Peacekeeping in Neo-Patrimonial Systems: The Examples of Burundi and Kenya', *Contemporary Security Policy* 38, 1: 109–28.

Brubacher, M., E. K. Damman, & C. Day 2017. 'The AU Task Forces: An African Response to Transnational Armed Groups', *The Journal of Modern African Studies* 55, 2: 275–99.

Cakaj, L. 2015. 'In Unclaimed Land: The Lord's Resistance Army in CAR', in Carayannis, T. & L. Lombard (eds.), *Making Sense of the Central African Republic*. London: Zed Books, 267–94.

Call, C. & V. Wyeth 2008. *Building States to Build Peace*, Boulder, CO: Lynne Rienner Publishers.

Carayannis, T. & L. Lombard (eds.) 2015. *Making Sense of the Central African Republic*, London: Zed Books.

Caspersen, N. 2012. *Unrecognized States: The Struggle for Sovereignty in the Modern International System*, Cambridge: Polity Press.

Cederman, L.-E., N. B. Weidmann, & K. S. Gleditsch 2011. 'Horizontal Inequalities and Ethnonationalist Civil War: A Global Comparison', *American Political Science Review* 105, 3: 478–95.

Cederman, L.-E., A. Wimmer, & B. Min 2010. 'Why Do Ethnic Groups Rebel? New Data and Analysis', *World Politics* 62, 01: 87–119.

Chabal, P. & J.-P. Daloz 1999. *Africa Works: Disorder as Political Instrument*, Oxford: International African Institute and James Currey.

Chandler, D. 2005. 'How "State-Building" Weakens States – the New Focus on the International Community's "Responsibility to Protect" Failing States Is External Meddling by Another Name', *spiked essays* [Online]. www.spiked-online.com/2005/10/24/how-state-building-weakens-states/ [Accessed 25 February 2013].

Chauvin, E. & C. Seignobos 2014. '"L'imbroglio Centrafricain": État, Rebelles et Bandits', *Afrique contemporaine* 248.

Checchi, F., A. Testa, A. Warsame, L. Quach, & R. Burns 2018. *Estimates of crisis-attributable mortality in South Sudan, December 2013-April 2018 A statistical analysis*, London: School of Hygiene & Tropical Medicine.

Cheng, C. 2018. *Extralegal Groups in Post-Conflict Liberia: How Trade Makes the Modern State*, Oxford: Oxford University Press.

Chojnacki, S. & Ž. Branović 2011. 'New Modes of Security: The Violent Making and Unmaking of Governance in War-Torn Areas of Limited Statehood', in Risse, T. (ed.), *Governance without a State? Policies and Politics in Areas of Limited Statehood.* New York: Columbia University Press, 89–114.

Clunan, A. L. & H. A. Trinkunas (eds.) 2010. *Ungoverned Spaces: Alternatives to State Authority in an Era of Softened Sovereignty*, Stanford, CA.: Stanford Security Studies.

Collier, P. & A. Hoeffler 2004. 'Greed and Grievance in Civil War', *Oxford Economic Papers* 56, 4: 563–96.

Collins, R. 2008. *Violence: A Micro-Sociological Theory*, Princeton: Princeton University Press.

Collins, R. 2012. 'C-Escalation and D-Escalation: A Theory of the Time-Dynamics of Conflict', *American Sociological Review* 77, 1: 1–20.

Cramer, C. 2006. *Civil War Is Not a Stupid Thing: Accounting for Violence in Developing Countries*, London: Hurst & Company.

Cramer, C., L. Hammond, & J. Pottier (eds.) 2011. *Researching Violence in Africa: Ethical and Methodological Challenges*, Leiden, Boston: Brill.

Daase, C. & C. Friesendorf (eds.) 2010. *Rethinking Security Governance: The Problem of Unintended Consequences*, London and New York: Routledge.

De Juan, A. & J. H. Pierskalla 2015. 'Manpower to Coerce and Co-Opt: State Capacity and Political Violence in Southern Sudan 2006–2010', *Conflict Management and Peace Science* 32, 2: 175–99.

De Vries, L. 2011. 'Négocier l'autorité : Les Micro-Pratiques Étatiques à la Frontière du Sud-Soudan et de la République Démocratique du Congo', *Politique Africaine* 122: 41–58.

De Vries, L. 2012. 'Facing Frontiers: Everyday Practice of State-Building in South Sudan', Doctoral dissertation, Wageningen University.

De Vries, L. 2013. 'Pulling the Ropes: Convenient Indeterminacies and the Negotiation of Power at Kaya's Border Checkpoint', in Vaughan, C., M., Schomerus, & L. D. Vries (eds.), *The Borderlands of South Sudan: Authority and Identity in Contemporary and Historical Perspectives.* New York: Palgrave Macmillan, 153–72.

De Vries, L. 2015. '"The Government Belongs to Other People": Old Cycles of Violence in a New Political Order in Mundri?', in Schomerus, M. (ed.), *Conflict and Cooperation in the Equatorias.* Juba: VISTAS.

De Vries, L. & P. H. Justin 2014. 'Un Mode De Gouvernement Mis En Échec: Dynamiques De Conflit Au Soudan Du Sud, Au-Delà De La Crise Politique Et Humanitaire', *Politique Africaine* 135: 159–75.

De Vries, L. & A. Mehler 2019. 'The Limits of Instrumentalizing Disorder: Reassessing the Neopatrimonial Perspective in the Central African Republic', *African Affairs* 118, 471: 307–27.

De Vries, L. & M. Schomerus 2017a. 'Fettered Self-Determination: South Sudan's Narrowed Path to Secession', *Civil Wars* 9, 1: 26–45.

De Vries, L. & M. Schomerus 2017b. 'South Sudan's Civil War Will Not End with a Peace Deal', *Peace Review* 29, 3: 333–40.

De Waal, A. 2014. 'When Kleptocracy Becomes Insolvent: Brute Causes of the Civil War in South Sudan', *African Affairs* 113, 452: 347–69.

Debos, M. 2008. 'Fluid Loyalties in a Regional Crisis: Chadian 'Ex-Liberators' in the Central African Republic', *African Affairs* 107, 427: 225–41.

Debos, M. 2011. 'Living by the Gun in Chad: Armed Violence as a Practical Occupation', *The Journal of Modern African Studies* 49, 3: 409–28.

Debos, M. 2016. *Living by the Gun in Chad: Combatants, Impunity and State Formation*, London: Zed Books.

Debos, M. & J. Glasman 2012. 'Politique Des Corps Habillés. État, Pouvoir Et Métiers De L'ordre En Afrique', *Politique Africaine* 4, 128: 5–23.

Diamond, J. 1999. *Guns, Germs, and Steel. The Fates of Human Societies*, New York: W.W. Norton & Company.

Doornbos, M. 2002. 'Somalia: Alternative Scenarios for Political Reconstruction', *African Affairs* 101, 402: 93–107.

Doornbos, M. 2010. 'Researching African Statehood Dynamics: Negotiability and Its Limits', *Development and Change* 41, 4: 747–69.

Doui-Wawaye, A. J. 2014. *Repenser La Sécurité En République Centrafricaine*, Paris: L'Harmattan.

Duffield, M. 2010. 'Risk-Management and the Fortified Aid Compound: Everyday Life in Post-Interventionary Society', *Journal of Intervention and Statebuilding* 4, 4: 453–74.

Elmi, A. A. 2010. *Understanding the Somalia Conflagration: Identity, Political Islam and Peacebuilding*, London: Pluto Press.

Elwert, G. 1999. Dynamics of Violence: Processes of Escalation and De-Escalation in Violent Group Conflicts. Sociologus/Beihefte, Berlin: Duncker & Humblot.

Engel, U. & A. Mehler 2005. '"Under Construction": Governance in Africa's New Violent Social Spaces', in Olsen, G. R. & U. Engel (eds.), *The African Exception*. London and Burlington VT: Ashgate, 87–102.

Erdmann, G. 2003. 'Apokalyptische Staatlichkeit: Strukturelle Probleme der Demokratie in Afrika', in Bendel, P., A. Croissant, & F. W. Rüb (eds.), *Demokratie und Staatlichkeit. Systemwechsel Zwischen Staatsreform und Staatskollaps*. Opladen: Leske + Budrich, 267–89.

Fearon, J. D. & D. D. Laitin 1996. 'Explaining Interethnic Cooperation', *The American Political Science Review* 90, 4: 715–35.

Fearon, J. D. & D. D. Laitin 2003. 'Ethnicity, Insurgency, and Civil War', *American Political Science Review* 97, 1: 76–90.

Fisher, J. 2017. 'Reproducing Remoteness? States, Internationals and the Co-Constitution of Aid 'Bunkerization' in the East African Periphery', *Journal of Intervention and Statebuilding* 11, 1: 98–119.

Förster, T. 2015. 'The Formation of Governance: the Politics of Governance and Their Theoretical Dimensions', in Koechlin, L. & T. Förster (eds.), *The Politics of Governance: Actors and Articulations in Africa and Beyond*. New York and Oxon: Routledge, 197–218.

Fukuyama, F. 2004. *State-Building. Governance and World Order in the Twenty-First Century*, London: Profile Books.

Galtung, J. 1969. 'Violence, Peace, and Peace Research', *Journal of Peace Research* 6, 3: 167–91.

Gandhi, J. & A. Przeworski 2007. 'Authoritarian Institutions and the Survival of Autocrats', *Comparative Political Studies* 40, 11: 1279–301.

Gatsi, É.-a. T. 2016. 'L'espace Judiciaire Commun CEMAC en Matière Civile et Commerciale', *Uniform Law Review – Revue de droit uniforme* 21, 1: 101–19.

Gerold, G. & M. Merino 2014. 'L'effondrement de L'état Centrafricain au Cours de la Dernière Décennie: Origines de la Crise et Quelques Idées Pour en Sortir', Fondation pour la Recherche Stratégique, April, 8.

Gerring, J. 2008. 'Case Selection for Case-Study Analysis: Qualitative and Quantitative Techniques', in Box-Steffensmeier, J. M., H. E. Brady, & D. Collier (eds.), *The Oxford Handbook of Political Methodology*. Oxford: Oxford University Press, 645–84.

Geschiere, P. 2013. *Witchcraft, Intimacy, and Trust: Africa in Comparison*, Chicago: University of Chicago Press.

Giddens, A. 1984. *The Constitution of Society: Outline of the Theory of Structuration*, Oxford: Polity Press.

Gidengil, E. L. 1978. 'Centres and Peripheries: An Empirical Test of Galtung's Theory of Imperialism', *Journal of Peace Research* 15, 1: 51–66.

Glawion, T. 2017. 'Field Research in Conflict Environments: Interviews, Focus Groups, and Observations in Somaliland and the Central African Republic', in Heucher, A., L. Linke-Behrens, & L. Schettler (eds.), *Measuring Statehood on a Sub-National Level: A Dialogue among Methods*. Berlin: SFB-Governance Working Paper Series, 35–9.

Glawion, T. 2018. 'Aufruhr in Zentralafrika: Proteste, Politik und Wege aus der Krise', *GIGA Focus Africa*, 3.

Glawion, T. & L. De Vries 2018. 'Ruptures Revoked: Why the Central African Republic's Unprecedented Crisis Has Not Altered Deep-Seated Patterns of Governance', *The Journal of Modern African Studies* 56, 3: 421–42.

Glawion, T., L. De Vries, & A. Mehler 2019. 'Handle with Care! A Qualitative Comparison of the Fragile States Index's Bottom Three Countries: Central African Republic, Somalia and South Sudan', *Development and Change* 50, 2: 277–300.

Gorur, A., J. M. Jok, & A. T. Mayai 2014. *Perceptions of Security in Aweil North County, South Sudan*, Washington, DC: The Stimson Center & the SUDD Institute.

Gurr, T. R. 1970. *Why Men Rebel*, Princeton: Princeton University Press.

Hagmann, T. & D. Péclard 2010. 'Negotiating Statehood: Dynamics of Power and Domination in Africa', *Development and Change* 41, 4: 539–62.

Hall, P. 2003. 'Aligning Ontology and Methodology in Comparative Politics', in Mahoney, J. & D. Rueschemeyer (eds.), *Comparative Historical Analysis in the Social Sciences*. Cambridge: Cambridge University Press, 373–404.

Hammond, L. 2013. 'Somalia Rising: Things Are Starting to Change for the World's Longest Failed State', *Journal of Eastern African Studies* 7, 1: 183–93.

Hansen, S. J. 2013. *Al-Shabaab in Somalia: The History and Ideology of a Militant Islamist Group, 2005–2012*, London: Hurst & Company.

Hansen, S. J. & M. Bradbury 2007. 'Somaliland: A New Democracy in the Horn of Africa?', *Review of African Political Economy* 34, 113: 461–76.

Hardin, R. 2011. 'Concessionary Politics: Property, Patronage, and Political Rivalry in Central African Forest Management', *Current Anthropology* 52, S3: 113–25.

Healy, S. 2011. 'Seeking Peace and Security in the Horn of Africa: The Contribution of the Inter-Governmental Authority on Development', *International Affairs* 87, 1: 105–20.

Heitz, K. 2009. 'Power-Sharing in the Local Arena: Man – a Rebel-Held Town in Western Côte D'ivoire', *Africa Spectrum* 44, 3: 109–31.

Helman, G. B. & S. R. Ratner 1993. 'Saving Failed States', *Foreign Policy*, 89: 3–20.

Helmke, G. & S. Levitsky 2004. 'Informal Institutions and Comparative Politics: A Research Agenda', *Perspectives on Politics* 2, 4: 725–40.

Hennink, M. M. 2007. *International Focus Group Research: A Handbook for the Health and Social Sciences*, New York: Cambridge University Press.

Herbert, S., N. Dukhan, & M. Debos 2013. 'State Fragility in the Central African Republic: What Prompted the 2013 Coup?', GSDRC Rapid literature review. GSDRC, University of Birmingham, UK.

Herbst, J. I. 2000. *States and Power in Africa: Comparative Lessons in Authority and Control*, Princeton: Princeton University Press.

Herbst, J. I. 2004. 'Let Them Fail: State Failure in Theory and Practice. Implications for Policy', in Rotberg, R. I. (ed.), *When States Fail: Causes and Consequences*. Princeton: Princeton University Press, 302–18.

Hilgartner, S. & C. L. Bosk 1988. 'The Rise and Fall of Social Problems: A Public Arenas Model', *American Journal of Sociology* 94, 1: 53–78.

Hills, A. 2014a. 'Security Sector or Security Arena? The Evidence from Somalia', *International Peacekeeping* 21, 2: 165–80.

Hills, A. 2014b. 'Somalia Works: Police Development as State Building', *African Affairs* 113, 450: 88–107.

Hills, A. 2016. 'Off-Road Policing: Communications Technology and Government Authority in Somaliland', *International Affairs* 92, 5: 1061–78.

Hobsbawm, E. & T. Ranger 1983. *The Invention of Tradition*, Cambridge: Cambridge University Press.

Hoehne, M. V. 2011. 'No Easy Way Out. Traditional Authorities in Somaliland and the Limits of Hybrid Political Orders', DIIS Working Paper No. 18.

Hoehne, M. V. 2015. *Between Somaliland and Puntland: Marginalization, Militarization and Conflicting Political Visions*, Nairobi: Rift Valley Institute.

Hoehne, M. V. 2016. 'The Rupture of Territoriality and the Diminishing Relevance of Cross-Cutting Ties in Somalia after 1990', *Development and Change* 47, 6: 1379–411.

Hoffmann, K. & T. Kirk 2013. 'Public Authority and the Provision of Public Goods in Conflict-Affected and Transitioning Regions', *LSE Justice and Security Research Paper* 7: 1–58.

Hönke, J. & M.-M. Müller 2012. 'Governing (In)Security in a Postcolonial World: Transnational Entanglements and the Worldliness of 'Local' Practice', *Security Dialogue* 43, 5: 383–401.

Howard, T. 2010. 'Failed States and the Spread of Terrorism in Sub-Saharan Africa', *Studies in Conflict & Terrorism* 33, 11: 960–88.

HSBA (Human Security Baseline Assessment). 2013. 'Pendulum Swings. The Rise and Fall of Insurgent Militias in South Sudan', Small Arms Survey No. 22, November.

HSBA (Human Security Baseline Assessment). 2016. 'Conflict in Western Equatoria', Small Arms Survey, July.

ICG (International Crisis Group). 2007. 'Central African Republic: Anatomy of a Phantom State', Africa Report No. 136, November.

ICG (International Crisis Group). 2010. 'Dangerous Little Stones: Diamonds in the Central African Republic', Africa Report No. 167.

ICG (International Crisis Group). 2014a. 'Afrique Centrale: les Défis Sécuritaires du Pastoralisme', Rapport Afrique No. 215, April.

ICG (International Crisis Group). 2014b. 'South Sudan: Civil War by Any Other Name', Africa Report No. 217.

ICG (International Crisis Group). 2015. 'Sudan and South Sudan's Merging Conflicts', Africa Report No. 223.

ICG (International Crisis Group). 2016. 'South Sudan's South: Conflict in the Equatorias', Africa Report No. 236, May.

ICISS (International Commission on Intervention, State, Sovereignty). 2001. *The Responsibility to Protect*, Ottawa: International Development Research Centre.

Jackson, P. 2003. 'Warlords as Alternative Forms of Governance', *Small Wars & Insurgencies* 14, 2: 131–50.

Jackson, R. H. 1990. *Quasi-States: Sovereignty, International Relations, and the Third World*, Cambridge: Cambridge University Press.

Jacobs, A. 2015. 'Process Tracing the Effects of Ideas', in Bennett, A. & J. T. Checkel (eds.), *Process Tracing: From Metaphor to Analytic Tool*. Cambridge: Cambridge University Press, 41–73.

Johnson, D. H. 2011. *The Root Causes of Sudan's Civil War*, Woodbridge: James Currey.

Johnson, D. H. 2014. 'Briefing: The Crisis in South Sudan', *African Affairs* 113, 451: 300–9.

Johnson, M. C. & M. Smaker 2014. 'State Building in De Facto States: Somaliland and Puntland Compared', *Africa Today* 60, 4: 3–23.

Jok, J. M. 2013. 'Mapping the Sources of Conflict and Insecurity in South Sudan', The SUDD Institute Special Report No. 1.

Joseph, R. 2014. 'Growth, Security, and Democracy in Africa', *Journal of Democracy* 25, 4: 61–75.

Justin, P. H. & L. De Vries 2019. 'Governing Unclear Lines: Local Boundaries as a (Re)Source of Conflict in South Sudan', *Journal of Borderlands Studies* 34, 1: 31–46.

Käihkö, I. & M. Utas 2014. 'The Crisis in Car: Navigating Myths and Interests', *Africa Spectrum* 49, 1: 69–77.

Kalck, P. 2005. *Historical Dictionary of the Central African Republic*, Lanham, MD: Scarecrow Press.

Kalyvas, S. N. 2003. 'The Ontology of "Political Violence": Action and Identity in Civil Wars', *Perspectives on Politics* 1, 3: 475–94.

Kalyvas, S. N. 2006. *The Logic of Violence in Civil War*, Cambridge: Cambridge University Press.

Kalyvas, S. N. 2008. 'Promises and Pitfalls of an Emerging Research Program: The Microdynamics of Civil War', in Kalyvas, S. N., I. Shapiro, & T. Masoud (eds.), *Order, Conflict, and Violence*. Cambridge: Cambridge University Press.

Kalyvas, S. N., I. Shapiro, & T. Masoud (eds.) 2008. *Order, Conflict, and Violence*, Cambridge: Cambridge University Press.

Kapiszewski, D., L. M. Maclean, & B. L. Read 2015. *Field Research in Political Science: Practices and Principles*, Cambridge: Cambridge University Press.

Kaplan, R. D. 1994. 'The Coming Anarchy: How Scarcity, Crime, Overpopulation, Tribalism, and Disease Are Rapidly Destroying the Social Fabric of Our Planet.' *The Atlantic* [Online]. www .theatlantic.com/magazine/archive/1994/02/the-coming-anarchy/304670/ [Accessed 26 January 2013].

Karlsrud, J. 2019. 'From Liberal Peacebuilding to Stabilization and Counterterrorism', *International Peacekeeping* 26, 1: 1–21.

Kasfir, N. 1976. *The Shrinking Political Arena: Participation and Ethnicity in African Politics, with a Case Study of Uganda*, Berkeley: University of California Press.

Kibble, S. & M. Walls 2013. *Swerves on the Road: Report by International Election Observers on the 2012 Local Elections in Somaliland*, London: Progressio.

Kindersley, N. 2019. 'Rule of Whose Law? The Geography of Authority in Juba, South Sudan', *The Journal of Modern African Studies* 57, 1: 61–83.

Kirsch, S. 2002. 'Rumour and Other Narratives of Political Violence in West Papua', *Critique of Anthropology* 22, 1: 53–79.

Konrad, K. A. & S. Skaperdas 2012. 'The Market for Protection and the Origin of the State', *Economic Theory* 50, 2: 417–43.

Kopytoff, I. (ed.) 1987. *The African Frontier: The Reproduction of Traditional African Societies, Bloomington*, Indianapolis: Indiana University Press.

Krahmann, E. 2003. 'Conceptualizing Security Governance', *Cooperation and Conflict* 38, 1: 5–26.

Krahmann, E. 2008. 'Security: Collective Good or Commodity?', *European Journal of International Relations* 14, 3: 379–404.

Krasner, S. D. 2004. 'Sharing Sovereignty: New Institutions for Collapsed and Failing States', *International Security* 29, 2: 85–120.

Krasner, S. D. & T. Risse 2014. 'External Actors, State-Building, and Service Provision in Areas of Limited Statehood: Introduction', *Governance*, 1–23.

Kraxberger, B. M. 2012. 'Rethinking Responses to State Failure, with Special Reference to Africa', *Progress in Development Studies* 12, 2–3: 99–111.

Kühn, F. P. 2011. 'Securing Uncertainty: Sub-State Security Dilemma and the Risk of Intervention', *International Relations* 25, 3: 363–80.

Lambach, D. 2007. 'Oligopolies of Violence in Post-Conflict Societies', *GIGA Working Papers* 2007, 62.

Langholm, S. 1971. 'On the Concepts of Center and Periphery', *Journal of Peace Research* 8, 3–4: 273–8.

Le Noan, A.-C. & T. Glawion 2018. 'Education Nationale en Territoire Rebelle: Le Cas du Lycée de Ndélé en République Centrafricaine', ABI Working Paper No. 10.

Le Riche, M. & M. Arnold 2012. *South Sudan: From Revolution to Independence*, London: Hurst & Company.

Leander, A. 2004. 'Wars and the Un-Making of States. Taking Tilly Seriously in the Contemporary World', in Guzzini, S. & D. Jung (eds.), *Contemporary Security Analysis and Copenhagen Peace Research.* New York and London: Routledge, 69–80.

Lederach, J. P. 1997. *Building Peace: Sustainable Reconciliation in Divided Societies*, Washington, DC: United States Institute of Peace Press.

Lederach, J. P. 2005. *The Moral Imagination: The Art and Soul of Building Peace*, Oxford: Oxford University Press.

Lefebvre, G. 2014 [1932]. *La Grande Peur de 1789*, Paris: Armand Colin.

Leonard, D. K. 2013. 'Social Contracts, Networks and Security in Tropical Africa Conflict States: An Overview', *IDS Bulletin* 44, 1: 1–14.

Leonard, D. K. & M. S. Samantar 2011. 'What Does the Somali Experience Teach Us About the Social Contract and the State?', *Development and Change* 42, 2: 559–84.

Leonardi, C. 2013. *Dealing with Government in South Sudan: Histories in the Making of Chiefship, Community and State*, Woodbridge: Boydell & Brewer.

Leonardi, C., L. N. Moro, M. Santschi, & D. H. Isser 2010. *Local Justice in Southern Sudan*, Washington, DC: United States Institute of Peace, Rift Valley Institute.

Lewis, I. M. 1961. *A Pastoral Democracy: A Study of Pastoralism and Politics among the Northern Somali of the Horn of Africa*, London: Oxford University Press.

Lewis, I. M. 2008. *Understanding Somalia and Somaliland: Culture, History, Society*, London: Hurst & Co.

Lijphart, A. 1969. 'Consociational Democracy', *World Politics* 21, 2: 207–25.

Lind, J. & R. Luckham 2017. 'Introduction: Security in the Vernacular and Peacebuilding at the Margins; Rethinking Violence Reduction', *Peacebuilding* 5, 2: 89–98.

Logan, C. 2013. 'The Roots of Resilience: Exploring Popular Support for African Traditional Authorities', *African Affairs* 112, 448: 353–76.

Lombard, L. 2012. *Raiding Sovereignty in Central African Borderlands*. (Unpublished.)

Lombard, L. 2013. 'Navigational Tools for Central African Roadblocks', *PoLAR: Political and Legal Anthropology Review* 36, 1: 157–73.

Lombard, L. 2015. 'The Autonomous Zone Conundrum: Armed Conservation and Rebellion in North-Eastern CAR', in Carayannis, T. & L. Lombard (eds.), *Making Sense of the Central African Republic*. London: Zed Books, 142–65.

Lombard, L. 2016a. *State of Rebellion. Violence and Intervention in the Central African Republic*, London: Zed Books.

Lombard, L. 2016b. 'Threat Economies and Armed Conservation in Northeastern Central African Republic', *Geoforum* 69: 218–26.

Lombard, L. & S. Batianga-Kinzi 2015. 'Violence, Popular Punishment, and War in the Central African Republic', *African Affairs* 114, 454: 52–71.

Long, N. 1990. 'From Paradigm Lost to Paradigm Regained? The Case for an Actor-Oriented Sociology of Development', *Revista Europea de Estudios Latinoamericanos y del Caribe / European Review of Latin American and Caribbean Studies*, 49: 3–24.

Luckham, R. 2017. 'Whose Violence, Whose Security? Can Violence Reduction and Security Work for Poor, Excluded and Vulnerable People?', *Peacebuilding* 5, 2: 99–117.

Luckham, R. & T. Kirk 2013. 'The Two Faces of Security in Hybrid Political Orders: A Framework for Analysis and Research', *Stability: International Journal of Security & Development* 2, 2: 1–30.

Lund, C. 2006. 'Twilight Institutions: Public Authority and Local Politics in Africa', *Development and Change* 37, 4: 685–705.

Lund, C. 2014. 'Of What Is This a Case?: Analytical Movements in Qualitative Social Science Research', *Human Organization* 73, 3: 224–34.

Lund, C. 2016. 'Rule and Rupture: State Formation through the Production of Property and Citizenship', *Development and Change* 47, 6: 1199–228.

Luttwak, E. N. 1999. 'Give War a Chance', *Foreign Affairs* 78, 4: 36–44.

Mac Ginty, R. 2010a. 'Gilding the Lily? International Support for Indigenous and Traditional Peacebuilding', in Richmond, O. P. (ed.), *Palgrave Advances in Peacebuilding* (Palgrave Advances). London: Palgrave Macmillan.

Mac Ginty, R. 2010b. 'Hybrid Peace: The Interaction between Top-Down and Bottom-Up Peace', *Security Dialogue* 41, 4: 391–412.

Mac Ginty, R. 2012. 'Against Stabilization', *Stability: International Journal of Security and Development* 1, 1: 20–30.

Mac Ginty, R. & O. P. Richmond 2013. 'The Local Turn in Peace Building: A Critical Agenda for Peace', *Third World Quarterly* 34, 5: 763–83.

Mahoney, J. 2000. 'Strategies of Causal Inference in Small-N Analysis', *Sociological Methods & Research* 28, 4: 387–424.

Malejacq, R. & D. Mukhopadhyay 2016. 'The 'Tribal Politics' of Field Research: A Reflection on Power and Partiality in 21st-Century Warzones', *Perspectives on Politics* 14, 4: 1011–28.

Mamdani, M. 1996. *Citizen and Subject Contemporary Africa and the Legacy of Late Colonialism*, Princeton: Princeton University Press.

Mampilly, Z. C. 2011. *Rebel Rulers: Insurgent Governance and Civilian Life During War*, Ithaca, NY: Cornell University Press.

Marchal, R. 2009. 'Aux Marges du Monde en Afrique Centrale', *Les études du CERI* 153–154, March: 1–50.

Marchal, R. 2015a. 'Being Rich, Being Poor: Wealth and Fear in the Central African Republic', in Carayannis, T. & L. Lombard (eds.), *Making Sense of the Central African Republic*. London: Zed Books, 53–75.

Marchal, R. 2015b. 'CAR and the Regional (Dis)Order', in Carayannis, T. & L. Lombard (eds.), *Making Sense of the Central African Republic*. London: Zed Books, 166–93.

Marchal, R. 2015c. 'Réconciliation, Stabilisation et Élections: Où en Est la RCA, 15 Mois Après L'intervention Internationale?', Mission Report in the CRA, 17 February–12 March 2015.

Marchal, R. 2016. *Brève Histoire d'une Transition Singulière: la République Centrafricaine de Janvier 2014 à Mars 2016*, Paris: ROSCA-G&D.

Martin, J. L. 2003. 'What Is Field Theory?', *American Journal of Sociology* 109, 1: 1–49.

Mbembe, A. 1996. *La Naissance du Maquis Dans le Sud-Cameroun (1920–1960). Histoire des Usages de la Raison en Colonie*, Paris: Éditions Karthala.

Meagher, K. 2012. 'The Strength of Weak States? Non-State Security Forces and Hybrid Governance in Africa', *Development and Change* 43, 5: 1073–101.

Meagher, K., T. De Herdt, & K. Titeca 2014. 'Unravelling Public Authority: Paths of Hybrid Governance in Africa', IS Academy Research Brief 10.

Mehler, A. 2004. 'Oligopolies of Violence in Africa South of the Sahara', *Nord-Süd Aktuell* 18, 3: 539–48.

Mehler, A. 2009a. 'Hybrid Regimes and Oligopolies of Violence in Africa: Expectations on Security Provision "from Below"', in Fischer, M. & B. Schmelzle (eds.), *Building Peace in the Absence of States: Challenging the Discourse on State Failure* (Berghof Handbook for Conflict Transformation. Dialogue Series No. 8). Berlin: Berghof Foundation, 57–66.

Mehler, A. 2009b. 'The Production of Insecurity by African Security Forces: Insights from Liberia and the Central African Republic', *GIGA Working Papers* 2009, 114.

Mehler, A. 2011. 'Rebels and Parties: The Impact of Armed Insurgency on Representation in the Central African Republic', *The Journal of Modern African Studies* 49, 1: 115–39.

Mehler, A. 2012. 'Why Security Forces Do Not Deliver Security: Evidence from Liberia and the Central African Republic', *Armed Forces & Society* 38, 1: 49–69.

Mehler, A. 2013. 'Consociationalism for Weaklings, Autocracy for Muscle Men? Determinants of Constitutional Reform in Divided Societies', *Civil Wars* 15, suppl. 1: 21–43.

Mehler, A. & B. Hoffmann 2011. 'Area Studies', in Badie, B., D. Berg-Schlosser, & L. Morlino (eds.), *The International Encyclopedia of Political Science*. Thousand Oaks, CA: Sage, 87–90.

Mehler, A., D. Lambach, & J. Smith-Höhn 2010. 'Legitimate Oligopolies of Violence in Post-Conflict Societies with Particular Focus on Liberia and Sierra Leone.' Research DSF, No. 23, Deutsche Stiftung Friedensforschung, Osnabrück.

Mehlum, H., K. O. Moene, & R. Torvik, 2002. 'Plunder & Protection Inc.', *Journal of Peace Research* 39, 4: 447–59.

Mengisteab, K. & C. Daddieh 1999. 'Why State Building Is Still Relevant in Africa and How It Relates to Democratization', in Mengisteab, K. & C. Daddieh (eds.), *State Building and Democratization in Africa*. Westport, CT: Praeger Publishers, 1–17.

Menkhaus, K. 2006. 'Governance without Government in Somalia: Spoilers, State Building, and the Politics of Coping', *International Security* 31, 3: 74–106.

Menkhaus, K. 2007. 'The Crisis in Somalia: Tragedy in Five Acts', *African Affairs* 106, 424: 357–90.

Messner, J. J. (ed.) 2017. *Fragile States Index 2017*, Washington, DC: The Fund for Peace.

Meyer, A. 2009. 'Regional Conflict Management in Central Africa: From Fomuc to Micopax', *African Security* 2, 2–3: 158–74.

Meyer, J. W. & R. L. Jepperson 2000. 'The "Actors" of Modern Society: The Cultural Construction of Social Agency', *Sociological Theory* 18, 1: 100.

Mkandawire, T. 2002. 'The Terrible Toll of Post-Colonial "Rebel Movements" in Africa: Towards an Explanation of the Violence against the Peasantry', *The Journal of Modern African Studies* 40, 2: 181–215.

Mogby, Z. & N. A. Moukadas 2015. 'Rapport Général des Consultations Populaires à la Base en République Centrafricaine.' Working paper, University of Bangui.

Molomo, M. G. 2009. 'Building a Culture of Peace in Africa: Toward a Trajectory of Using Traditional Knowledge Systems', *Journal of Peacebuilding & Development* 4, 3: 57–69.

Moore, S. F. 1973. 'Law and Social Change: The Semi-Autonomous Social Field as an Appropriate Subject of Study', *Law & Society Review* 7, 4: 719–46.

N'diaye, B. 2009. 'Security Sector Reform in the Central African Republic', in Born, H. & A. Schnabel (eds.), *Security Sector Reform in Challenging Environments*. Berlin: LIT, 39–68.

Nathan, L. 2005. 'The Frightful Inadequacy of Most of the Statistics: A Critique of Collier and Hoeffler on Causes of Civil War.' Crisis States Discussion Paper No. 11, LSE.

Nathan, L. 2006. 'Domestic Instability and Security Communities', *European Journal of International Relations* 12, 2: 275–99.

Öhm, M. 2014. *War and Statehood in South Sudan*, Baden-Baden: Nomos.

Olson, M. 1993. 'Dictatorship, Democracy, and Development', *The American Political Science Review* 87, 3: 567–76.

Ottaway, M. 2002. 'Rebuilding State Institutions in Collapsed States', *Development & Change* 33, 5: 1001–23.

Owen, T. 2004. 'Human Security – Conflict, Critique and Consensus: Colloquium Remarks and a Proposal for a Threshold-Based Definition', *Security Dialogue* 35, 3: 373–87.

Paris, R. 2010. 'Saving Liberal Peacebuilding', *Review of International Studies* 36, 2: 337–65.

Péclard, D. & D. Mechuloan 2015. 'Rebel Governance and the Politics of Civil War', Swiss Peace Working Paper No. 1.

Pegg, S. & M. Walls 2018. 'Back on Track? Somaliland after Its 2017 Presidential Election', *African Affairs* 117, 467: 326–37.

Pendle, N. 2014. 'Interrupting the Balance: Reconsidering the Complexities of Conflict in South Sudan', *Disasters* 38, 2: 227–48.

Phillips, S. G. 2016. 'When Less Was More: External Assistance and the Political Settlement in Somaliland', *International Affairs* 92, 3: 629–45.

Pinaud, C. 2014. 'South Sudan: Civil War, Predation and the Making of a Military Aristocracy', *African Affairs* 113, 451: 192–211.

Pouligny, B. 2009. 'Supporting Local Ownership in Humanitarian Action', *Humanitarian Policy Paper Series* 9, 1: 1–32.

Prunier, G. 1998. 'Somaliland Goes It Alone', *Current History* 97, May: 225–28.

Randeria, S. 1999. 'Jenseits von Soziologie und Soziokultureller Anthropologie: Zur Ortsbestimmung der Nichtwestlichen Welt in einer Zukünftigen Sozialtheorie', *Soziale Welt* 1999, 50: 373–82.

Rathbun, B. C. 2008. 'Interviewing and Qualitative Field Methods: Pragmatism and Practicalities', in Box-Steffensmeier, J. M., H. E. Brady, & D. Collier (eds.) *The Oxford Handbook of Political Methodology*. Oxford: Oxford University Press, 685–701.

Read, B. L., L. M. Maclean, & M. Cammett 2006. 'Symposium: Field Research: How Rich? How Thick? How Participatory?', *Qualitative Methods* 4, 2: 9–18.

Renders, M. 2007. 'Appropriate "Governance-Technology"? Somali Clan Elders and Institutions in the Making of the 'Republic of Somaliland', *Africa Spectrum* 42, 3: 439–59.

Renders, M. 2012. *Consider Somaliland: State-Building with Traditional Leaders and Institutions*, Leiden: Brill.

Renders, M. & U. Terlinden 2010. 'Negotiating Statehood in a Hybrid Political Order: The Case of Somaliland', *Development and Change* 41, 4: 723–46.

Reno, W. 1998. *Warlord Politics and African States*, Boulder, CO: Lynne Rienner Publishers.

Reno, W. 2002. 'The Politics of Insurgency in Collapsing States', *Development and Change* 33, 5: 837–58.

The Resolve LRA Crisis Initiative & Invisible Children. 2015. 'Tracking Joseph Kony: A Rebel Leader's Nine-Year Odyssey', Security Brief, LRA Crisis Tracker.

Rice, C. 2005. 'The Promise of Democratic Peace.' *Washington Post*, 11 December.

Richards, P. (ed.) 2005. *No Peace No War: An Anthropology of Contemporary Armed Conflict*, Athens, OH and Oxford: Ohio University Press and James Currey.

Richmond, O. P. 2011. 'De-Romanticising the Local, De-Mystifying the International: Hybridity in Timor Leste and the Solomon Islands', *The Pacific Review* 24, 1: 115–36.

Rigterink, A. S. 2015. 'Does Security Imply Safety? On the (Lack of) Correlation between Different Aspects of Security', *Stability: International Journal of Security & Development* 4, 1: 1–21.

Risse, T. (ed.) 2011. *Governance without a State? Policies and Politics in Areas of Limited Statehood*, New York: Columbia University Press.

Risse, T. & U. Lehmkuhl (eds.) 2007. *Regieren Ohne Staat? Governance in Räumen Begrenzter Staatlichkeit*, Baden-Baden: Nomos.

Rolandsen, Ø. H. 2015a. 'Another Civil War in South Sudan: The Failure of Guerilla Government?', *Journal of Eastern African Studies* 9, 1: 163–74.

Rolandsen, Ø. H. 2015b. 'Small and Far Between: Peacekeeping Economies in South Sudan', *Journal of Intervention and Statebuilding* 9, 3: 353–71.

Rolandsen, Ø. H. & M. W. Daly 2016. *A History of South Sudan: From Slavery to Independence*, Cambridge: Cambridge University Press.

Rotberg, R. I. (ed.) 2003. *When States Fail: Causes and Consequences*, Princeton: Princeton University Press.

Rothschild, E. 1995. 'What Is Security?', *Daedalus* 124, 3: 53–98.

Rubin, B. R. 2005. 'Constructing Sovereignty for Security', *Survival* 47, 4: 93–106.

Ryan, K. E., T. Gandha, M. J. Culbertson, & C. Carlson 2014. 'Focus Group Evidence: Implications for Design and Analysis', *American Journal of Evaluation* 35, 3: 328–45.

Samatar, A. I. 1989. *The State and Rural Transformation in Northern Somalia, 1884–1986*, Madison: University of Wisconsin Press.

Saulnier, P. 1998. *Le Centrafrique: Entre Mythe et Réalité*, Paris: Harmattan.

Schäferhoff, M. 2014. 'External Actors and the Provision of Public Health Services in Somalia', *Governance* 27, 4: 675–95.

Schlee, G. 2013. 'Customary Law and the Joys of Statelessness: Idealised Traditions Versus Somali Realities', *Journal of Eastern African Studies* 7, 2: 258–71.

Schlichte, K. & A. Veit 2007. 'Coupled Arenas: Why State-Building Is So Difficult', *Working Papers Micropolitics* 2007, 3.

Schneckener, U. 2010. 'Unintended Consequences of International Statebuilding', in Daase, C. & C. Friesendorf (eds.), *Rethinking Security Governance: The Problem of Unintended Consequences*. London and New York: Routledge, 62–81.

Schomerus, M. 2012. '"They Forget What They Came For": Uganda's Army in Sudan', *Journal of Eastern African Studies* 6, 1: 124–53.

Schomerus, M. & L. Aalen 2016. 'Considering the State: Perspectives on South Sudan's Subdivision and Federalism Debate', Overseas Development Institute (ODI) Research Report, August.

Schomerus, M. & L. De Vries 2014. 'Improvising Border Security: "A Situation of Security Pluralism" Along South Sudan's Borders with the Democratic Republic of Congo', *Security Dialogue* 45, 3: 279–94.

Schomerus, M., L. D. Vries, & C. Vaughan 2013. 'Introduction: Negotiating Borders, Defining South Sudan', in Vaughan, C., M. Schomerus, & L. D. Vries (eds.), *The Borderlands of South Sudan: Authority and Identity in Contemporary and Historical Perspectives*. New York: Palgrave Macmillan, 1–22.

Schroeder, U. C. 2010. 'Unintended Consequences of International Security Assistance: Doing More Harm Than Good?', in Daase, C. & C. Friesendorf (eds.), *Rethinking Security Governance: The Problem of Unintended Consequences*. London and New York: Routledge, 82–101.

Schroeder, U. C. & F. Chappuis 2014. 'New Perspectives on Security Sector Reform: The Role of Local Agency and Domestic Politics', *International Peacekeeping* 21, 2: 133–48.

Scott, C. 2017. *State Failure in Sub-Saharan Africa: The Crisis of Post-Colonial Order*, London: I.B.Tauris.

Scott, J. C. 2009. *The Art of Not Being Governed: An Anarchist History of Upland Southeast Asia*, New Haven, CT and London: Yale University Press.

Simojoki, M. V. 2011. 'Unlikely Allies: Working with Traditional Leaders to Reform Customary Law in Somalia', in Harper, E. (ed.), *Working with Customary Justice Systems: Post-Conflict and Fragile States*. Rome: International Development Law Organization, 33–50.

Simons, C., F. Zanker, A. Mehler, & D. M. Tull 2013. 'Power-Sharing in Africa's War Zones: How Important Is the Local Level?', *The Journal of Modern African Studies* 51, 4: 681–706.

Skaperdas, S. 2001. 'The Political Economy of Organized Crime: Providing Protection When the State Does Not', *Economics of Governance* 2, 3: 173.

Smith, D. L. 2014. 'Lining up for the Presidency in the Central African Republic', ISS Central Africa Report No. 2.

Smith, S. W. 2015. 'CAR's History: The Past of a Tense Present', in Carayannis, T. & L. Lombard (eds.), *Making Sense of the Central African Republic*. London: Zed Books, 17–52.

Southward, F., Y. Weyns, L. Hoex, & F. Hilgert 2014. 'Diamonds in the Central African Republic', International Peace Information Service (PIS) Insights Report.

Spanger, H.-J. 2007. 'Staatszerfall Und Staatsbildung: Eine Bestandsaufnahme Der Internationalen Theoriebildung', in Weiss, S. & J. Schmierer (eds.), *Prekäre Staatlichkeit Und Internationale Ordnung*. Wiesbaden: Springer, 85–105.

Spittaels, S. & F. Hilgert 2009. *Mapping Conflict Motives: Central African Republic*, Antwerp: IPIS.

Spittaels, S. & Y. Weyns 2014. *Mapping Conflict Motives: The Sudan–South Sudan Border*, Antwerp: IPIS.

Stedman, S. J. 1993. 'The New Interventionists', *Foreign Affairs* 72, 1: 1–16.

Tilly, C. 1990. *Coercion, Capital, and European States, AD 990–1990*, Cambridge, MA: B. Blackwell.

Titeca, K. & T. Costeur 2015. 'An LRA for Everyone: How Different Actors Frame the Lord's Resistance Army', *African Affairs* 114, 454: 92–114.

Tull, D. M. & A. Mehler 2005. 'The Hidden Costs of Power-Sharing: Reproducing Insurgent Violence in Africa', *African Affairs* 104, 416: 375–98.

UNMISS (United Nations Mission in South Sudan). 2016. *Executive Summary of the Independent Special Investigation into the Violence Which Occurred in Juba in 2016 and UNMISS Response*.

Utas, M. (ed.) 2012. *African Conflicts and Informal Power: Big Men and Networks*, London: Zed.

Valentino, B. A. 2014. 'Why We Kill: The Political Science of Political Violence against Civilians', *Annual Review of Political Science* 17, 1: 89–103.

Van Munster, R. 2007. 'Review Essay: Security on a Shoestring: A Hitchhiker's Guide to Critical Schools of Security in Europe', *Cooperation and Conflict* 42, 2: 235–43.

Van Tongeren, P. 2013. 'Potential Cornerstone of Infrastructures for Peace? How Local Peace Committees Can Make a Difference', *Peacebuilding* 1, 1: 39–60.

Vandekerckhove, N. 2011. 'The State, the Rebel and the Chief: Public Authority and Land Disputes in Assam, India', *Development and Change* 42, 3: 759–79.

Vaughan, C., M. Schomerus, & L. D. Vries (eds.) 2013. *The Borderlands of South Sudan: Authority and Identity in Contemporary and Historical Perspectives*, New York: Palgrave Macmillan.

Veit, A. 2010. *Intervention as Indirect Rule: Civil War and Statebuilding in the Democratic Republic of Congo*, Frankfurt am Main: Campus.

Verhoeven, H. 2009. 'The Self-Fulfilling Prophecy of Failed States: Somalia, State Collapse and the Global War on Terror', *Journal of Eastern African Studies* 3, 3: 405–25.

Vircoulon, T. 2017. 'La Reconstitution de L'armée Centrafricaine: Un Enjeu à Hauts Risques', IRSEM Research Note 36, April.

Vitturini, E. 2017. 'The Gaboye of Somaliland: Legacies of Marginality, Trajectories of Emancipation', Doctoral dissertation, University of Milan-Bicocca.

Walls, M. 2009. 'The Emergence of a Somali State: Building Peace from Civil War in Somaliland', *African Affairs* 108, 432: 371–89.

Walls, M. & S. Kibble 2011. *Somaliland: Change and Continuity. Report by International Election Observers on the June 2010 Presidential Elections in Somaliland*, London: Progressio.

Wassara, S. S. 2015. 'South Sudan: State Sovereignty Challenged at Infancy', *Journal of Eastern African Studies* 9, 4: 634–49.

Weber, M. 1922. *Wirtschaft und Gesellschaft. Grundriß der Sozialökonomik*, Tübingen: J.C.B Mohr (Paul Siebeck).

Weber, M. 1992 [1919]. *Politik Als Beruf*, Stuttgart: Reclam.

Weinstein, J. 2005. 'Autonomous Recovery and International Intervention in Comparative Perspective', Center for Global Development Working Paper No. 57, April.

Welz, M. 2014. 'Briefing: Crisis in the Central African Republic and the International Response', *African Affairs* 113, 453: 601–10.

Welz, M. 2016. 'Multi-Actor Peace Operations and Inter-Organizational Relations: Insights from the Central African Republic', *International Peacekeeping* 23, 4: 568–91.

Weyns, Y., L. Hoex & S. Spittaels 2014. *Mapping Conflict Motives: The Central African Republic*, Antwerp: IPIS.

Whalan, J. 2017. 'The Local Legitimacy of Peacekeepers', *Journal of Intervention and Statebuilding* 11, 3: 306–20.

Williams, P. D. 2016. 'AMISON under Review', *The RUSI Journal* 161, 1: 40–9.

Wimmer, A. 2008. 'The Making and Unmaking of Ethnic Boundaries: A Multilevel Process Theory', *American Journal of Sociology* 113, 4: 970–1022.

Wimmer, A. 2013. *Ethnic Boundary Making: Institutions, Power, Networks*, New York: Oxford University Press.

Wimmer, A., L.-E. Cederman & B. Min 2009. 'Ethnic Politics and Armed Conflict: A Configurational Analysis of a New Global Data Set', *American Sociological Review* 74, 2: 316–37.

Wolff, S. 2012. 'Consociationalism: Power Sharing and Self-Governance', in Wolff, S. & C. Yakinthou (eds.), *Conflict Management in Divided Societies: Theories and Practice*. London and New York: Routledge, 23–56.

Woodfork, J. 2006. *Culture and Customs of the Central African Republic*, Westport, CT and London: Greenwood Press.

Worrall, J. 2017. '(Re-)Emergent Orders: Understanding the Negotiation(S) of Rebel Governance', *Small Wars & Insurgencies* 28, 4–5: 709–33.

Young, J. 2012. *The Fate of Sudan: The Origins and Consequences of a Flawed Peace Process*. London: Zed Books.

Zanker, F., C. Simons & A. Mehler 2015. 'Power, Peace, and Space in Africa: Revisiting Territorial Power Sharing', *African Affairs* 114, 454: 72–91.

Zartman, I. W. 2000. 'Ripeness: The Hurting Stalemate and Beyond', in Committee on International Conflict Resolution (ed.), *International Conflict Resolution After the Cold War*. Washington, DC: National Academy Press, 225–50.

Zartman, I. W. 2001. 'The Timing of Peace Initiatives: Hurting Stalemates and Ripe Moments', *The Global Review of Ethnopolitics* 1, 1: 8–18.

Index